The Present Lasts a Long Time

CRITICAL CONDITIONS: FIELD DAY ESSAYS AND MONOGRAPHS

Edited by Seamus Deane

The Present Lasts a Long Time

Essays in Cultural Politics

Francis Mulhern

UNIVERSITY OF NOTRE DAME PRESS
in association with
FIELD DAY

Published in the United States in 1998 by
UNIVERSITY OF NOTRE DAME PRESS
Notre Dame, IN 46556
All Rights Reserved

and in Ireland by
CORK UNIVERSITY PRESS
University College Cork, Ireland

Library of Congress Cataloging-in-Publication Data

Mulhern, Francis.
    The present lasts a long time : essays in cultural politics /
    Francis Mulhern.
        p.   cm. — (Critical conditions : 7)
    Includes bibliographical references and index.
    ISBN 0-268-03861-9 (pbk. : alk. paper)
        1. Europe—Intellectual life—20th century. 2. Political culture.
    I. Title. II. Series.
    D1055.M84 1998
    306.2'.094—dc21   98–42849
                                                          CIP

CONTENTS

PREFACE

The governing concerns of these essays are set out in the first part of the opening essay, with which the collection shares its title, and need not be trailed here. For now, I will only say two things about their status and form. If they can plausibly claim a disciplinary home, it is in intellectual history. All the essays deal with 'ideas' rather than, say, organizations and events, though in my own practical understanding, discourse is precisely a mode of organization and eventuality in indivisible historical processes. They deal with 'ideas' rather than the putatively contrasting practice called 'literary', though my academic formation in literary studies accounts for the matter or emphasis of most of them – and also, as friendly philosophers and historians cannot always forbear to tell me, for marked features of their approach. I describe them as essays in 'cultural politics', which is not a discipline, actual or aspirant, but a commitment and a perspective, in which each term is explored as a condition of the other. This interest was shaped by a subsequent education over a decade of editorial activity in a journal of socialist politics and ideas, *New Left Review*. That education was quite fundamental, but, of course, non-official, and when I speak directly of politics – the politics of Britain, Ireland and Europe – I claim no disciplinary authority whatever, merely the ordinary entitlement of a citizen.

The essays are diverse in their form and circumstances of origin. Some were commissioned as articles or chapters; some began as introductions to the work of others, or as public lectures, or as reviews that then developed lives of their own; another defends an earlier text against critical attack. Most were written in the nineteen-nineties. They represent the kind of writing that is often termed 'occasional'. In truth, all writing is occasional, not only in that it can be dated and placed, but in the stronger sense of assuming a context – a specific field of reference and interest, a specific audience – that is actually internal to it, giving it shape and sense. The stylistic effort to write for eternity – for no one and nowhere – is a special case of the general rule, not an exception to it. However, the signs of occasion can be particularly evident in the normally short kind of text called 'the essay'. The etymology of the term – *essai*, 'attempt' – survives in the practice of the form, which is said to suggest provisionality; and even where a writer's subjective disposition is not at all provisional, circumstance insists on its due: such texts are written relatively quickly, in a few weeks or months, perhaps with rather little premeditation, and usually with a quite practical awareness of venue and audience. In the essayists I most admire, these conditions are acknowledged, and accepted as secular disciplines rather than creaturely blemishes. I have tried to learn from their example, and now, in putting the essays together as a book, to keep faith with the occasions for which they were written.

Most of them have been amended, to deal with confusing or inappropriate or merely trivial reminders of circumstance. At the same time, however, I have not attempted to suppress their differences of register, which are part of their substance. Each essay now carries a date – in most cases, that of publication. Although I have deleted or tried to moderate plain anachronisms (with some obvious, unyielding exceptions), I hope to have denied myself any secret backdating of knowledge or judgement, any unannounced change of position. In the one case where text has been cut and replaced on substantive grounds, the alteration is declared and accounted for. Other changes have been made for the sake of information, clarity or readability. In sum, I have tried to re-present the essays, to acknowledge their original contexts without taking refuge there, to reiterate them, with all necessary qualifications made, as contributions to discussion in the here and now.

The biggest revision of all could have been made without a single stroke of the pencil. The chapters of a book are written in full awareness of one another; memory and anticipation shape every page. But a collection of essays is a book after the fact, something that probably was not meant to be. No doubt the consciousness of this new occasion has governed my local revisions in many ways. The most important aspect of the occasion is that the book appears in a Field Day series, part of a project in which the ideas of context and intellectual purpose – a cultural politics and a public sphere to be entered, questioned and redefined – have acquired special edge and point. I am glad of the opportunity so granted me to see these writings afresh, and especially to return, as I do in the later parts of my opening essay, to dwell a little further on the politics and culture of Ireland, the North and then the South, where their commitments both positive and negative took early shape.

In the upside-down accountancy of intellectual exchange, solvency is the aspiration of fools; I am pleased to owe so much. My warm thanks go to all the friends and colleagues who have been good enough to help me with these essays, at one time or another: Tariq Ali, Perry Anderson, Michèle Barrett, Neil Belton, Homi Bhabha, Robin Blackburn, Peter Bush, Clara Connolly, Mehmet Ali Dikerdem, Terry Eagleton, Gregory Elliott, John Kraniauskas, Rachel Malik, Franco Moretti, Patricia Mulhern, Aoibhinn O'Kane, Peter Osborne, Tony Pinkney, Jonathan Rée, Lynne Segal, Stan Smith. Sara Wilbourne's support, as publisher, has been indispensable.

I owe a special debt, not for the first time, to Seamus Deane, whose generous encouragement and advice were the making of this book.

ACKNOWLEDGEMENTS

I wish to acknowledge the editors and publishers of the books and journals in which the following pieces first appeared: 'Marxist Literary Criticism: Past and Future' was first published as the Introduction to Francis Mulhern, ed., *Contemporary Marxist Literary Criticism* (London: Longman, 1992). 'Reading Althusser' was first published as 'Message in a Bottle: Althusser in Literary Studies', in Gregory Elliott, ed., *Althusser: a Critical Reader* (Oxford: Blackwell, 1994). 'Intelligentsia and Their Histories' was first published as the Introduction to Régis Debray, *Teachers, Writers, Celebrities* (London: Verso, 1981); it also appeared in *New Left Review*, 126, 1981. 'Intellectual Corporatism and Socialism' originated as a paper for a conference, 'Matthew Arnold and the Fate of Critical Humanism 1888–1988', Oxford English Limited, Oxford, 1988; it was first published in *News From Nowhere*, 5, 1988. 'Towards 2000, or News From You Know Where' was first published in *New Left Review*, 148, 1984; it also appeared in Terry Eagleton, ed., *Raymond Williams: Critical Perspectives* (Oxford: Polity, 1989). 'A Welfare Culture?' was first published in *Radical Philosophy*, 77, 1996. 'English Reading' was first published in Homi K. Bhabha, ed., *Nation and Narration* (London: Routledge, 1990). 'A Nation, Yet Again' was first published in *Radical Philosophy*, 65, 1993. 'Postcolonial Melancholy' was first published in *Radical Philosophy*, 72, 1995. 'Translation: Rewriting Degree Zero' was first published in *In Other Words: the Journal for Literary Translators* 6, 1995. 'A European Home?' originated as a contribution to a panel discussion, with Stuart Hall and Doreen Massey, on 'The Political Geography of the Future', part of the BLOCK conference 'Local Cultures, Global Change', London Tate Gallery, 1990; it was first published in Jon Bird, Barry Curtis, Tim Putnam, George Robertson and Lisa Tickner, eds., *Mapping the Futures: Local Cultures, Global Change* (London: Routledge, 1993).

THE PRESENT LASTS A LONG TIME

The present lasts a long time: I offer this proposition, with just a little irony, as a synopsis of some general assumptions and concerns that shape the essays gathered here. In one respect, it is always true, but in another respect, never. Always, because the present is what actually exists, past and future figuring only as the representations of memory and anticipation; never, because as the point through which future becomes past, the present cannot be said to last at all. However, my formulation is better seen as dialogic, marking an effort to resist the generically 'modern' tendency to trivialize what it too readily classifies as past and the specifically 'postmodern' tendency to banalize what can no longer, in perfect consistency, be called the future – taking a position in what Peter Osborne calls 'the politics of time'.[1] The times that concern me in these essays are those of theory and politics, of intellectual formations and the cultures they serve or seek to fashion, of nations and nationalisms.

1

The historical situation we inhabit is less obviously new than old, in that its primary structures and processes – those of generalized commodity production on the basis of a radical separation of capital and labour – have been dominant in the making and re-making of social and cultural relations for some two hundred years. Innovation continues, of course, but this has always been the necessary discipline of capitalist competition; even where its novelties are not bogus or destructive, their forms and applications observe the dominant logic of capital; and the foremost novelty of these years is the reinvigoration of the system internationally, through the reconfiguring of capital and labour processes, the opening up of territories once sheltered from the rigours of commodification by the continuance of anterior forms (peasant agricultures), reforming social policy (welfare states, education) and experiments in the construction of a post-capitalist order (historical communism). Already old in this sense, our historical situation is also blocked, in that its oppositional forces have never, in the past hundred years, seemed so weak or so confused. The weakness promotes the confusion, which is potentially the graver state. Faced with the disappointment of immediate political hopes, and with the involution or disintegration of projects and movements that, however much and deservedly reviled, were at least dependable points of reference, the left, and above all the intellectual left, has proved itself strikingly vulnerable to rationalizing solutions. Communists settle for social democracy, whose latter-day ideologists have meantime converted to liberalism – and usually in the name of new understanding and a new situation. Yet these understandings are not 'new' in the only senses that seriously count: they are demonstrably not original, and there remain strong, unanswered objections to their claims to be more nearly adequate to the problems they address. Nor is the situation new in the required sense: capitalism has certainly created unprecedented kinds of crisis, but without surmounting any of the older kinds. Petty apocalypse is the house genre in market cultures, where every mode must imagine itself the last one, and also in the bourgeois academy, where the idea of progressive inquiry, itself now marketized, both emulsifies fundamental differences and privileges the signs of novelty; today, in too much left culture, such flourishes set off the plain realities of adaptation and regression. In these ways too, the present lasts a long time.

This evaluation of historical probabilities is in the first and last instance political; but its underlying reasons find their premises in general theory, and are thus more than strictly political in their applications. Historical time does not answer to received ideas of progress; it is not simple in composition or uniform in rate, not merely directional, let alone one-directional, in mode. What we conventionally singularize and measure as history is a complex, a mutually irreducible plurality, of times, different and variable in their tempos, rhythms and modes. Discrepancy and complication are not time's nuisances, then, nor do they succour the literary-liberal resistance to the thing called 'theory': they are the normal phenomena of history properly understood, the unmisleading appearances of what Louis Althusser termed 'differential historical time'. Two of these essays include direct discussion of this concept as a matter of cultural and general theory; I should not rehearse what is said there, and cannot now develop it in an adequately critical way.[2] However, the concept plays a more general role in the book, as one formative condition of its substantive critical interests and procedures, and in this guise it calls for some further comment.

One manifestation of differential time is perfectly familiar in literary and cultural studies: the apparent capacity of certain works – classics, as we say – to perdure in time and space, so that, as the Russian Formalists maintained, they never lapse into the past tense, but remain contemporaneous elements in successive literary 'systems'. The terms of contention over these appearances are equally familiar: they were set, for English critical culture, in the early 1950s, by F. R. Leavis and F. W. Bateson.[3] For Leavis, a critic in the humanist tradition, the appearances are real: they signify the discoverable truth that the finest uses of literary language mediate a best self whose moral intimations engage us all, as properly human beings. For Bateson, this is the principle and practice of wilful historical nescience and critical subjectivism, which can be controlled only by strict attention to the formative context of literature. Over the nearly fifty years since that exchange, the balance of professional opinion has shifted to the advantage of contextualism. The strong varieties of this style of reading have grown only more impressive in their ability to trace, in the details of literary utterance, the iterative weaving of temporally and locally specific meaning – in an old word that deserves greater currency, the 'contexture' of writing. The evidences of the universal have been reinterpreted as constructions of specifically humanist practices of reading, which can themselves be subjected to historicizing contextual analysis and judgment. These norms of reading, understood in specifically Marxist terms, govern all the essays in the book, and figure as subject-matter in about half of them, including 'English Reading' and 'Marxist Literary Criticism: Past and Future'. The earlier essay set out to elucidate the condensation of 'human' and 'English' values in Leavisian discourse; to trace the part of specifically social and sexual meanings in its formation; to show the complementary work of rhetorical force in binding it; and, finally, to analyse the historical conditions that shaped this paradoxical cultural entity, an exclusivist universalism, and favoured its moral ascendancy in mid-century England. At the same time, however, the essay signalled doubts about one of its own categories of analysis, posing the question that recurs with hardened emphasis in other writings here: that is, whether anti-humanism – inasmuch as it tends to regard any appeal to common human norms or goods as a pseudo-universalist imposition – is not a useless passion condemned sooner or later to self-contradiction. This is most obviously a moral and political question; but, as I argue in the essay on Marxism, it bears also on matters of historical analysis.

Anti-humanism has a natural affinity with strong varieties of historical contextualism, to which it imparts something of its own performative irony. If meaning is so radically contextual, how can it be reconstructed from a distance? And if, in spite of the apparent obstacles, such contextualizing reading is possible, what is the meta-context that makes it so? Contextualist analysis can offer a more or less cogent account of the real specificities of a text, and more or less incisive criticisms of the assumptions that govern universalizing traditions of reading, but it hobbles itself if it cannot also think the objective conditions that make those traditions not only possible but plausible. The case I make in 'Marxist Literary Criticism' is that the regulative idea of context must not be simplified, as it very often is, to a hyper-historicist valorization of change. The prized continuities of the humanist tradition are indeed constructed in one sense or another, but their conditions of possibility include, as well as present social interests, the slow times, the *longues durées*, as Fernand Braudel termed them, that always invest the fast-moving temporalities of concrete historical situations.[4]

The cognitive and political stakes in play here become easier to evaluate if we turn from the abstract consideration of discourse-as-meaning to its real functioning as performance – from 'ideas' to intellectuals. Or rather, 'intellectuals', for the whole purpose of the two essays here given to this matter is to quote and examine: to acknowledge the objective reality of a phenomenon but to hold it at a distance, not claiming or accepting its voice as mine. This has nothing to do with the psychic syndromes that so often ruin attempts at serious discussion in this area – I have no difficulty with the description 'intellectual' as an index of my place in the social division of labour. The issue is theoretical, historical, and, in critical moments, political.

Contemporary culture inherits two modes of discourse on intellectuals. The older and better-known is, broadly speaking, ethical; it foregrounds notions of responsibility, and usually specifies moral and political terms by which that may be judged to be honoured or scanted. The second is sociological, and purports to characterize intellectuals not essentially as ethical-psychological substances but as a social category. The choice of mode has no necessary evaluative implication. The defence of intellectual mission, what I call at one point the 'affirmative' tradition, or the tradition of 'self-declaration', quite naturally tends to the ethical mode – Julien Benda's *La Trahison des clercs* is the iconic instance, and Edward Said's *Representations of the Intellectual* furnishes a notable latter-day case – but sociology, in the person of Karl Mannheim, has also offered to serve that end.[5] The objectivist register of sociological writing is well adapted to more sceptical purposes, such as those of Joseph Schumpeter; but Paul Nizan's assessment of Benda and French academic philosophy, although Marxist in inspiration, was a moral indictment rather than a social analysis.[6] (Vulgar anti-intellectualism can relieve itself in either mode, caricaturing the intellectual's ethical mission as highbrow presumption or exploiting social categories as a form of muck-raking.[7]) Nevertheless, there seems to be an underlying logic of alternation at work here, such that a certain self-representation of the intellectual must be either confirmed (with or without approval) or dissolved into an alien social category (usually a class). In either case, the objective specificity of the phenomenon – its element of compulsive repetition and its real, though limited effectivity – eludes conceptual capture.

Sixty years ago, the Italian Marxist Antonio Gramsci proposed a distinction that has become classic, between 'organic' and 'traditional' intellectual types, the former being culturally specialized members of their respective social classes, the latter evincing a corporate solidarity and separateness. This taxonomy seems to me to reinforce the problem it seeks to resolve. Its formal symmetry is misleading. What Gramsci offered, in reality, was a theoretical claim – that intellectuals emerge 'organically', in a quasi-biological process of functional specialization – and its vexing empirical remainder – the phenomenon of 'traditionality', or in Western parlance, intellectuals *tout court*. (It is very striking that Said, invoking Gramsci and then Benda, should in effect read the distinction as one between independent and compromised forms of intellectual practice, and thus domesticate it for the missionary tradition.[8]) Gramsci persisted with this crux, which held specific political value for him, but without resolving it. My own attempts, which would be unimaginable without his example, set out from the concept of 'intellectual corporatism', through which I try to re-write the binary dialogue of ethical self-representation and sociological reductionism as a singular historical question: in what conditions and with what effects do ideologies of corporate solidarity and independence take shape in the social category whose objective role is the production and circulation of meaning, the intelligentsia?

The question has more than one kind of interest. Seen in the most general terms, it marks one attempt to explore a conspicuous and commanding instance of the problem of perdurance in cultural history, a repertoire deeply established and a performance that recurs; or, in a psychoanalytic analogy, to explore the formation of a cultural 'imago', an unconscious figure that determines the apprehension and self-apprehension of its real counterparts. I suggest in one of these essays that imagos of 'the intellectual' take shape as specific effects of state forms and their associated political orders.[9] However, the states I discuss are in no case more than three centuries old; some scholarly studies – such as mine is not – trace the formation of modern intellectuality much further back.[10] It seems likely that the present dynamics of the phenomenon summarized as 'the intellectuals' arises not only from specifically modern conditions, but from the far slower history of one of the oldest of all social structures, the *longue durée* of the division of 'general' and 'particular' labour.[11] Intellectuals are often figured, romantically, as critics of 'the eternal yesterday'; but the reality may be that, even in their most oppositional or avantgardist moments, their social performance has, in this objective sense, depended upon it.

Anachronism appears differently in this light, and not only as a category of historical description and judgement; it can be, on occasion, a political resource. The essay 'A Welfare Culture?' puts this thought self-consciously to use. It is in one respect a study in intellectual history, reviewing the diffusionist liberalism that was the dominant cultural formula in post-war Britain, and the varieties of socialist cultural thinking that emerged in that context. At the same time, however, it intervenes in the present, arguing that the terms of critical engagement proposed at that time remain actual, and in key respects qualitatively more advanced than the better-adjusted styles of resistance now current in much of the left. That past is future now, or may be, if we resist the facile identification of time with development, of chronological sequence with desirable change – if, without nostalgia, we can summon up 'the courage of our anachronisms'.[12] And if, in this, the most general problems of 'culture' and 'intellectuals' have special claims to attention, it is because of their foundational role. For intellectuals – the kind of person who might write a book like this one, and is more likely than others to read it – these categories are the inescapable grounds of practical self-definition, and of what we agree or decline to know as our politics. I assign these essays to the genre called 'cultural politics' – a familiar phrase marking an important, difficult, contentious encounter of meanings, over which it is worthwhile to pause.

Where these essays approach this question, they back into it, more conscious of existing problems than of fair prospects. Explicitly or at least in practice, they try to identify and outrun two kinds of reductionism: culturalism, the generic tendency of the liberal critical tradition, and latterly of cultural studies, which asserts the moral primacy of culture over politics;[13] and instrumentalism, the error both fairly and falsely associated with socialist traditions, which elevates existing political priorities as the test of cultural legitimacy. The inborn drive of the first is to dissolve political reason; the predictable outcome of the second is regimentation and self-inflicted inanition. These contrasting tendencies differ in their historical distribution and weight: instrumentalism certainly enjoys the greater notoriety, though above all in the eyes of those who sponsor the alternative, which has been the more prolific.[14] In formal terms, however, they are specular opposites founded on a common inability to think the necessarily discrepant character of the politics-culture relation. The issue, as I argue later, does not concern the proper classification of orders and substances.[15] If the cultural, in the broad definition, is the moment of meaning in social relations, then it is coextensive with historical sociality as such, which can have no sense, political or other, beyond its powers of expression and representation. And if politics deals in the maintenance or transformation of social relations, then there is no cultural matter that may not enter its discursive range. The difference is one of function, and so of discursive mode. The specificity of political practice consists in the work of determining the shape of social relations: as discourse, it is necessarily deliberative and injunctive in mode, and – for this is the specificity of states and revolutions – may avail itself of force. Cultural practices, understood specifically as those whose principal function is to produce and circulate meaning, are not of this kind. They move in a common world of sense; they cannot eschew political suggestion; but they lack, have no need of, the specialized characteristics of the political. This difference grounds the relation of discrepancy between cultural and political judgement. Culture may tacitly privilege any or all differences as absolute; politics, committed to securing this or that general condition of existence, cannot follow suit. In other circumstances, but for the same reason, political interest may entail the effort to create division in a field of cultural affinity. In the perspective of any given cultural interest, a political demand is normally too much or too little; and the political complaint against culture is of the same kind. In the terms I use later, each, with regard to the other, is *both* ecumenical *and* sectarian.

One sympathetic but potentially grave objection to this theoretical construction is that it disables the very idea of cultural politics. I believe this is not so. Two familiar varieties of cultural politics are no less easily recognized in these terms: that in which matters and interests agreed to be political are thematized in specifically cultural practices – novels, plays, films – and another in which the conditions of cultural practice become matters of public policy debate – censorship, for example, or arts funding, or the regulation of media ownership. And there is a third sense of cultural politics, perhaps more interesting than either of these, which this theoretical analysis not only admits but implies. Cultural formations are necessarily more diverse and prolific in meaning than the political discourses active within them. Political practices, whose defining object is the conditions of implementation of what is possible and desirable in a given social perspective, can find no positive use for much of what their ambient culture may suggest. Culture is always excessive, in this precise sense. This excess – call it the surplus or, with a different nuance, the remainder – is not constant from one time-space to another, nor is it homogeneous in its social implication. Forty years ago, in metropolitan capitalist discourse, it included both 'outmoded' neo-liberal economics and 'romantic' political ecology; no longer ago, in contrast, Catholic doctrine was a touchstone of political legitimacy in Southern Ireland, as was the principle of collective welfare provision in Britain. What the cultural excess represents, in any case, is an array of unchartered versions of the possible, everything that moves in the space between enforceable judgement and negative certainty. This is the space of cultural politics. One of the necessities of any bourgeois political formula, as it strives for electoral legitimation, is to suppress the discrepancy between programme and imagination, to represent its optional version of the possible as the only one. One of the marks of an emancipatory politics, in party or governmental form, would be the ability to acknowledge that discrepancy, which must always be present, as the difficult, changeable condition of its moral authority. The English Conservative R. A. Butler, of all people, popularized a phrase that we might well expropriate and redeploy as a gloss on the idea of cultural politics: it is 'the art of the possible'.

2

Complex time, intellectuals, cultural politics: these themes have particular relevance in the setting of nations and nationalisms. Modern nationalist cultures are narrative cultures: the taxonomies of difference they organize are always in movement, caught up in stories of loss and recovery, or destiny, or decline, as the case may be. It has often been claimed – by Schumpeter, among others – that socialism is the paradise of intellectuals, but if that zone has any historical existence, its coordinates are those of nations. Intellectuals figure awkwardly in socialist, including Marxist, political traditions, because their relationship with labour movements is elective, not fatal; but nationality is inborn, and intellectuals may express its spirit as fully as any of their people. More fully, indeed, for cultural elaboration has been a crucial political mode in national movements, which accordingly not only embrace but exalt their poets, journalists and scholars.

Cultures of nationality are the primary matter of the five essays that complete this volume, and, above all, those of England and Ireland. Their general spirit is Marxist, but even within that theoretical and political range they have provoked negative reactions. The English and Irish essays have alike been charged with what the Communist tradition called 'national nihilism', or a denial of positive value to any putatively national element in a social formation. There is something in this accusation, though I think of it more specifically as a habit of abstraction that is not conditioned only by deliberate theoretical and political choices. Another kind of criticism helps to clarify my meaning. Writing about Ireland, it has been observed, I stress the distinct reality of Southern society, but then, writing from and about Britain, I disregard the part of Ireland that is still included in the Ukanian state – a curious absence in a socialist, and especially curious in someone who comes from there. There is truth here too. Indeed, these criticisms illuminate each other's grounds, though not in the most obvious of ways. Considering them together, I believe I can better understand what I guessed long ago: that the abstraction was fostered by a certain experience of Northern Ireland, and has been, for me, a way of signifying the place – a motif in my own cultural politics.

From London, now, through Dublin, and northwards by the express bus to Donegal – a direct route involving a detour through another state, to stop at Enniskillen. The view, in the approach to the western bridges, is generally found imposing. The foreground, which on a calm night the river takes like a polaroid, is occupied by the Watergate, the facade of the seventeenth-century castle. Rising away from it, towards the centre of the island, a church spire and then a campanile; and, high above them, beyond the bridges on the far side, a column with statue. Follow those landmarks, then, and climb to the top of the column for another perspective. Low, clustered hills, nearly all built upon, shape the horizon on both shores. Some of these structures are old – a military hospital, or the column itself – but most are not: the view, all the way round, is of housing estates and schools. Look downwards, finally, into the middle distance. See the car parks that have replaced the old neighbourhoods on the island, slums all; see the new building, observing a codified historicist norm of local style, and facilitated greatly by an alternative practice of urban renewal, car-bombing; see the spanking-new superstore where the cattle market used to be; and trace the handsome roads that link these things to one another, the shopping mall to the dormitory villages, hotels and marinas to airport and ferry.

These things coexist as factually as may be, but not in homogeneous time. The perspectives I recall now support distinct, discrepant narratives, each with its own terms of identity and antagonism, its own imaginative range. These narratives register one another's presence, but they cannot simply coexist; in choosing one as primary, you re-write the others.

The high points on the first skyline are the monuments of an old Plantation. The castle was a forward base in the Williamite Wars; the spire tops a Protestant cathedral, the campanile the old town hall; and the column honours one of the Coles, a family of landowners, soldiers and parliamentarians.

They are thus signs of endurance and achievement, reminders of the trials that won the town its place in the regimental histories and a special mention in 'The Sash My Father Wore'. Or they are symbols of colonial oppression: landlordism, a rotten borough, a Protestant Ascendancy, a system of local government that gave half the population a permanent two-to-one council majority and even greater privilege in the allocation of jobs and other material necessities.

The second perspective is 'British' too, but its time and sense are different. Here, in the estates and schools, are the plainer monuments of a welfare state. The estates were, with one exception, deliberately segregated, so that the gerrymandered electoral field would not thoughtlessly be levelled along with the slums. The view from the mainly Catholic northern hills showed the fourth, less charming eminence on the island skyline: the communications tower of the RUC barracks. The new Catholic schools were only partly financed from government budgets, the balance being met through long-running parish subscription schemes. But these basic securities and this extension of opportunity gave grounds for believing that not even Unionists could have everything their own way.

The phenomena of the middle distance do not make a third skyline, only a way of seeing the others. They discourage vexatious political interpretation, and only diehards will persist. The narrative they sponsor is that of development and the humanizing discipline of the tourist trade; their horizon, as Chambers of Commerce like to say, is peace and prosperity. Resolutely oriented towards the future, this narrative is nevertheless tender in its embrace of the past. A favoured image circulates in postcard form, and shows, across the river, a castle, with spire, campanile and column.

The Second World War ended seven years before I was born, but I grew up thinking of 1945 as the beginning of the world around me, and phrases like 'since the war' continued to mark my sense of historical time until well into the teenage years. The traces of the war itself were everywhere. The RAF and US army bases had been left intact, and now accommodated National Service units. Items of army surplus – berets, greatcoats, canvas shoulder-bags – were in common use among working-class men. At Halloween, the man next door would make up as Hitler (he was, as it happened, a house-painter) and goose-step into our kitchen with a half-dozen bottles of stout for the evening. What he talked about I no longer remember, but my father's stories would be about his student days in London during the Blitz. My schoolmates' fathers included English ex-servicemen who had stayed on to marry and settle in Enniskillen. We spent our last year of infant school in a converted air-raid shelter.

But it was not so much the war itself, except when we played the game oddly constructed as 'Japs and Germans'. It was the great change that came with it: Beveridge, Butler, Bevan, the social security and education reforms and a national health service, everything that went by the name of 'the wel-fare state'. Children had few reasons to like this still-developing world: it meant injections, cod liver oil, an infinity of schooldays and, in cases like mine, the final humiliation of spectacles. But I had no room to doubt that it was the pattern of a decent life, and that we owed it to Britain and Labour.

Our estate seemed the model of it all. Begun in the later forties, the build-ing went on for decades, houses and flats spreading over one, then another of the northern hills and down to the river and lough shores around them. Hun-gry Hill was its name in the old Catholic back streets on the island, where the reasoning was that the rents must eat the wages, leaving nothing for food. It never seemed like that. The real poverty was over there, in fact, and the real money was somewhere else again. The estate was mostly working-class, with a sprinkling of teachers, a few shopkeepers, and married police; unemploy-ment was, by the town's wretched standard, low enough, even among Catholics. The nearest things to posh were a new car or full make-up on a weekday or, as I was made to understand in time, a weakness for big words.

Alone among the town's estates, this one was owned and managed by a statutory trust, not the local council; its design standards were better than the average, and, by the same fluke of post-war planning, it was mixed. The majority were Catholics; the shortage of decent housing was far more acute among them, and the gerrymander dictated where they would go. But the Protestants made a substantial minority, and in my part of the estate neared parity. Relations varied, in most cases, from the warm to the pragmatically tol-erant. My family was close to the people next door, and on easy terms with other Protestants around. Of course, the children quickly learned to trace a border in their lives. Halloween was everybody's night, but not Guy Fawkes, when parents kept us in. There was some issue about the presence of Catholic veterans in the Remembrance Day parade. The woman three doors along was a decent neighbour every day of the year except one, the day the racket of the bands came up from the island, imposing itself on everything, and we became unrecognizable. And then there were the 'black' ones, the real bigots, whose children always had something else to do. Some Catholics thought them typ-ical, but they were not, those hatchet-faced bastards for whom a half-dis-tracted greeting was a wanton expense and a come-on to the devil. They disapproved of other Protestants nearly half as much as they hated us. There was something of a shared life around them, but they wanted none of it. The common advice was 'Ignore them', and I mostly did.

There were other things to ignore – to notice, yes, but from a distance. The B-man opposite setting out, after a first day's work, with his black uni-form and a .303 rifle on his shoulder; the sound of gunfire clattering over the water from the barracks, and the searchlight sweeping the river-bank after dark; the day I found a clip of live ammunition in the road, or the night the street outside my aunt's house filled up with tenders come to take neighbours' sons for a hammering and a trial, a jail sentence and then internment. This was the time of the IRA's Border Campaign, six years of bombing, mostly of bridges and customs posts, and shoot-outs around isolated police stations. Nothing in my context stirred me in its favour. In my mother's family, the dominant political feeling was Labour, and there was a record of trade-union activity. I had heard from my father about the doings of the old generation in the War of Independence, and about the terrors of his childhood in the Lower Falls Road in the twenties, but those were stories. There were Catholic neighbours whose evening entertainments were self-consciously 'Irish', a swapping of stories and ballads and rebel songs beneath the picture of the Sacred Heart; I winced at this culture, finding it quaint and countrified, the more embarrassed because it claimed me. I couldn't quite turn these things away, but the only place they found in my head was a lead-lined box marked 'the past'.

In the conditions of the early sixties, these intuitions stiffened into a personal programme. The IRA had ceased fire in 1962, the year I passed the eleven-plus. I detested the good life as expounded by the priest who taught us both religion and Irish, a village arcadia with the national language, national games and, always and everywhere, so sure of their welcome, God's smiling busybodies, our own men in black. I detested it, and my brattish resistance found its justifying terms in the changing conditions of British politics and popular culture. With Labour back in office, the work of 1945 could be resumed; teenage experience was not an apprenticeship in the ways of the elders, but the test by which they were found wanting. This was modernity, and we too could have a part in it. The Unionist regime had to be defeated, but the Nationalist Party would not lead the attack. Dull counterparts of the Orange bloc that ruled over them, these local notables – self-appointed committees of businessmen, footballers and the indispensable priest – had no language in which to speak what I could guess of social need and possibility. A member of a religious order, posted from the South to a school in Enniskillen, summarized his dismay at the locals' lack of national passion in a phrase that still raises chuckles today: here, he said, was 'a garrison town with garrison people'. Here, I say, was a classic nationalist misperception. Catholics took the name of nationalist more or less as a matter of course. But the reality, as I came to see it, was that the experience of 1945 had in many cases weakened, if not quite severed, that identification, and at any rate complicated the practical meanings of 'Britain'. Unionism was the problem, but nationalism was no solution. As Labour and Liberals were beginning to show, there was scope now for a realignment across the communal line, and a new struggle for political and social reform.

The change came soon, and with an explosive force of which those electoral initiatives had given little sign. Militant civil rights agitation, persisting in the face of repressive edicts and police violence, precipitated a crisis of the Stormont regime. The Unionist bloc began to disintegrate, and in the camp of the mass opposition the old leadership was elbowed aside. This could not go on for long, people agreed; no state, no society could live at this pitch of crisis. Political argument became the common passion: everyone found a voice and insisted it be heard. One night late in 1968 I stood in the crowd below the campanile. Civil rights organizers spoke, then the student leftists from the university, and finally, the local Nationalist MP. At a loss, I suppose, to match the language of the platform – fascists came from Catholic Italy, didn't they, and what in God's name was a Green Tory? – he made no effort at a speech, but just gave us one of the old songs.

That was it. They were finished, all of them, now.

There was something else about the speakers that night and the many other nights like it. They were in all senses popular – in social origin, in politics, in appeal – and most of them were highly educated. Among Northern Catholics, the belief in education was something akin to land hunger. Work was scarce and often insecure, and the better jobs were more or less reserved for Protestants, as a matter of custom or policy; capital was for the few who possessed it. But education opened the prospect of a way out: a bright youngster might get a position in an Irish bank, or in the Inland Revenue (which, alone among civil service departments, was controlled from London, not Stormont, and did not discriminate against Catholics); or become a teacher, and make a career in the parallel school system Catholics were creating as their most formidable apparatus of resistance. Orange prerogatives counted for less here, because education had been reformed from London, through the Butler Act and the government of 1945.

Of course, the reforms were strongly class-differential in their general effects, which were there to see in these schools too. There were those who quickly and correctly learned that education for them was a course in failure and self-blame: one primary-school classmate, from a slum so vile it caused a public scandal, was beaten, day after day, because he came to school late and dirty. In the later stages of schooling, working-class boys would often leave at the first sign of decent work, and sometimes quite suddenly. The suddenness went to the heart of the social logic. There would be a real money crisis – a lay-off or sickness or a death – such that the family could no longer do without a possible wage; or an imaginary one, provoked by a father whose masculine honour was offended by the idle son with the big appetite and a bigger head. Then there was the farmer who refused to bear the expense of his daughter's grammar school, maintaining that the money was wasted on someone whose future lay with housework and chickens. (His wife confounded him, selling eggs and chickens from door to door to pay the bills.) But these pressures acted within a fiercely affirmative culture of education, which, in a town like Enniskillen, could also be facilitated by the pattern of class relations. This was a market town, and now a centre for schooling and public services, on the edge of an urban-industrial economy, and family class histories could be complex. In my own family network, which was not unique, a random gathering might include a casual labourer and his sister-in-law, an old domestic who wasn't sure whether the language we spoke was Irish or English, a builder who also kept cattle, bus conductors, shopworkers, a teacher, a car mechanic who had been to grammar school, and a cabinet-maker who would eventually make a small fortune in construction and real estate. Framed in this way, the division of mental and manual labour, the difference between property and the lack of it – the objective structures of alienation and antagonism in a class society – could seem easily negotiated, as fact or value. The common condition of Catholic, the political dominant in our lives, fostered the narrative implicit in such situations, lending it generality and point. Getting on was desirable, possible, and also unthreatening, and the high road was education.

The high road, and the destination too: for the children of propertyless homes, the farthest reach of social mobility is normally a graduate profession, and very often – since the training is cheap and the market relatively large – teaching. Britain might have served Unionism well by financing a new generation of Catholic businesses: a Conservative time-traveller from the eighties would have urged that course, and warned of the danger of welfarist options. As it turned out, the new generation – Butler's children – formed a new Catholic intelligentsia. Years after leaving Northern Ireland, I found myself absorbed in Gramsci's 'organic intellectuals', and wondering whether the concept might not be more strictly understood if it were more widely applied, taking in social categories other than the basic social classes that had been Gramsci's primary concern. The case closest to hand was feminism, and that is what I wrote about. But it came to me that I had known the phenomenon long before I learned the idea, that I had grown up in the midst of it. The local leaderships of the Civil Rights movement were to a striking degree highly educated, with teachers, present, past or future, most prominent in them. These people enjoyed a conventional authority, but unlike an earlier generation of their kind they were not a rarity; and unlike the Nationalist notables they now displaced, they wore their class difference lightly. Most of them would have been first-generation graduates, the children of workers who had returned to educate their younger counterparts, and to resume scarcely modified participation in a familiar collective identity. Their political language was untraditional and sometimes disturbingly anti-traditional; and, as I remember from conversations offstage, they were also versed in the standard intellectual topic of 'the masses'. But they spoke this language of rights and justice and even socialism in familiar accents, with egalitarian self-confidence, and a fluency that dumbfounded Unionists. These people were not only Fenians and hotheads and subversives and outside agitators and all the other things that disturb the peace; they were, as the Ulster Defence Association complained, with an air of real cultural grievance, 'silver-tongued devils'. Or, to revert to Gramsci's terms, they were organic intellectuals, intellectuals from and for their social group – which was not a class, in his strict sense, but the Catholic popular majority. A state-wide education reform, worked through in the regional conditions of oppression and resistance, gave rise to a new intellectual formation, from which came the new politics of Northern Ireland's 1968.

That's it . . . finished . . . new politics. Yes, but no. Reading the fifties and sixties in the way I recall here, in that narrative perspective, in those images of Enniskillen, I was hardly likely to forecast what really did come next, much less adjust to it. In an immediate practical respect, this came to matter less – I left the North in late 1969, a few weeks after the Loyalist pogrom in Belfast, to study first in Dublin and then, five years later, in Cambridge, and have not lived there since. But it could never matter less, as an internalized moral demand or as a formative and still controlling experience of politics. Twenty years later, on the Remembrance Day when my old primary school turned into a bomb and buried a group of Protestants, including some who had been neighbours on the estate, that sentimental education seemed a training in illusion.

There was illusion all right, but to say only that would be to stop short of proper criticism, not only of myself but also of those I have gone on arguing with since the sixties. The error lay in staring at one skyline, privileging one narrative; framing the older skyline as the picturesque and reading its narrative as a story of the past; levelling this complex time and the situation it defined.

The sovereign objective of the British intervention was not justice but pacification. The promise of reform was only one instrument among others in the effort to quell this embarrassing, costly, dangerous – and of course irrational – disorder. That, whatever nationalist tradition may assert, was by then the only 'British interest', though in fact the lack of a deeper interest made the crisis worse. Repression can be the more wanton when it imagines itself as doing no more than policing the long approach to constitutional good sense. In the borrowed words of an English literary specialist in civil unrest, Matthew Arnold, 'Force till right is ready'.[16] That failure to reform, the complacent, philistine reliance on 'peace-keeping', restored the authority of traditional nationalist analyses – which the intellectual formation of 1968, 'organic' not least in this, soon adopted as its own. Westminster's civilizing army reanimated the old story, which became the future. Nationalists understood that without a resolution of the residual national question, there would be no lasting resolution at all. That fact put paid to the leftist imaginings of the sixties, just as it now passes judgement on the crasser visions of trickle-down business confidence – the car parks, the superstore – and disciplines the miserable, near-universal longing for a credible peace. The peace process begun in 1994 has given the proof of this, depending as it has done not merely on the self-restraint but also and crucially on the creativity of the political untouchables, 'the men of violence'.

However, nationalists of all kinds have been slow to understand, or at least to acknowledge, the implication of the other story: that the cultural sensibilities of Catholics – like Protestants – have been far more complex than their voting habits suggest. The diplomatic talk of Northern Ireland's divided 'traditions' reaches for a possible political gain at the risk of eternalizing, as 'culture', the antagonism it seeks to overcome. The historical memory of the Catholic majority has assigned more than one meaning to the British connection; the everyday stereotypes of the South were an open secret; and it may be that in more open political conditions, where voting choices are not only expressive – aspirational or solidaristic – but deliberative, these complexities will begin to tell. It is a little soon to say. Any constitutional arrangement that evolves in the new century will be a nonesuch, unsettling to all tradition in those six counties which are no longer quite a colony but have not yet become anything else. If Northern options begin to be refigured in a European perspective (something the last Conservative government could not risk, for narrowly English political reasons) and in a political context defined, as now seems more rather than less likely, by the shaping of a more democratic, more lucidly post-imperial constitution for the neighbouring island, then the range of productive uncertainty will widen, intensifying traditionalist reactions, doubtless, but also validating other terms of coexistence and identity. The place I grew up in did not really exist: I know that now. But it may be possible.

3

This may look stubborn, or merely sentimental – not the most familiar of emigrant romances, but belonging to that genre nevertheless. Perhaps the Brechtian 'solution' I sardonically recommend to others at the close of my second Field Day essay is in truth the final absurdity of my own position, not theirs. Perhaps it is Marxists of a certain nihilistic bent, not nationalists, who must dismiss the real Ireland and appoint a historically correct society. I do not think so. However, to say that and no more would be too easy. The record of Marxist theory and politics in Ireland has been uncompelling, and in important respects questionable, not least for Marxist themselves, and consistency alone demands renewed efforts towards understanding why it has been thus, and how it might be otherwise. If personal recollection and conjecture are no kind of historical science, they may yet contribute something to a worthwhile purpose.

Ireland is different. But in relation to what putatively normal society? There is none. Ireland is different, and in that respect the same as anywhere else; if Marxism seems defeated by it, there must be a problem in the general theory, for which any social formation is an exceptional case; Ireland or no Ireland, we have to adjust the theory or find a better one. If, however, Ireland really is special, in a way that oddities like Britain or Brazil or Germany are not, then it will frustrate all social theory, not only the Marxist variety, which need not accept particular responsibility for its inability to read the island's *sui generis* discourse upon itself. What is truly 'special' here is the special pleading. My own view is that Marxist understanding of Irish realities, North and

South, is limited chiefly in so far as it assimilates the dominant discourses of its environment, thus tending to reproduce what it should be striving to displace. I would like to consider the matter of Marxism and Ireland in appropriately specific historical terms, by recalling the politico-intellectual complexion of the left I grew up in, after leaving the North.

Dublin was a revelation, in good part the one I wanted, and, for the rest, an enlightenment I could not deny. What I wanted was the whole experience of the student 1968. University College offered its own version of that. The committed left was of course no match, in scale, for its instant legend, but it was precocious, argumentative and venturesome, and the main mobilizing themes of the day, a typical combination of international causes – Vietnam, South Africa – and student-specific grievances, had wide appeal. Then, sharpening the edge of this everyday revolutionism, and making difficult but unignorable demands on the formal studies themselves, was the theoretical challenge of Marxism: the classics, in the first place, but also the writings of the contemporary Western tradition – above all, in my own case, as a conventional but increasingly anxious student of literature, those of Sartre and Althusser. Beyond its official and alternative curricula, UCD offered a third kind of education, an informal civics of Southern society. My first mass meeting, in the autumn of 1969, did not go according to script. Called by the veterans of the previous year's battles, attended by an audience of the eager and the curious, it was captured within twenty minutes by two newcomers, who transfixed us with their confident, articulate case against socialism and the student movement. The convenors (who, as it happened, had come to bury studentism for the opposite political reasons) were quickly reduced to formulaic bluster. That some of the formulae seemed apt was small consolation; this was frustrating, and also confusing. Even my Southern friends, who had been schooled with people like these and understood far more of what was going on than I did, were impressed. That was my first sighting of a generation self-consciously in training for high office. To describe them as aspirants would be bland: those teenagers, like the others with whom they pursued well-judged associations or necessary rivalries, simply knew – so guiltless and lucid was their ambition they did not hope, they actually knew – that they would one day assume elite positions in the ruling bloc. (And so they have done, as part of the new liberal ascendancy of the nineties. That meeting saw further into the future than it could have believed at the time.) Other, more settled styles of authority were conspicuous too: the political dynasties, one of which clustered like ivy in the Arts Faculty; the Church, whose demesnes were education and philosophy; in my own area, the studied aristocratism for which a certain version of literature – Yeats, Eliot, the US Agrarians, Catholicism in the high manner – furnished a spacious repertoire. Then framing these, inside the university and outside it, were the public authorities proper, whose manner I found hard to trace: undistant and fluent, assuming kinship with the audience in a way that could seem egalitarian but was more often merely affable, and, together with this, a habit of arrogance and arbitrariness so plain it could look innocent.

These rambling observations of a half-strange country were put in order by the worsening crisis in the North. The events of August 1969 led to a split in the IRA and mined the British road to reform; as open mass struggle faltered and armed politics assumed the leading role, so the North became dominant in the life of the Irish left. I cannot hope to reconstruct the factional theatre of the early seventies with the same energy of discrimination we brought to it then; all I venture is the outline of a discursive order, with its structured propensities of thought. 'The national question' was the conventional Marxist parlance for the crisis that now returned to claim us, and in that innocent misdescription lay the greater part of our perplexity. For the fundamental 'question' came always-already answered, leaving us to fight over derivative uncertainties. Ireland was a historic nation, for long wholly colonized and still partly alienated in the Anglo-British imperial interest – that was the first proposition of Irish nationalism, and a commonplace more or less widely honoured in every register of public discourse. The second proposition, which was already more clearly questionable, eliciting much piety but also increasing cynicism, was social. Any definition of 'the nation' condenses and naturalizes a representation of social relations in the population it identifies, and the distinction of the Irish national character was its spontaneous deviation from the international bourgeois norm. Neither proposition could simply be adopted by a Marxist left, and especially not the second; yet neither seemed easily rejected, and especially not the first. What happened was that most tendencies on the left took a course of critical self-differentiation, within shared terms whose provenance was local but also, it is worth emphasizing, cosmopolitan.

Imperialism rather than capitalism was the named object of revolutionary-socialist attack in the sixties and seventies. Wars of national liberation continued in Asia and Africa, and most of the independent Third World seemed trapped in the poverty and dependence of what was widely understood as neo-colonialism, from which the only effective liberation was socialism. Thus, except in a handful of metropolitan states where specifically anti-capitalist strategies were appropriate, socialism and national liberation were the mutually translating goals of popular struggle against imperialism. Viewed in this international perspective, the matter of Ireland was soon settled, in thought if not yet in fact. For the most important formation on the left, the then 'Official' majority faction of the republican movement, which was making its way, in the vehicular language of anti-imperialism, from revolutionary-nationalist to para-Communist positions, the category of 'the Irish people' furnished the dialectical resolution of nation and class. Such populism was not available to Trotskyists, who in their majority supported the IRA's armed campaign and at the same time insisted on the specificity of proletarian social interests, but the principle of all-purpose intransigence served just as well. There was scope for real and consequential political difference here, and even lethal feuds. It was of course necessary to repudiate the confessional and Anglophobic tendencies of traditionalists, including their Provisional comrades-in-arms; to explain that the British interest was economic, not a primordial urge to make croppies lie down, and that, in any case, other imperialist interests were even more heavily involved; to promote working-class unity in the North, where that seemed possible, and to insist, unsentimentally, on the reality of indigenous class struggle in the South. It was necessary at the same time to stress the dependent, comprador character of the Southern Irish bourgeoisie, its symptomatic complicity with British policy and anti-national embrace of Brussels, and to elucidate the objectively anti-imperialist, and therefore national, dynamic of trade-union struggles against corporate capital. In such ways, with such qualifications, Marxism achieved a morganatic union with Ireland, finding its duly 'critical' but deeply *uncritical* place within the discourse of the nation.

A minority faction, with which I associated myself, rejected the founding propositions of nationalism. Our defining assertion was that Ulster Protestants constituted a second Irish nation, and had the right to maintain a separate politico-juridical existence if that was their democratic will; while the oppression of the Northern minority was, by the same principle, a wrong that must be redressed, the conditions of reform included the withdrawal of irredentist claims of right, which were ill-founded. The historical analysis underlying this political position stressed the unequal regional development of capitalism in nineteenth-century Ireland, and it was unsurprising, then, that we should also attack the populism of much of left-wing anti-imperialism in the South: thus, most of us opposed the spontaneous rally against Dublin's application for entry to the EEC, insisting, here as in other matters, on specifically proletarian, not presumptively national-popular, terms of political alignment. I have no wish to rehearse these arguments now; readers may judge for themselves how far, and with what wisdom, I have maintained or adjusted the positions I supported in the early seventies. The more interesting thing now is to note the fate of that political variety over the next twenty-odd years, to trace the unwilled dialectic of that kind of enlightenment. The risk inherent in the so-called 'two nations theory' – or, as our critics believed, the iron consequence of it – was that it could deteriorate into an abstract politics of working-class independence and unity, effectively assuming the solution it sought to achieve, and adopting, through exasperation or simple default, a posture of quietism or cynical indulgence towards Unionism and state policy, North and South. As it became clear – though to some, even now, it is not clear – that armed nationalism was not merely an atavistic sport of Irish historical nature, or a spoiling faction kept alive only by scheming politicians and sentimental expatriates, those tendencies grew from hypothesis into fact. The cognate risk, for Marxists already in revolt against national pieties, was that the insistence on the dominance of capitalist relations in the Irish economy, and on the presence within it of a weak but otherwise perfectly ordinary local capital, could deteriorate into a hard-boiled 'progressive' defence of capital accumulation as such. This too happened, as the post-republican left became something like old Russia's 'legal Marxists', cold-eyed critics of narodnik fantasy in the service of a liberal tomorrow. Neither of these evolutionary outcomes was necessary, though, in the given conditions, they were probable; in any case, they represented political failure. Setting out to break the inherited discursive order of the Irish nation, to discover a consistently socialist theory and politics for Ireland, anti- or post-nationalist Marxism was largely confined within it, providing an *a contrario* demonstration of its unspent authority.

In 1975 I left Ireland to continue my studies in England, and have been since then – by fact of residence if not of nationality – a member of the British left. My working interests, partly already formed, lay in Marxist theory and specifically in intellectual history – an area in which I could try to turn my literary education against itself, to understand it as a historical formation of cultural interest and authority, and, in that way, start to unlearn its intuitions of social virtue. My everyday political interests were those of my new context – in which Ireland had a prominent place. This is the left of which it has come to be said, with strong feeling but little expectation of dissent, that it neglected its political duties in respect of the crisis there. It will seem unimaginative to disagree, but that is one justified response. The numbers involved in 'Irish work' – a common phrasing in the organized left – were always small, but so were they in any specified political sector, as distinct from generic activity in trade unions, which was expected from any in a position to pursue it. But the attitudes of the left in Britain were conscious, decided and emphatic, and if some on the Irish left did not perceive them sufficiently clearly, did not see and hear what lay in sight and earshot, it is because those attitudes so closely replicated their own. The British left in the seventies had a great deal to say about Ireland, and scarcely a word was new.

Of course, there is more than one definition of political duty, and therefore more than one response to the criticism. Distance, objective and subjective, always makes a difference. There were more than enough English revolutionaries with a vicarious passion for the war, hardly knowing that they would not have to do the bleeding and mourning – but all causes have these fools in their rear. The more serious effect of distance was that those who were sceptical of conventional pro-republican orientations, or whose simple optimism was drained over time, were able, as their counterparts in Ireland were not, to fall silent, and to occupy themselves elsewhere: if they appeared, to frustrated observers, to be indifferent towards the activity of their own state, in its own territorial annex, this was because they had counted the pragmatic cost of seeming, in the eyes of their comrades, to indulge it. Conviction, posturing, scepticism and discouragement all made for conformism. Dissident arguments were not much tolerated, appearing 'objectively' counter-revolutionary. Efforts at sustained rethinking usually came to nothing, at least in public.[17] One publishing non-event epitomizes my own experience as a dissenting Irish socialist in the British left. Together with a like-minded Dublin friend, I devised a book-length symposium on Ireland, for a mass-paperback series.[18] Our idea was to bring together serious, not merely platform-standard, exponents of every position in socialist controversy over Ireland, with strict procedural equity, and thus to create a resource for honest, informed discussion. The commissioning publisher – a salient figure in the industry and a good friend to the left – declined our offer with feeling: he had published numerous books about Ireland, 'all of them left-republican' in commitment, and he wasn't in favour of publishing anything different now. There may have been a murmur of objection, or just disappointment, among those present at our meeting; I don't remember saying anything. It seemed no time until the chair called next business.

'Next business' might have made an ironic slogan for a certain kind of anti-nationalist Marxism. For if the majority of Irish socialists articulated their politics within the discourse of anti-imperialism, with its crucially ambiguous conjugations of nation and class, their critics could fall prey to another kind of ventriloquism. Nationalist discourse, in its various forms and registers, had been the cultural dominant in Ireland, assigning identities and interests, legitimate or spurious, throughout its social space. By the end of the sixties, however, this was no longer quite so. The greater impetus, though not yet the greater social authority, was now commanded by a discourse of modern times – which, at that juncture, was itself undergoing a generic mutation from a 'national' to a 'post-national' form. In the succeeding decades, that discourse has become the dominant, the first official language of Southern society, the preferred code of all advocacy and dissent.

In what sense, now, would the times be modern? The concept of modernity is inherently paradoxical, and Ireland conjured its own tricks of the light. Modernity as such has no necessary social content: it is a form of 'temporalization', an invariant production of present, past and future that 'valorizes the new' and, by that very act, 'produces the old', along with the characteristic modes of its embrace, the distinctively modern phenomena of traditionalism and reaction.[19] Here, surely, is the master-trope of the new South. But perhaps not. It is part of the pathos of specific theories and projects of modernity that they can sooner or later be dated, and in this case the relevant time-span is some three decades – not those just past, however, but the thirty-odd years of the middle century. Ireland's foremost modernist was de Valera; the historical project he embraced and sought to implement was *sinn féin*, ourselves alone. This was hardly stock futurism. The Irish revolution was 'new' in one simple sense: it inaugurated the anti-colonial history of the twentieth century, and became an inspirational example for nationalists around the world. It was in familiar, expected ways 'modern', in that it honoured the ideals of bourgeois revolution – territorial sovereignty, representative government, a national economy and the dissolution of semi-feudal property in land. In the light of other, equally familiar standards, however, it appeared programmatically traditionalist, or even reactionary. The official imagery of the emerging society was ruralist, as in the imposing case of sport, where organizational principles valorized county and provincial identities, and all but effaced the social reality of urban settlement; and the state not only shunned the liberal cultural heritage of the Enlightenment but harried those who claimed it, subordinating public and private life to the mysteries and disciplines of the Holy See. But to dwell on the ostensible taxonomic oddity of de Valera's Ireland, to try to estimate the ratio of good and bad in its new-and-old constitution, is to mistake that occasion, and our own. This was a coherent modernist project. It was new, a configuration of political, economic and cultural relations without precedent in the island's history; and its rationale, which governed its purportedly traditional as well as its canonically modern elements, was a leap from the past as colonial oppression and dependence, *the past-as-Britain*, into a wholly contrasted Irish future.

Seen in this perspective, the dominant culture of the North, in those decades and since, was distinct not only in allegiance but in the very form of its historical being. If modernist time-consciousness has a perfect antitype, its Irish embodiment has been Orangeism. The Irish nationalist project detonated a crisis in the north-eastern counties, but there was no Protestant counter-project, merely the determination that nationalism must not prevail. The Northern state took shape as a crisis stiffened into a system. Hence the seemingly ungovernable repetition-compulsion in Orange culture: the rites of origins (Derry, Aughrim, Enniskillen and the Boyne), and the exaltation of liberties that, like the front parlours, are too good to make actual use of, let alone open to the neighbours. Hence too the stilted style of Unionist discourse, which, at its most pained, could seem to mark a radical alienation from speech itself – a kind of symbolic death. It was not only the Irish nationalist future that was unspeakable, but futurity itself. Protestant Ulster prided itself on the greater wealth and dynamism of its regional economy, yet the dominant culture of Orangeism was a ritual denial of all change: what we have we hold. Meanwhile, appearances notwithstanding, modern Ireland had launched itself in the priest-ridden rural South.

However, the phrase 'modern Ireland' commonly describes the society that began to take shape from the sixties, after the abandonment of that autotelic nationalism, and the supporting evidence can seem ample and plausible enough to deter questioning of it. Economic policy was reconstructed on Keynesian – later, neo-liberal – bases. With the growth of industry, through organized inward investment, came a population shift from the country to the towns. The South first reported an urban majority at the turn of the seventies, and today industrial production engages twice the numbers involved in agriculture. Emigration levels fell dramatically, for a time to zero. Accession to the

Treaty of Rome secured these changes, transferring significant subsidy and development costs to Brussels; perhaps equally importantly, it also favoured the cultural conditions of escape from a collective identity cramped in defensive bipolar relations with the old colonial power – Ireland as not-Britain. The nationalist claim to the North, though remaining a constitutional tenet and a residual and serviceable theme in public discourse, was in practice rewritten to mean a diplomatic duty of care in respect of the minority there. The clerical prerogative could no longer be exercised without challenge; secularism at last became a tenable option in official political life, and, by the nineties, a successful one – largely thanks to determined and resourceful radical campaigning, led by feminists, but in part also because of the moral discomfiture of a Church whose hidden history is now indelible shared knowledge. Today, Ireland is a media byword for cultural energy and confidence; traditional imageries, including much that is newly minted, now bear a euphoric charge, referencing a social landscape they hardly resemble. De Valera's 'comely maiden' has become the darling of Europe.[20]

Here, then, is really modern Ireland, whose historic other is that surmounted national project now called traditional – and among its most telling cultural features is precisely the salience of those binary abstractions as terms of self-description. The object of de Valera's modernism was 'Ireland'; the object of latter-day Ireland, its official good sense, is 'being modern'. The cultural dominant of the nineties is 'modernization'. 'National' and 'modernizing' values are not inherently opposed, but economic development on a world scale has forced them into mutual alienation, not only in once-colonized countries like Egypt or Ireland but also in the old imperial seats of Europe, which is undergoing its own kind of 'structural adjustment'. The themes of 'nation' and 'modernity' are pervasive in contemporary politics and culture, so much so that they appear adequate as categories of analysis, and even – grand narratives permitting – meaningful as terms of practical choice. My own view is that they are neither, that they are, as categories, functionally alternative forms of disavowal. I have said something, here and in the body of this book, about the discourse of the nation; there remains the far more powerful discourse that now subsumes and reproduces the national as the traditional other – decorative or sullen – of our properly modern times.

The discourse of modernization is itself no longer new. Forming as a theory of historical process in the European centres, it duly expanded into the colonized world, to offer a model account of the future there; latterday versions function similarly in the zones of historical communism and social-democratic welfarism. Its thematics are partly variable, and even reversible, the good sense of one phase becoming the outworn dogma of the next. Yet it persists as a general form of understanding, promoting a determinate mode of representation of social structure, dynamics, interest and agency. Modernizing discourse homogenizes social formations and reinscribes their differences as sets of technical functions – industry, urbanism, literacy and the rest – which, once quantified, indicate relative states of backwardness and progress. The complex time-space of social relations within and among states resolves itself into a simple narrative whose actors are moving, with varying degrees of luck, judgement and resolve, towards a common end, the pragmatically 'modern' condition. Singularizing social development, modernizing discourse also naturalizes it. Progress is not merely what happens next – that is the critical tenet of all modern advocacy. However, modernization is specifically a process of catching up – with a modernity that cannot stand still – and as such is prone to fetishize chronology and the natural reality it calibrates. No one will be found to defend this civilized animism, but the junk-language of governments and media – call it 'chronobabble' – testifies to its hold on the collective imagination: modernization appears not as a specific project or ensemble of projects, serving identifiable and contestable social interests, but as the ineluctable demand of time itself.

Modernizing discourse is a twentieth-century variety of the bourgeois ideology of progress. But that judgement implies, by contrast, a degree of cultural self-possession that the Marxist tradition may not uncomplicatedly claim. Marx saw capitalist modernity as innately contradictory in its process and effects, but in so far as that history was conceived as progress there would always be scope and temptation to edulcorate it. Legal Marxism had a more imposing counterpart in the leading theoretical tendency of German Social Democracy, which propagated an evolutionist scheme of ascent through capitalism to the necessary higher stage of socialism; Communist parties in the Third World sponsored a developmentalist Marxism envisaging national class partnership in the necessary, first-stage drive towards the gates of Western social modernity. The conceptual difference between those historical formats, 'metropolitan' and 'peripheral' respectively, is not the crux it once appeared to be, as Irish experience can show. The evolution of left republicanism and its successor formations, from an appropriately nationalist version of the second to an appropriately modernized version of the first, illustrates the continuity between them.[21] The syndicalist element in the Irish Marxist character – a propensity, shared with the British left, to model socialist politics rather narrowly on organized labour and its primary forms of struggle – has favoured unsentimental recognition of local capitalist development but also strengthened its appeal, as a key condition of release from the post-Treaty political order. The oppressive clericalism of official Southern culture has confirmed, by negation, the value of development in itself, the general critical appeal of the 'modern'. But it is precisely for the sake of the truth in such perceptions that the category should be resisted. Modernity and tradition, the new and the old, are unstable as descriptions, obtuse as terms of analysis, and mystifying as norms of social judgement.

The protectionist, dirigiste strategy of mid-century Ireland was modern in relation to *laissez faire* tradition, which, however, has now returned to trump it, there and elsewhere, as the last word in policy. The tiger economy of the nineties has been fashioned politically by the 'traditional' post-Treaty formations, which the smaller, 'modern', class-ascribed parties (Labour is in fact the oldest of the constitutionalist parties) seem destined to renovate rather than supersede. The culture is unquestionably 'modern' in canonical senses: increasingly liberal and secular, and pragmatic in its appraisal of available styles of consumption and recreation. But novelties like these were once old, the signs of an inauthentic, dependent existence that the national modernism would redeem. Ireland's colonial history, by virtue of its sheer duration, is more like a history of colonization itself, and the cultural repertoire of the island includes something of all the diverse colonial and ex-colonial futures it fell short of: as a West British principality like Wales, a second Scotland, a creole republic like those of the Americas, or a pilot version of Algeria. Such images persist, or have been reclaimed, as tropes of imaginable futures.

Facile as description, the stock sociological narrative of tradition and modernity is actively confusing as a scheme of explanation. Even at its most plausible – where it records a process of technical innovation and increasing productivity of labour – it is insufficient as an account of social relations and their dynamics. Linear scales of progress and affluence cannot explain the pattern of an economic formation, which is determined, rather, by its forms of property and labour. Southern society, in its formative decades, was shaped by its articulation of two compatible but nonetheless distinct modes of production. A modest capitalism led the urban economy, at a low level of industrialization, and an important sector of agriculture. But the greater part of Irish rural space was dominated by a class of smallholding farmers, who, indeed, were only partly (and sometimes not at all) involved in commodity production. Thus, most Irish economic property was not capitalist, and the salient labouring class was not proletarian: the social dominant was a free peasantry. That kind of production is typologically anterior to capitalism, but this peasantry was the opposite of residual: it was in fact the youngest of the Southern social classes, the cause – motor and object – of the anti-colonial struggle, with a special role in the self-definition of the new nation.

This constellation of property and labour governed the traditionalist modernity of culture and politics in the independent state. Catholicism would have had a salient role in any version of the new society: it was, along with sport, the main mark of collective severance from Anglo-British cultural norms. But Vatican teaching also validated the modal social experience of the countryside, sanctifying the habitus of a class constitutively dependent on family labour services, reproving material acquisitiveness and affirming the frugal equality of the spirit, deploring the antagonism of capitalism and labour in the name of a higher authority. Land and religion confirmed the kinship-household bond as the cell and model of social existence: the nation-as-family. Although Southern democracy has been impressive by international standards, the familiar tropisms of public discourse suggest a different model of civic virtue. Personalist, to the point of indulging cussed anarchism, but also conformist; given to plain speaking but not to a commensurate tolerance; easy-going yet prone to resentment and panic: these have been collective character traits of an Irish populism, not so much democratic or egalitarian as familistic, in keeping with the patriarchal custom of the country.

They have been correspondingly marked features of official political life, promoting and rationalizing the practice of clientelism and patronage, and a historic weakness for charismatic leaders. The formal symmetry of the two major parties, Fianna Fáil and Fine Gael, shaped in factional warfare, and the shared mock-heroism of their nomenclature have often been construed as signs of fixation and archaism – the Irish *misère*. But here is a textbook illustration of the way in which stock expectations of the modern generate their own mysteries. Dublin's political formula has not been symmetrical or socially schizoid or, least of all, immobilist. It formed in conditions where capital-labour antagonisms were structurally secondary to the differentiated interests of property as a whole. One party – Fianna Fáil, Ireland's version of the Indian Congress – dominated the new state and society, according to a national-populist formula that subsumed the lesser producing class under the greater – waged labour under proprietary labour – and consolidated one kind of property as a secure political base for the expansion and eventual superordination of another. The only crucial test of a bourgeois party is whether it can create a secure and fertile environment for capital, and by that measure the formula has held good. The post-Treaty parties have not merely survived in spite of some normal demand of history: they prosper, now with negotiable support from liberal formations to their right and left, as loyal stewards of a class society that shaped them and which they, at length, remade.

The party order as a whole, like the culture, is a living palimpsest of a history that notions of the modern and the traditional cannot adequately describe or explain – or, it then follows, evaluate, in whatever sense. The attempt to judge in those terms quickly turns metaphysical, as the course of argument forces one after another discrimination between what is really or not really modern or traditional or Irish. The heterogeneous social interests that move in that discursive space can seldom, in any concrete situation, be identified and judged in that way. What are the main meanings of Ireland's modernity? It has become a more liberal society, legalizing contraception and divorce, setting an advanced standard in its statutory acknowledgement of equality for homosexuals, and admitting the further reproductive right of abortion as a crux that cannot forever be wished abroad. These changes are basic gains in the long march towards a fully secular public life – a goal made the more, not the less, necessary by Catholic demographic advantage. However, this civic liberalism progresses in irregular step with another kind, the canonical neo-liberalism of late-twentieth century capitalist economics, which sponsors altogether less appealing forms of freedom and diversity: desublimated corporate aggression, deepening insecurity in employment, increasing social inequality, the stripping of public assets and the withering of collective provision, the raw anarchy of existence in the margins of affluence: the commodification of social relations as a whole. This second kind of liberalism – it has to be said – has favoured the first, though not in a systematic, let alone committed way: its moral substance is the practical indifference of everyday capitalism. Membership of the European Union has greatly facilitated both. And in a small country, once 'British' and now 'European', where the typical neo-liberal turn of recent decades has coincided with a late, primary consolidation of capitalism as such, producing an accelerated modernization, the new cultural constellation has been bewitching. With the decline in smallholding agriculture and the increasing generality of commodity relations, the family has lost its old potency, both as a material discipline and as the template of the social bond. The image of the nation-as-family, evoking a world of custom and duty, has now been over-printed by the brighter, colder image of the nation-as-market, in a world of rights and opportunities. The crisis of the old patriarchal legality in the sphere of gender and sexuality is an organic part of the restructuring of the society's economic relations, and the figure that condenses them is 'youth'. This is perhaps the key term in media chronobabble about the new South, and although demographic realities encourage its use, they do not justify its functioning as a Barthesian myth.

Youth rather than *young*, for the meaning is social, not biological, and the implicit contrast is not *old* but *parent*, or *father*. The ascendancy of youth then figures the historical recession of a privileged popular class whose legendary 'self'-reliance depended on the labour of biddable women and children, and the new-found legitimacy of individual autonomy as a social value. Autonomy, perhaps, but more precisely individualism, for youth *culture* is arguably more intensively commodified than any other. As a popular phenomenon, it is not more than a half-century old; prior to that, only the children of the well-off might expect a youth in the relevant sense: a discretionary interlude between the attainment of psycho-physical maturity and the entry into adult obligations. Youth culture is, then, a genuine creation of capitalism, and also one of its most lucrative and ideologically potent: it is a Chinese market in desire.[22] This welcome decompression of sensibility, with all its liberating impulses, is a literal index of consumer-capitalist share values, for which, willy-nilly, it furnishes politico-ideological insurance in the form of a new post-patriarchal market populism. The cultural foregrounding of youthfulness idealizes an achieved process of economic and social change, while mystifying its character and further possibilities. 'Youth' is a time-honoured symbol of renewal – but nothing more than that. In one way valorizing historical uncertainty, the trope of youth-as-change also trivializes its possible outcomes. Youth passes quickly, even now, and its likelier social effect, akin to its modal biological function, is not transformation but adaptive reproduction: more and more of the never quite the same. In this way, change is naturalized – imaged as irresistible, in its persistence but also in its character and limits, which are, rather evidently, those of the capitalism that now powers it. Ireland's richly unruly, eclectic youth culture, as appropriated for the dominant imagery, is indeed mythic, a sensuous emblem for the ideology of modernization. The nation as market, the market as youth, youth as the spirit of the new nation: this festive ring-dance of meanings is Irish capital's rite of spring.

The appeal to the modern may help to broaden the campaigning fronts of feminist and other reforming social movements; it may ease the guilt of those who inflict generational wounds, and numb the pain of those who suffer them; but above all it serves the purposes of the dominant classes and their political and cultural élites. Much like the autotelic nation of an earlier socioeconomic phase, Irish modernity encodes a specific order of interests and possibilities, whose historical space is that of an emancipated capitalism. There is the promise, and there is the iron limitation. The considerable hegemonic value of the emerging culture lies in its availability as a transfiguring representation of capitalism, which is the only unambiguously emancipated agency in the new order, in so far as its historic momentum goes unresisted, and 'modern' is the word that turns the trick. The more garrulous the talk of the 'youthful', 'dynamic', 'progressive' new Ireland, the greater the need for the left to attend to the discrepant, contradictory realities of a small, in some ways vulnerable European capitalism, and to clarify the terms of a discoverable socialism beyond its old and new oppressions. Here is an exercise for all of us. Define your situation, interests, goals and means; name your allies and your adversaries; do this, but without once saying 'modern'.

4

I say 'exercise' rather than 'test', because it may be that success is beyond our present power of imagining. A last recollection comes to mind. The preceding section of this essay was partly written in Brazil, during a visit to the University of São Paulo, where I was teaching a course on the British New Left and the Formation of Cultural Studies. My students were appropriately attentive to the politico-intellectual history I was trying to construct, but far more interested in the cultural concepts themselves, which they insisted on striking against what they called 'Brazilian reality'. Again and again, they sounded the theme of 'misplaced ideas', the coinage of the literary critic Roberto Schwarz, from a famous essay in which he elucidated the incongruous functioning of European liberalism in the culture of slave-owning Brazil.[23] Schwarz's principal literary interest, over some thirty years, has been the novelist Machado de Assis, and, as it happened, the third and final volume of his study appeared during my stay in São Paulo. The event was marked by a long newspaper interview in which, as well as elucidating Machado's 'poisoned dialectic', he offered a long-awaited assessment of Brazil's once-Marxist, neo-liberal president, Fernando Henrique Cardoso, suggesting, by this sly collocation, that modernization Brazilian-style was yet another misplaced idea, that Cardoso was, as it were, a real-life character out of Machado.[24]

The broader collage of circumstances in which I now found myself had something novelistic about it too, renewing the force of the old paradox about realist art, that only reality is allowed to exaggerate. I had not expected that the ideas of Raymond Williams and the rest could simply travel to Brazil, like so many English tourists, and find their new environment either perfectly familiar or perfectly other, though, characteristically, I seldom foresaw the likely points of disturbance. Although I half-knew what I wanted to write about Ireland, I expected difficulty, and was not pleasantly surprised. What I could not have foreseen was how these matters would be linked and thematized by Schwarz's ironic commentary on contemporary Brazilian culture and its misplaced ideas. Should Irish modernization not be read in the same way, as a decorative ideology ill-adapted to the local reality? What might Marxism have to say about that, or that about Marxism? Part three is my semi-improvised response to those questions.

Modernization Irish-style is not a misplaced idea: it has a recognizable social logic and mediates an appropriate array of social effects, in the reconfigured economy of the later century. It is rather an idea that *misplaces us* – all of us, Irish or not, in one sense or another – in relation to our historical practice. We may not confidently infer from this that it can simply be set aside, as a falsified claim. Modernity, as a form of temporalization, a way of experiencing history, was born with capitalism and will live at least as long as it – that is to say, it is not about to disappear. However, even if it is insurmountable as a category of practical subjectivity, the modern may still be known and criticized from within – not dissolved, but suspended – and that is the promise of Marxism, which, in so far as it holds on to the difficult idea of a countermodernity, resists progress and custom alike, in the name of a liberating uncertainty. The modern, with its self-consuming future, is the enemy of the contemporary, which is all we ever really have. As we might say, the present lasts a long time.

1998

MARXIST LITERARY CRITICISM
Past and Future

'Marxist literary criticism' seems a plain enough description, yet none of its terms is self-explanatory. 'Literature' and 'criticism' no longer mark off a stable community of interest and procedure; and the meanings of 'Marxism' continue to be the most disturbing in twentieth-century culture. Some preliminary clarifications are necessary, therefore, both for practical guidance and as tokens of interest and intent. *Literary criticism* is used colloquially here, referring to any kind of discourse on written texts – mainly those made for reading but also texts written for oral delivery or performance, and above all the kind of text conventionally assigned to 'literature'. It includes theoretical, historical and sociological styles of work as well as the various kinds of textual analysis, avoiding strict classification or discrimination of rank. *Marxism* might be encapsulated in the manner of the later Engels as (i) a general theory of modes of production, the forms of their development, crisis and transformation, and their structuring role in human history; and specifically (ii) a theory of the capitalist mode of production, its fundamental classes and their antagonisms, and of the organic relationship between working-class struggles against capital and the historical possibility of socialism.[1] These have been the constitutive themes of historical materialism, the 'real foundation' upon which the specifically cultural constructions of Marxist thought have been raised. They are the minima of a Marxist identity, the core elements that make it meaningful to speak of a tradition at all. Yet they have never had the character of a singular, univocal doctrinal code: even in the darkest years of the twentieth century, diversity and contention did not disappear from Marxist intellectual life. And besides, a Marxist culture is always something more than its inherited canon, various and evolving as this may be. Marxism is historical not merely because it is subject to change but because it is itself fully a part of the history it seeks to understand and act in.

History is as much a part of Marxism as Marxism is of it; they inhabit one another, in unending tension. This proposition has general force, as a principle of theory and method; and in today's conditions, where the idea of a *contemporary* Marxism – that is, a Marxism that does not merely linger – may be thought at least oxymoronic, its challenge is also ethico-political, and even existential. The critical culture of the past quarter-century has been, by any comparative reckoning, a turbulent one. The merest inventory of the ideas, forces, projects and institutions whose time has come or gone since 1968 is a sufficient index of this. Wholly involved in this turbulence, contemporary

Marxist literary criticism has not been and is not a stable entity, or even a phase in the history of a settled lineage. It is a field of forces drawn and redrawn by the shifting contentions of all four defining terms. The decades ahead will be especially testing for Marxism in all its forms and areas of engagement, including this one. Marxism has not, after all, 'arrived' – nor yet has it departed. It persists, theoretically and practically, in a continuing history whose outcome is uncertain.

The past is the prehistory of the present, and, as tradition, it is itself an actor in the present; without historical understanding we can neither explain our own situation nor evaluate the options it offers us. In returning, as I do in this essay, to analyse the courses of Marxist literary thinking over the past 150 years, I am attempting to clarify the conditions, terms and purposes of future work in a collective development of thought. This history is not easy to construct. Even a brief reminder of its outlines – all that is offered here – must proceed by caveat. Three phases of initiative and elaboration can be distinguished, but it is misleading to imagine these as stages in an upward movement, or even as separable periods in a less triumphalist sequence. All the familiar schemes of history occur here: development and decline; continuation, but also break and recombination; supersession, but also stasis and return. With such cautions kept in view, it is possible to mark a *classical or scientific-socialist* phase, initiated by Marx and Engels and continuing strongly into the first half of the twentieth century; a self-styled *critical* phase originating in the 1920s, maturing and diversifying over the next three decades and establishing, by the 1960s, a curious 'norm of heterodoxy'; and then a phase at first pledged to a *critical classicism*, announced in the early 1960s and vigorously propagated in the succeeding decade, but then rapidly and variously redefined under such spacious headings as 'materialism' and 'anti-humanism', in a process that continues today.

Classical Perspectives: Towards Scientific Socialism

Marx and Engels were deeply cultivated men, interested in the implications of their theory for the status and practice of literature. The standard compendium of their writings 'on literature and art' runs to some 500 pages (and the authoritative account of Marx's personal literary culture is nearly as long).[2] No developed theory emerges from them. A number of latter-day theorists have maintained that the basic categories of historical materialism themselves imply an aesthetics, but in substantive terms so deeply contrasted that, paradoxically, they serve mainly to emphasize the philological fact of absence.[3] However, a general theory of social structures and their transformations bears with the utmost logical force on our understanding of the cultural practices within them; and the associated politics, assessing every kind of cultural commitment in the terms of classes and their struggles, can scarcely forgo comment on the actual and possible courses of literary production. These minimum considerations framed Marx and Engels's diverse writings on culture, and while they do not amount to a theory, they defined a perspective that has held ever since.

The terms of the perspective were both analytic and political, and in both senses *critical*. Historical materialism would refound the knowledge of cultural life, asserting its own basic theses and their implications against received understandings; and would clarify and promote cultural tendencies favouring the objectives of socialism as theory and movement. Engels's writings furnish the plainer and more systematic instances of this commitment. In a text like *Ludwig Feuerbach and the End of Classical German Philosophy* (1886), he set out to illustrate the material reality of 'spirit' as one activity among others in an integrated social-historical process governed ultimately by the dynamics of modes of production. His late sequence of letters to Bloch, Schmidt, Mehring and others sought to defend and enhance the explanatory claims of historical materialism, distancing Marx and himself from any belief in mechanical determinism and arguing that the evidence of autonomy in intellectual life, far from controverting their basic claims, was itself a specific effect of historical development in their sense.[4] A structured culture was not necessarily a passive one, Engels maintained, and such episodes in constructive aesthetics as his letters to Lassalle and Harkness bear witness to the quite practical spirit of his claim. The broad realism he advocated here (as did Marx in his own response to Lassalle's play) was not a matter of 'reflection', nor simply an animated version of theoretical abstractions, but a project of historical construction achieved in a critical deployment of the repertoire of dramatic and narrative forms.[5]

However, the single most telling adumbration of the classic perspective occurs in the closing passage of Marx's draft 'Introduction to the Critique of Political Economy' (1857), where he turns from his main concern to reflect on a crux in literary history:

> In the case of the arts, it is well known that certain periods of their flowering are out of all proportion to the general development of society, hence also to the material foundation, the skeletal structure as it were, of its organization. For example, the Greeks compared to the moderns or also Shakespeare. It is even recognized that certain forms of art, e.g., the epic, can no longer be produced in their world epoch-making, classical stature as soon as the production of art, as such, begins; that is, that certain significant forms within the realm of the arts are possible only at an undeveloped stage of artistic development. If this is the case with the relation between different kinds of art within the realm of the arts, it is already less puzzling that it is the case in the relation of the entire realm to the general development of society. The difficulty consists only in the general formulation of these contradictions. As soon as they have been specified, they are already clarified.
>
> Let us take e.g. the relation of Greek art . . . to the present time. It is well known that Greek mythology is not only the arsenal of Greek art but also its foundation. Is the view of nature and of social relations on which the Greek

imagination and hence Greek [mythology] is based possible with self-acting mule spindles and railways and locomotives and electrical telegraphs? What chance has Vulcan against Roberts & Co., Jupiter against the lightning-rod and Hermes against the Crédit Mobilier? All mythology overcomes and dominates and shapes the forces of nature in the imagination and by the imagination; it therefore vanishes with the advent of real mastery over them. . . . Greek art presupposes Greek mythology. . . . This is its material. . . .

But the difficulty lies not in understanding that the Greek arts and epic are bound up with certain forms of social development. The difficulty is that they still afford us artistic pleasure and that in a certain respect they count as a norm and as an unattainable model.

A man cannot become a child again, or he becomes childish. But does he not find joy in the child's naiveté, and must he himself not strive to reproduce its truth at a higher stage? . . . Why should not the historic childhood of humanity, its most beautiful unfolding, as a stage never to return, exercise an eternal charm? . . . The charm of [Greek] art for us is not in contradiction to the undeveloped stage of society on which it grew. [It] is its result, rather, and is inextricably bound up, rather, with the fact that the unripe social conditions under which it arose, and could alone arise, can never return.[6]

The very occasion of these sentences is eloquent: a study in political economy turns suddenly towards cultural analysis, illustrating the inborn drive of a strong general theory to assert itself throughout its domain of application. That this drive is critical rather than dogmatic is attested by the distinctive movement of Marx's reflection. There is little here of Engels's didactic manner. Rather, Marx opens with an evocation of a basic materialist analysis, which he takes to be persuasive, and then presses on to 'the real problem' presented by his exemplary case: not the historical conditions of *formation* of a culture but those of its *persistence*. Writing in the months before 'the materialist conception of history' received its first, classic formulation, Marx was already imagining the analytic agendas of his posterity a century on. But the bathos of his conclusion tells a less heroic story. The appeal to 'the historic childhood of humanity', a mystified trope bearing no substantive relation to his own concepts, prompts a second look at the concrete terms of his particular case, which in truth was less a piece of evidence than a preconstituted cultural topic. Marx's theoretical insight was valid and important: the problem of persistence (or active anachronism, or tradition) is central to any history of politics or culture. But his phrasing of this 'real problem' in fact rewrote one of the great commonplaces of literary culture in his day: the belief that ancient Greek culture was 'a norm and an unattainable model'.[7]

That truth has long since passed away, as has the genre of explanation that it called forth; the theoretical issue remains. The fusion of the two in Marx's prose illustrates a general point about the terms and conditions of Marxist intellectual work. Here, as in the areas of their more emphatic concern, Marx and Engels drafted a prospectus of theoretical and historical inquiry: what is implied in the iconoclastic thesis that literature, like all cultural phenomena, is fundamentally determined by its economic conditions of existence? How can this claim be substantiated, and in what kind of analytic procedure? And what would be the corresponding bent of a socialist literary politics concerned not only to explain and interpret but also to develop a partisan tendency in the practical life of culture? As rational ventures, such questions are properly tackled in the light of critical reason alone. However, any intellectual practice internalizes its cultural conditions of existence to some extent – even when, like Marx's, it aims at 'the unsparing criticism of all that exists', the political and cultural conditions in and against which it moves are always already a part of its own being.

So it was that as a succeeding generation pursued the effort to extend and systematize the theoretical work of Marx and Engels, they did so under the banner of 'science'. The intellectual project that they sought to further – perhaps to complete – was irresistible in its grand, simple ambition. The middle years of the nineteenth century had witnessed decisive advances in the historical sciences of nature – Lyell's geology and Darwin's evolutionary biology. They also saw major initiatives in the scientific study of social organization, in its oldest forms (Morgan's ethnology) and its most modern (Mill's *Principles of Political Economy* or Marx's *Capital*). Against a background of prolific capitalist development and as yet unbroken liberal confidence, an entrancing – and attainable – horizon came into view: it now seemed possible to make a concerted scientific assault on all history, to devise a scheme of knowledge unified in method and integrated in its results, capable of mastering the evolutionary and structural ascent from protein to poetry in a single cognitive operation. This positivist goal was pursued in more than one kind of philosophical or political conviction – Spencer's *Evolutionary Sociology* and Duhring's *System* are two of its better-remembered initiatives – and in Marxism, too, the spirit of scientific encyclopaedism worked strongly. The great expression of Marxist positivism was by all standards a latecomer: Kautsky's *Materialist Conception of History* (1927). However, in its very *passéisme* and its status as the culminating effort of fifty years' intellectual labour, this treatise of nearly 2,000 pages bore witness to the deep, early formation of its author.

Art found its necessary but modest place in this macroscopic scheme; while the nature of the work dictated some consideration of it, the bent of Kautsky's personal interest ensured that this would be minimal. The cultural temper of late-nineteenth-century Marxism is more fully illustrated in the writings of his Russian peer and co-thinker G. V. Plekhanov. The rhetorical mode of his *Unaddressed Letters* (a sequence begun in 1899 and never completed) itself embodies the didacticism of much Marxist work in this period: suasion is as important a goal as discovery. Plekhanov takes for granted the power of art as a value and so sees it as a particularly rewarding test of his 'general view of history': a science that can raise its standard on the highest ground of culture must be recognized as a great intellectual power. His analysis recapitulates the putative order of life, beginning with the natural world as seen by Darwin, moving on to an ethnological account of early social forms, and thus to a materialist social psychology in which art appears as a primarily 'utilitarian' activity conditioned by the 'mentality' appropriate to a given 'situation', whose determining component is the forces and relations of production. Plekhanov's contribution to 'scientific theorizing on aesthetics' was ambiguous in outcome. The manner and substance of his analysis were at odds with the prevailing ethos of art, but its political suggestions were quite unthreatening. Positivism in theory led, here as also in the later *Art and Social Life* (1912), to fatalism in practice. The idea of intervention in the course of artistic practice did not arise.[8]

Within years, however, intervention had become the leitmotiv of Marxist discourse on art. The scientific encyclopaedism of Kautsky and Plekhanov was conventionally honoured by the younger generation of theoreticians, but not much imitated. Political organization, the strategy and tactics of revolutionary struggle and the awesome novelty of socialist construction were the fated preoccupations of Lenin, Trotsky, Luxemburg and their peers: the topics of their most important writings and the determining context of their thinking about art and culture. Lenin's articles on Tolstoy (1908–11) were polemical in character, political interventions in the ideological controversies of the anti-Tsarist revolution. Trotsky's later *Literature and Revolution* (1923) was a more ambitious work, by someone in whom artistic interests ran more deeply; but again its guiding concerns were the practical ones of cultural orientation and policy in the new revolutionary society. The cultural vision of the Proletkult movement was indeed bold and systematic, but in a spirit that Kautsky and Plekhanov expressly repudiated: with its voluntaristic commitment to a 'proletarian' culture wholly new and disconnected from the past, it was antithetical to the positivism of the elders.

The most significant literary-theoretical initiatives of these years were not Marxist in origin, though their bearers were often actively revolutionary in sympathy and in some cases worked for an intellectual rapprochement with Marxism. These were the work of the trend that came to be known as Formalism. The shaping context of Formalism was the brilliant culture of late Imperial Russia, with its pattern of innovation and departure right across the sciences and arts. Its specific identity emerged in the confluence of two such currents of innovation: linguistic and literary research and the avant-garde poetry of the Futurists. Led by such figures as Viktor Shklovsky, Yuri Tynjanov, Boris Eikhenbaum and Roman Jakobson, the Formalists fashioned a 'scientific' agenda for poetics: a new object ('literariness') with its specific modes of existence and change, a distinctive cultural motivation ('making strange'), and, implicitly, a new canon of criticism and literary practice. Formalist themes made their contribution to the extraordinary intellectual and artistic turbulence of early Soviet Russia, and were in turn remade by it; towards the end of the 1920s there emerged a current of 'post-formalism' associated with the names of Bakhtin, Vološinov and Medvedev, deeply critical of its parent tradition and closer to historical materialism. But the time for free debate had passed. Marxism was being reduced to a code of intellectual rectitude, as Stalin moved to eliminate what remained of political opposition and cultural pluralism in party and society. The new orientation was both exclusive and traditionalist, fusing the cultural traditions of the Tsarist state with those of its intellectual opponents in an official doctrine of ('socialist') realism.

By the middle 1930s, the situation of Marxist culture had been transformed. The corpus of revolutionary political thought had been expurgated and codified as 'Leninism', Marx's theory of history had achieved the metaphysical finish of 'dialectical materialism' – and both were in the keeping of a state now embarked on a course of domestic terror. In response to the gathering European crisis, the Communist International called for the creation of people's fronts whose overriding purpose would be to oppose fascism and war. This was the narrow and deceptive setting in which the important intellectual radicalizations of the 1930s occurred. Popular-frontism promoted the etiquettes of open cultural dialogue but did little to renew the spirit of rational debate. At worst, the studied forbearance of Communist 'humanism' was a sectarian's gambit, the tax that truth must pay to circumstance. The truly critical intelligences of the Communist tradition worked far from its authorized venues, victims of Stalin's purges (Trotsky) or fascist repression (Gramsci). Airless and embattled, this was not an environment in which intellectual energies ran strong and free. But let the life of Christopher Caudwell serve as a cameo of how much was ventured and how much lost in those years.

Caudwell was perhaps the last notable encyclopaedist in the Marxist tradition. Reprocessing the enormous yield of his reading in natural sciences, philosophy, anthropology, psychoanalysis and literature by means of his new-found theoretical apparatus, he attempted to synthesize a Marxist vision of reality. Physics and poetry – the fundamental science and the most elevated art of language – were, significantly, the matter of his most elaborate studies; a book on the novel and two volumes devoted to the logic of capitalism's 'dying culture' stood beside them. All this and more in something like four years. But Caudwell was a devoted rank-and-file Communist, not merely a radicalized literatus; and so he joined the International Brigades in Spain, where, within weeks, he died in action, not yet thirty years old.

Critical Departures

However, Marxism was already something more than the theoretical outlook of organized communism (official or other). Numerous intellectual varieties had emerged in the revolutionary climate of 1917–23 and survived, sometimes in the margins of party life but more often in quite different settings, where they followed distinctive lines of development. Similar episodes of diversification were to occur after the Second World War. The generic resemblance in these minority Marxisms was their avowedly *critical* character, and this in two senses. They offered a philosophical critique of what was now commonly known as 'orthodox' Marxism; and their intellectual energies were devoted primarily to culture, above all to art and literature. Whereas Plekhanov's generation had tended to address 'the literary question' (a label it might aptly have borne) as a dramatic test case for a general theory, the exponents of 'critical' Marxism made it their special concern. Out of their various initiatives came a wealth of theoretical, historical and textual analysis; entire modes, genres, periods and movements were studied; 'culture' was anatomized, both as an idea and as a changing historical formation; there was recurring controversy over the ethics and politics of contemporary art. The long reign of party dogmatism, through the decades of Stalinism proper and beyond, was also a golden age of Marxist aesthetics.[9]

To generalize further than this is to risk error. 'Critical Marxism' is at best an ideal-typical construction with no perfect incarnation, at worst a legend. The short-list of its variably ascribed membership is itself a caution: Georg Lukács; the so-called Frankfurt School of Theodor Adorno, Herbert Marcuse and others; Walter Benjamin; Jean-Paul Sartre; Lucien Goldmann – and, sometimes, the earlier Raymond Williams. Not a great deal unites these heterogeneous thinkers except their distance from 'orthodoxy'; and even then it must be added that the distinction between 'critical' and 'orthodox' Marxism has commonly been broadcast in deeply uncritical ways. However, there are real relationships and affinities here, defining important shifts in Marxism's cultural sensibility.

The 'critical' tradition yielded nothing to the 'orthodox' in the measure of intellectual ambition, but its projects were normally conceived in a different register. The temper of Plekhanov's time had been positivist: the paragon of knowledge was natural science imagined as the progressive disclosure, by induction, of a law-bound reality. The answering appeal of the 'critical' tradition was to the philosophical legacy of Hegel – less to 'materialism' than to 'dialectics'. 'The truth is the whole', Hegel had declared, so epitomizing his vision of history as a dynamic unity. The method proper to Marxism, Lukács continued, in the inspirational text of this tradition, *History and Class Consciousness* (1923), is 'the point of view of totality'.[10]

Lukács was in important respects a deviant among 'critical' Marxists. He was a lifelong Communist, notoriously willing to pay a heavy intellectual price for his party membership when circumstances demanded it; and the signature of his literary studies from the later 1920s onwards was an exclusive sponsorship of realism, which intensified the appearance of conformism. Yet the pattern of his intellectual development suggests a different emphasis. Lukács came to Marxism as a relatively mature professional intellectual with already-formed commitments in the philosophical and artistic arenas of his day; his early writings belong, by his own account, to the late-Romantic culture of 'despair'. Similarly, Walter Benjamin's idiom was lastingly shaped by his early interest in Judaic theology and French symbolism. Herbert Marcuse's political conversion came early, through involvement in the German revolutionary crisis of 1918–19, but his counterpart intellectual orientations were to avant-garde art and Heidegger's phenomenology. Theodor Adorno learned musicology from Berg and Webern and wrote a critical study of Kierkegaard before gravitating to Marxism in the later 1920s. Lukács's aggressive anti-modernism was less egregious than it may appear to have been in this setting. Modernism, as it featured in his historical design, was the subjectivist other of a more enduring negative preoccupation: the para-scientific culture of *naturalism*. His advocacy of realism was, among more familiar things, a modified continuation of his early rebellion against bourgeois positivism.

Just as once Marxist theory had been forwarded as the culmination of a wider movement of scientific enlightenment, so now it was reconstrued in the terms of a far less confident, more conflict-ridden cultural phase. 'Critical' Marxism took shape in the tumult of Europe's second Thirty Years War.[11] It is normally, and correctly, maintained that the privileged phenomena of 'critical' reflection were those to which any alert and responsible Marxism would have turned its attention. The containment and reversal of revolution; the anti-thetical novelties of avant-gardism and 'the culture industry'; the dialectics of liberal traditions in the era of fascism; the courses of subjectivity in landscapes of organized happiness, and the meaning of reason itself in conditions of 'scientific' barbarism: these historical realities explain and vindicate the agendas of the new Marxisms, and the ethos of paradox and tragedy that set their characteristic tone. What must be added, however, and with equal emphasis, is that bourgeois culture thematized its crises for itself, in philosophical and aesthetic modes that actively formed the intellectuals who went on to create the new 'critical' repertoire. The achievements of Lukács, Adorno, Benjamin and Marcuse – to cite only these – are unforgettable. To them twentieth-century Marxism owes its boldest synopses of intellectual and artistic history, its most acute assessments of culture in developed capitalism, its whole sense of what liberation from such a condition might demand and promise. But this work should not be abstracted as the reward of a heroically unorthodox insistence on the moment of the new; rather, it made articulate the internalized dialogue of historical-materialist tradition with self-critical bourgeois culture in a distinctively modernist Marxism.[12]

Frankfurtian Critical Theory, the leading form of this tradition, remained productive long after the Second World War, and became deeply influential both on its native ground, where Adorno – returned from wartime exile in New York and California – taught and wrote for a further twenty years, and in the USA, where Marcuse went on to do his most important work (becoming, for a season, notorious as the 'prophet' of the student revolt). The post-war period also saw new critical departures, this time originating in France, in the work of Jean-Paul Sartre and Lucien Goldmann. Goldmann was a direct descendant of the inter-war tradition. For him, still more than for Adorno or Benjamin, Lukács's early writings were a key reference. Drawing on these and on his engagement with Piaget's psychology, he elaborated an expressly 'anti-scientistic' historical sociology of literature and culture, to which he gave the name 'genetic structuralism'.[13] Sartre's affiliations were distinct, but the pattern of his relations with Marxism was, if anything, hyperbolically typical. He entered the field of Marxist culture as a formed and distinguished philosopher and novelist of 'existence'; the constant sense of his intervention was a militantly anti-positivist insistence on human freedom; his philosophical summa, the *Critique of Dialectical Reason* (1960), derived a Marxist anthropology from the rigorously individualist premises of his early thought, and his culminating achievement was a study of Flaubert, whose ethos was not merely an old preoccupation in Sartre's writing but – arguably – an element in its distinctive personality.[14]

English-language culture can claim to have contributed to the 'critical' tradition in the person of Raymond Williams. Expressly at odds with the perceived positivism of historical-materialist tradition and unconcerned to claim the title of Marxist, deeply attentive to Romantic and other ethical lineages of social criticism and particularly engaged with the positions of F. R. Leavis, Williams's earlier writings are indeed a part of this mid-century constellation. But the ulterior logic of his work led beyond its common terms, as was to become apparent in a new phase, whose opening may be marked by the symbolic date of 1968.

Critical Classicism and Since

The main intellectual energies of 'scientific socialism' were directed to the positivistic goal of demonstrating the laws of social nature. The 'totality' of the later phase, in contrast, was philosophically conceived, not so much the last horizon of discovery as the precondition of validity in critical analysis and judgement. Both kinds of work continued well after their defining periods, in both pure and hybrid forms, and neither tradition is spent. However, by the later 1960s, the culture of Marxist theory was entering a new, and fateful, phase of reconstruction. The signature of the third phase, as of the first, was 'science', though now without the cosmological inflection of the nineteenth century; like the second, the new phase was to be 'critical', though not in the spirit of Hegel, who now assumed the role of ceremonial outcast. The intellectual agenda announced by the French Communist philosopher, Louis Althusser, dictated a 'return to Marx', or, precisely, to the science of history that must at last be disengaged from the heterogeneous mass of Marx's writings and their posterity of unrigorous commentary – in a phrase, a *critical classicism*.

The motives and conditions of this new departure were in significant measure political. Althusser's unfamiliar, often scandalizing Marxism – an 'anti-humanist', 'anti-historicist' 'theoretical practice' formed and sustained in a 'break' with the ordinary world of ideology – was deliberately pitched against what he saw as the mistaken bearings of official communism at home and internationally. But its main register was philosophical, and its decisive effects were felt in the intellectual sphere. Althusser's most important substantive intervention in historical materialism was a new analysis of the canonical 'base-superstructure' relation, an abiding crux in literary and other cultural theory.[15] Marx's 'totality' was structurally complex, he insisted. It contained no master contradiction to which all social reality could be reduced, whether along a chain of mechanical effects (the positivist error) or as simple expression (the characteristic assumption of left Hegelianism). It was, rather, a dynamic ensemble of 'relatively autonomous' practices, each possessing a 'specific effectivity' and entering with all the others into 'overdetermined' configurations (or 'conjunctures'), which the economy determined only 'in the last instance'. The immediate implication and the promise of Althusser's rereading were obvious. It was unnecessary, and probably mistaken, to analyse literature as the complicated appearance of the essentially simple reality of classes and their struggles. Rather, it must be grasped as a distinct practice, carried on by specific means and with specific ideological effects, within an always complex social history. The further implication, half-silenced by the characteristic apocalypticism of Althusserian discourse but soon to make itself heard with lasting effect, was that while historical materialism was the general science of history, it was not therefore theoretically competent to construct the 'regional' sciences of specific historical practices: the definitive entry into scientificity entailed renunciation of the belief in Marxism as a self-sufficient world view.

Althusser's opening was quickly taken. His collaborator Pierre Macherey ventured a specific theory of literary production, and Terry Eagleton followed, at a critical distance, with a more comprehensive analysis centred on the notion of the literary as work in and on ideology.[16] An Althusserian pattern of intellectual dependency was also visible in these ventures. Where Althusser had paid some attention to structural linguistics and was substantially committed to psychoanalysis, so both Macherey and Eagleton appealed to structuralist and kindred traditions in linguistics and poetics, and to a Freud who seemed exemplary as a reader of texts born out of antagonism. Of course, such borrowings were neither so new nor so distinctive as legend would have it. The history of Marxist attraction to psychoanalysis is a long and varied one: reference to Freud was canonical in the Frankfurt tradition (which seeded a remarkable synthesis of Marxist and psychoanalytic theory in the form of Marcuse's visionary *Eros and Civilization*[17]). Italy witnessed a wholly independent, and rather earlier, development of anti-Hegelian Marxism under the aegis of Galvano Della Volpe, whose aesthetic treatise *Critique of Taste* (1960) made systematic use of structural linguistics.[18] And Franco Moretti, a critic of Della Volpean background whose early work coincides with these Althusserian excursions, was from the outset closely, though quite differently, engaged with formalist and structuralist poetics and with psychoanalysis.[19] Nevertheless, it was only in the early 1970s, and most often in Althusserian accents, that reference to linguistics and psychoanalysis became habitual in Marxist literary theorizing. The 'return to Marx', in this intellectual zone, meant a turning out into a new phase of inquiry and debate.

The work that now began to appear was, by any comparative standard, remarkable in its versatility and ambition. The analytic potential of a Marxist-psychoanalytic-semiotic trinity, promoted in France by the influential *Tel Quel* group, was explored with greatest concentration and impact in the collaborative work of the London quarterly *Screen*, which also reassessed the legacies of German and Russian revolutionary culture, in the context of its central concern with the dominant and oppositional cinemas of the present. The contrasting 'Hegelian' coloration of much North American Marxism was visible in the project of the *Telos* group, and remains so in the writings of Fredric Jameson, who, though lastingly shaped by the example of Lukács's *History and Class Consciousness*, has sustained a strong, resourceful relationship with French avant-garde theory.[20] On Hegel's home territory, meanwhile, the Frankfurt tradition was forwarded by a new generation of theorists, among them Peter Bürger, whose *Theory of the Avant-garde* renews a central concern in the work of Adorno and Benjamin.[21] The dramatic return of feminism, initially in the form of the Women's Liberation Movement, confounded every kind of common sense, not exempting that of left culture, where groups like the Marxist-Feminist Literature Collective set out to reconstruct inherited analytic and political perspectives. Within instituted literary studies, Raymond Williams's work reached a crucial point of development in the formulation of a Marxist 'cultural materialism'.[22] And the gathering significance of these eddies and currents of thought – as, in effect, a collective re-formation – was given concrete and sustained form in such journals as *Literature and History*, *Red Letters* and *Radical Philosophy*.

There were familiar ways of describing the new critical styles: they were 'sociological', 'historical' and 'political' in 'approach'. But these were reductive (and often defensive) characterizations. The diverse undertakings of this phase were far more radical in their implications – in truth, fateful for the old world of literary criticism. At their most concerted, they undermined the deep taxonomy and criteriology that founded the discipline and in this way – fitting climax in a literary battle – unmade its corporate imagination. 'Literature' and 'criticism' themselves were called into question – as, for example, in Tony Bennett's *Formalism and Marxism* and *Outside Literature*.[23] The *domain* of inquiry was now reconstructed by the inclusion of other written materials, non-'literary' or 'popular', and the formulation of wider, more demanding notions of historical 'context' – Said's mapping of orientalism or Jameson's Marxist conceptualization of postmodernism.[24] New analytic *objects* were proposed, displacing the literary as self-evident value or genus: the social formations of writing, to which Williams gave primary emphasis in his later work, or the historical-spatial morphology of its great modes.[25] The basic *norms* of analysis – say, explanation, interpretation, evaluation – were redefined or reordered or displaced altogether, in new strategies of reading. An enlarged domain, new objects, revised norms, and, framing these, new terms of identity. The emerging formation of (post-)literary studies was, in all its varieties, theoretically 'materialist'; its ethos was 'political'; and its summarizing commitment, polarized against the sovereign value of bourgeois culture, was 'anti-humanist'.

But these last paragraphs smack a little of Whig history . . . They exaggerate the institutional strength and, more important, the intellectual authority of the emerging formation – as many of its exponents have been symptomatically prone to do. And they are written as if from the confident centre of the new collective identity – which, however, has been ever less inclined to think of itself as Marxist. For those of us who remain so inclined – others will judge according to their different lights – the pattern of this third phase has been thought-provoking in more ways than one.

The defining initiatives of the new formation were launched, in Britain and the wider Anglophone world, by Marxists, with expressly Marxist intellectual and political motives. The general project of *New Left Review*, whose publishing initiatives were decisive in this, was to foster a left culture informed about its past and unbewitched by it, versatile and capable in its own socialist and other contexts; and, in doing so, to help free and focus intellectual energies for the development of a contemporary revolutionary politics. The call to 'theory', the broad rubric of 'materialism' and the always more controversial slogan of 'anti-humanism' were, in an important respect, the keywords of an ecumenical terminology intended to facilitate productive, though duly critical, exchanges with other radical movements and with the human sciences. Marxist cultural theory benefited significantly from this conjuncture of ideas and activity, learning to explore aspects of subjectivity and signification that were, with good but still limiting cause, only partially conceptualized within historical materialism strictly understood. Hybridization was one natural consequence of all this, and – irrespective of the widely differing merits of particular instances – a sign of general growth; Marxism, and more so its individual adherents, could not expect to emerge unchanged from engagements with unfamiliar ideas and demands. At the same time, it was to Marxism that the new formation owed its widest perspectives. In so far as anything united the proliferating critical culture of the early-to-middle 1970s (not only the specifically theoretical trends but also the new movements of social emancipation, and notably feminism), it was a spontaneous orientation to one or another variety of Marxist historical reason and politics. Out of this came the recognizable collective idiom of radical literary and cultural studies; but the continuity of such phatic signals as 'materialism', 'theory', 'anti-humanism' and the rest served mainly to ease a steady reordering of investments. Historical materialism was not only hybridized; it was relativized, marginalized or simply anathematized, as the heterogeneous intellectual avant-gardes of the preceding decades (eponymically: Barthes-Derrida-Foucault-Lacan) were recruited to a new canon of subversion, the counter-enlightenment thematics of 'post-struc-turalism'. The 'return to Marx' was not only a salutary turning out from Marx-ist autarky; for many it was a roundabout turning away.

As a passage of intellectual debate, this shift must be evaluated in properly conceptual terms. But as a collective tendency it calls rather for historical inter-pretation, and in this perspective, the new formation of radical literary studies appears as a creature of paradox – the paradox of its legendary moment of ori-gin, May 1968. For a whole generation of intellectual radicals, the French May was the blazing symbol of revolutionary possibility. The Cold War had ended. Imperialism was weakening, fought to a standstill in the revolutionary theatres of the Third World, challenged in its heartlands by a dramatic renewal of work-ing-class combativity and an international explosion of student revolt. Repres-sive political structures were at the point of collapse all along the periphery of bourgeois Europe, from Ireland to Greece – and perhaps also in the East, where the crisis of Stalinism was overt. In such conditions, socialist revolution seemed a quite concrete, short-term possibility. Such was the widespread expectation (and for too many of this generation, it has to be said, the crux of a tacit personal deal with history), and it proved false.

Flatly reckoned, May 1968 was after all a defeat, And the modal political experiences of its intellectual progeny were hope and set-back, misadven-ture, poisoned victories, moderated ambition encountering still more painful rebuff – a pattern that continues today. Thus, the cultural innovation of 'sixty-eight' – the making of a numerous and versatile leftist intelligentsia – was unmatched by any comparable political advance of the left or workers movement generally, with results that became unambiguous in the worsened conditions of the 1980s. Dismayed by the lengthening experience of politi-cal frustration and supported less and less by independent cultural struc-tures and practices (which, inevitably, were directly affected by the general downturn), left intellectuals became increasingly exposed to the norms and priorities of the dominant order, and particularly those of the academy, where so many of them worked. Rightly determined to master and criticize bourgeois culture on its own best terms, to challenge and, where possible, reconstruct the given order and substance of learning, at the same time they were now vulnerable to an academic remaking of their politics. In effect, political and academic desiderata became hard to distinguish. The political demand for fresh thinking could be recoded as the academy's positivistic requirement of 'progress in research'; and this, recoded in reverse, facilitated an inappropriately abstract valorization of political revision (always in the sense of greater moderation). The ambient culture of the capitalist market, in years largely voided of general challenge to its values, then sealed this com-pact in the vacuous idiom of fashion.

And so it came about that 'new' and 'old' began to circulate, tendered and accepted without irony or shame, as terms of intellectual and political judge-ment. The denominator of 'materialism' remains current but (except in the case of the 'cultural materialism' deriving from Williams) with little differential meaning other than 'not liberal-humanist but not or not really or no longer Marxist'. The 'political' posture of radical literary studies is, at worst, a residual group mannerism; more often, it combines a fanciful belief in 'subversion' *ordinaire* with a knowing disdain for revolutionary ideas, in a mutant creed that might be called anarcho-reformism. And at the centre of this subculture stands its legendary achievement, a thing that no one, of whatever particular persuasion, would have thought to design: the institutional chimera named Theory.

Theoretical work is indispensable to all fruitful inquiry, and must be defended as such. But the latter-day culture of Theory is an academic mystification, a factitious singular that tends to relativize and equalize the heterogeneous ideas it entertains, to inhibit understanding of the antagonisms and sheer incommensurabilities of the real world of theories (plural). Rational theories submit only to stronger theories, which may but also may not be newer ones, and almost certainly will not be more accommodating. But Theory, mistaking professional collegiality for a meaningful consensual standard of judgement, beckons its votaries into a 'politics' of adaptive novelty. This must seem an ungenerous summary; its net justification is that it emphasizes the need to assert the distinct identity and purposes of Marxism within radical literary studies, whose spontaneously evolving life in a narrow, unyielding environment is not necessarily a story of progress and not ever a binding pattern of conduct.[26]

Results and Prospects: Notes for Now

The historical impression offered here is of a tradition that, though strong, is not autarkic. The sub-culture of Marxism, like any other, is intertextual in character.[27] And in so far as it acts consistently in the spirit of science, Marxism acknowledges its necessary cognitive incompleteness – as Freud once observed, 'world views' are theological, not scientific goals.[28] Marxism's claim has to do with modes of production and their functioning in the structure and courses of social history. This is its power and its self-defined limitation: the first in so far as it therefore asserts a critical check on all theses concerning the social; the second in that it is, at the same time, not competent to generate an exhaustive knowledge of the social from within its own conceptual resources. Marxism has always drawn on other knowledges, whether avowedly or not. It fares better when it acknowledges its cognitive dependencies, and understands its appropriate 'world view' not as the acme of self-elaboration but as the changing horizon of sciences in critical solidarity.[29]

The same anti-triumphalist qualifications apply in internal affairs. There is no unalloyed truth of Marxism, against which to measure the deficiencies of other aspirants. Marxism's history has been irreducibly various and agonistic; nothing in that history is simply over, and the temptation to judge and act as though it were otherwise bespeaks a damaging parochialism of spirit. So then, in going on to sketch some orientations in Marxist literary studies in the years ahead, I do not claim either certainty or consensual authority. It would of course be legitimate to propose a distinctive programme, but that suggests a measure of originality that I cannot claim either. All I offer here are some annotations – at times commonplace, at others idiosyncratic – of our current theoretical culture. Their manner will seem to belie the profession of modesty. But this is partly the effect of brevity, and partly a mark of the belief that discussion is served better by clear statements, vulnerable though they may be, than by a fog of defensive qualifications.

Rhetorics in history is an inclusive but still pointed definition of our field. Rhetoric is often remembered, in this post-Romantic literary culture, as taxonomania, a tireless cataloguing of schemes and tropes, as the art of mere eloquence. But in its full ambition it was, simply, the study of language in action. Of *language* and thus of forms and meanings; of language in *action* and thus also of its occasions, purposes and effects. Invoked in this sense, the tradition of rhetoric is not merely the depository of a certain knowledge; it furnishes a critical example for the present. Specifically, it displaces without simply liquidating two persistent literary-critical cruces, which Marxism has not been spared.

The first concerns the relation between 'form' and 'content'. Everyone has learned the correct response to this metaphorical couple; yet the received solution – 'the unity of form and content' – is either gestural or tendentious. 'Form' and 'content' are alternative analytic abstractions from a singular signifying practice; the idea that they could be other than a 'unity' is the merest fiction of uncertainty, an ideological feint. What is really in question is whether the text is – or can be – in either aspect unitary in the required sense. In the tradition of rhetoric, forms are always-already meaningful and meanings are always-already shaped; discursive practice is intertextual, working in and across existing formations of sense (the topics and commonplaces, the fallacies and so on), *specific organizations of social meaning*, whose variable ratios of unity and disorder must be understood in that sense.

The second, which is the first in another aspect, concerns the relation between the text and its exterior. The notion of textual autonomy has been a tenet of literary culture in this century, and for Marxism, the chief mystification. But it is not sufficiently countered by efforts, however sophisticated, to demonstrate a relationship 'between' the text 'and' history. Textual practice is internal to history, which inhabits it. The tradition of rhetoric assumes just this: linguistic practice is discourse, situated and motivated utterance, organized in and organizing specific relations of culture. To explore the historicity of the text is, then, not simply to relate a frail singularity to the broad design of a period; it is also to investigate its direct social relations, the formations of writing and reading – and these not as 'context' or 'background' but as substantive elements of the practice itself.[30]

This theoretical orientation implies a distinctive pattern of inquiry and exposition. Marxist criticism has characteristically paid special attention to the larger units of literary history, privileging period and genre in contrast with the dominant preference for individual texts and corpuses. Lukács's *The Historical Novel* and Benjamin's *The Origin of German Tragic Drama* are classic instances. Other, less familiar objects, collective or intertextual in character, must also be written into a developing Marxist scheme: the *conventions*, as Williams terms them, the 'techniques' or topics which, forming an order distinct from the received classification of literary kinds, are the deeper organization of the culture; and the *repertoire*, the changing array of conventions, of possible and spontaneously preferred writing options, which is arguably the true actor in literary history.[31] Such undertakings tend to displace the individual text from its traditionally central position, and in doing so, disturb one of the strongest and 'politically' most serviceable intuitions of the critical profession. That is, the conviction that the normal mode of critical attention – inquiry and *also* commentary – is the reading of a given text: this *form* of discourse is the visible sign and the indispensable warrant of 'relevance'. This is, in Barthes's sense of the term, a myth, whose operation deserves a little homeopathic close reading.[32] The presiding trope in this critical convention is metaphor: the elementary distinction between the order of research and the order of exposition, familiar from all intellectual work, is occluded, the latter dissolved into the former in an expository mode that simulates a primal act of discovery. Thus, the exposition validates itself and in the same gesture naturalizes its underlying norms of inquiry. Reading is reading, and its protocols are given and validated by the kind of text being read – a text embodying the distinctive quality conveyed in one word: literature.

Literature, in its ordinary sense of an inherently valuable canon of imaginative writing, has been and remains a potent cultural value. As a norm, it has been institutionalized in public bodies and internalized by countless individuals, organizing the whole culture of writing and reading, inflecting the course of practice in other media, and validating major traditions of discourse. An enormous amount of important work has been done under its sign. The historical force and productivity of 'literature' are not in dispute; the interesting question is, rather, whether it can make a legitimate claim of privilege either as an object of analysis or as a norm of subjectivity. Balibar, Macherey, Eagleton, Bennett and Williams have been notable in maintaining – correctly – that it cannot.[33] The claim that the study of written culture should continue as the study of 'literature' is dogmatic and obscurantist. Literary studies so conceived are an authoritarian defence of certain received cultural values, within preset limits of debate and discovery. 'Literature gives us wisdom', goes one definition-cum-defence I have personally encountered. It is memorable as an act of self-exposure: the verb erases reading as an active process; 'wisdom' displaces debatable knowledge in favour of humbling revelation; and the appeal to an indeterminate 'us' simply cancels the existing order of human relations and interests. Procedural openness to the whole field of writing and a pluralist corporate ethos are the minimum conditions of genuinely 'critical' literary study. It may be that there are important and very general qualitative distinctions to be made within the material range of writing, yet it is doubtful whether 'literature' will feature among them. The scientific search for the objective properties and functions of the poetic has run a paradoxical course. 'Literariness' is both too general and too variable to fulfil its all-important specifying role: it may indeed exist and flourish in language but it does not vindicate the received hypothesis of 'literature'.[34] On the other hand, the function of 'the literary' as a norm of subjectivity seems clear. 'Literature' (more generally, 'art') is, in Freud's sense, fetishistic. Exactly in the manner of its profane counterpart, 'entertainment', it mediates a disavowal, acknowledging a process of meaning in the practice it designates, yet suggesting that such meaning is somehow not really implicated in the secular divisions of sense that are the ordinary substance of culture. The conventional riposte to the onset of 'ideological' questioning ('but as *literature* . . .') is seldom if ever the formalism that it might decently be (on the contrary: formalism in literary studies is scarcely less barbarous than 'sociology'). It is, rather, an appeal to an ideological 'elsewhere' – in literal translation, an *alibi*.

The material sign of this elsewhere is 'form', and the essence of form is 'unity' or 'closure'. The moral integrity of 'literature' is incarnated as material ('aesthetic') completeness. Again, there is no need to doubt the potent reality of this modern tradition of the aesthetic. Eagleton accords it a key role in the constitution of bourgeois culture as such, and it has been taken over and indeed reaffirmed by many Marxists, most notably Herbert Marcuse.[35] Rhetorical closure, connoting unity, harmony, reconciliation, has been the sovereign norm of most artistic practice for two centuries or more, as also of the world of critical commentary and valuation in which it lives. Deviant rhetorics are recent and minoritarian, or, in one sense or another, primitive, and in all cases disturbing to deep collective intuitions. But closure is, in strict principle, unattainable. The practical infinity of language and the intertextual character of signifying processes forbid it, in aesthetic as in all other sense-making activity. Even the most concentrated trope of language, the pun, is, precisely, equivocal: it is, according to perspective, a binding of meaning, or an uncontrollable accretion of it – like a tryst made awkward by unwanted company. The action of 'the aesthetic' has been valued by Marcuse and, latterly, Jameson for its utopian moment – the closure effect as anticipating a healed existence. It can be interpreted, less grandly, as a privileged occasion of unconscious desire – artistic language as a recovery of infantile pleasures. But such proposals give no comfort to traditionalism. 'The aesthetic' and 'the literary', so defined, are non-identical with the canons defended in their name. Anything but norms, they bear witness rather to the inextinguishable strain of perversity in social life.[36]

Reading as well as writing is implicated in the vicissitudes of 'closure'. The notion of a 'correct' reading, in its simplest form, is philosophically humanist, presupposing a shared essence that guarantees the possibility of perfect communication between writer and reader. But subjectivity is mobile and self-divided, composed and recomposed in ways that it seldom chooses and often does not or cannot recognize. Even where writerly deliberation is at its most consequential, the text is necessarily deficient in authority over the reader – who, reciprocally, is condemned to read without the warrant of innocence and propriety. Extrapolated over the ordinary distances of history, the necessary discrepancies of the writing-reading relationship become marked. Texts are 'iterable': they function in spaces and times quite remote from their primary conditions of existence, and, in doing so, are in effect rewrittenreread, acquiring further or different meanings, undergoing alterations in status, suffering fluctuations of imputed value. Textual productivity is unending, as is the variability of reading. There is no 'text-in-itself' and no 'reader-assuch' to appropriate it.[37]

The difficulty with this now-familiar view is not that it is false – in its own terms it is persuasive – but that it is abstract and, at worst, trivial. To insist on the constitutional non-identity of writing and of subjectivity is to be returned, as though by counter-suggestion, to the abundant historical evidence for stability and continuity in culture. It may be true in principle that 'you(?) can't read the same text twice'; but what is then all the more striking is how relatively little, and how weightlessly, this enforced liberty is exercised in concrete cultural relations. Meaning and inter-subjectivity have no absolute ground, yet they are orderly, strongly consensualist in tendency and rather predictable in their patterns of antagonism and discrepancy. They are shaped and held in historical formations of writing and reading that constrain textuality, that are, precisely, *authoritative*.

If the idea of a perennially self-identical text is a humanist dogma, the antithetical idea of an ever-self-differing text is an academic-libertarian trifle. Neither is adequate for the purposes of historical inquiry, for which some notion of *context* is indispensable. Yet to say only so much is to say very little: everything depends on how 'context' is understood. The generic claim that meaning is context-determined is uninteresting: it amounts to saying that there is no culture without society, a truism for all but the most other-worldly perennialist. What, then, counts as an interesting context? A characteristic response (familiar not only in recent literary studies but also, and over a longer period, in the history of political thought[38]) is to privilege the most limited contexts, beyond which a text is quickly self-estranged, and thus to assert an extreme relativism of meaning – and again, but this time for sheer want of plausibility, to weaken the challenge to common-sense perennialism. The preference for narrow contexts reproduces the misapprehension of the generic claim: both rest on a tacit reduction of *history* to *change* – a kind of hyper-history. This is the most understandable of polemical habits, but it perpetuates a confusing half-truth. History is also – and decisively, for its greater part – *continuity*. The historical process is differential: it is patterned by a plurality of rhythms and tempos, some highly variable, some very little so, some measured by clocks and calendars, others belonging to the practical eternity of 'deep time'. Historical structures and events – the substance of what we invoke as 'contexts' – are thus necessarily complex in character, never belonging to a single mode (continuity/discontinuity) or temporality. Contexts are brief and narrow (a generation, a political crisis) but they are also long and wide (a language, a mode of production, sex-gender privilege), and all of these at once.[39] Perennialist reading – across continents and centuries – is no more pure fancy than hyper-historicism is pure enlightenment. The appeal to 'context' does not suffice either to discredit the one or to establish the other. The concept of 'context', putative determinant of meaning, is itself under-determined, acquiring critical value only within a specific understanding of history.

History, and so, for good or for ill, historical materialism. All contemporary reflection on history is a declared or tacit response to the legacy of Marx. That this should be so testifies to the crucial character of Marx's theoretical claims, but also to their ambiguities. Thus any statement on behalf of historical materialism is, at the same time, an intervention within it.

The oldest ambiguities – and in the present connection, the most stressful – inhere in the very notion of a *materialist* conception of history. 'Materialism', in the Marxist tradition, is a complex idea, incorporating three variably related claims. The first asserts an ontological monism: reality is homogeneous, without residue, consisting of so many modes of materiality. The second claim is already historical in implication, positing a reality so structured that its 'lower' modes constrain its 'higher' ones, which, though irreducible as systems, are none the less consubstantial with them: biological existence does not outstrip physico-chemical regularities, nor human sociality the biological. Finally, as these claims imply, 'materialist' epistemology is broadly realist, affirming the existence of an object-world independent of thought and accessible to it. These three claims have shared the common space of 'materialism' since the 1840s, peaceably for much of the time but often, and certainly in recent years, in a state of antagonism.

'Materialism' in the first sense has motivated – or at least glossed – significant developments in Marxist thinking about culture. Ideology as material practice; meaning as the effect of work in language, as textual production; the notion of culture as, quite literally, *making* sense – these have become common themes in Marxist discourse, in some cases through initiatives within the tradition, in others through the assimilation of various kinds of semiotic theory. Marxism's habits of theory and analysis have been residually dualist, it is said (by Williams, for example).[40] Historical materialism has redefined the *social status* of culture but has not been commensurately active in rethinking its specificity as a *practice*; the old cultural spirituality lingers, humbled but not banished, in a theory which, to that extent, remains unequal to its own materialist rule of life. That this has often been so is undeniable, even if the historical record as a whole is more varied, and less flawed, than some latter-day generalizations admit. Marxist cultural analysis has, in the past twenty years, finally come to terms with its 'erstwhile philosophical consciousness', thinking through and beyond essentialist understandings of the literary and the aesthetic and displacing such equivocal categories as 'expression' and 'reflection' in new forms of attention to discourse and representation in their material specificity.

However, 'materialism' in this sense has often been taken to imply a further critical objection – one which, pursued to a finish, strikes Marxism at its theoretical core. If cultural practice is truly understood as material (the monist thesis), then perhaps there is no longer any strong reason to endorse the structural-historical thesis ('materialism' in its second sense) that social reality is subject to a hierarchy of constraint. Marx's privileging of the economic, the notorious theory of 'base and superstructure', itself embodies the old dualism. Althusser's attempt to resolve its cruces through the notion of 'relative autonomy' was a late, and insufficient, improvisation; 'determination in the last instance' is no determination at all; as he himself conceded in his famous quip, 'the last instance never comes'.

This appeal to consistency is itself fallacious and philosophically inconsistent. 'To say . . . that an object is material is still to say nothing,' Lucio Colletti once wrote: 'materiality as such does not specify, it is rather a *generic* attribute, a property common to all things.'[41] In other words, to say that a given reality is material is merely to assert its ontological unity with other realities, not to imply anything, one way or another, about its relations with them. Even if the notion of a social hierarchy of constraint is misconceived, it cannot be rebutted by an appeal to ontological 'materialism' – which, as deployed on occasions like this, betrays its own kind of dualism. The literary 'materialism' of recent times remains true to custom in its tacit special pleading on behalf of humanity. Arguments over the relations between cultural and economic practice are conducted in abstraction, as though humans, whether as poets or as farmers, were not wholly a part of nature – where the reality of hierarchical constraint, of 'relative autonomy', in effect, is manifest, and understood as such in the materialist knowledge of the sciences generally. 'Relative autonomy' – or, more precisely and tellingly, *conditional* autonomy – encapsulates that unity of specificity and generic dependence that characterizes the relationship of more to less complex modes of nature. Thus, animal behaviours are specific, but effectively so only in and in conformity with physico-chemical nature. Human history exhibits unique specificities, but is not exceptional. Biological self-reproduction is the permanent condition of all social practice, whose real and effective power of variation is correspondingly limited. The historical means of self-reproduction – the organization of economic relations – are, for any given place and time, a 'second nature' that systematically favours certain social variations over others, and, as an essential part of this, fosters a 'common sense' which, though never homogeneous and always contested, is the given substance of our perceptions, imaginings and valuations – which is, in a word, the historically specific reality of our *culture*, in its ordinary and specialized modes alike. Culture is omnipresent, it is pointed out, as a necessary element of all social practice: the idea that it is determined by 'something else' is confused. It is indeed omnipresent, and for just that reason can *not* be represented, contrariwise, as a strong independent variable. It is, moreover, subject to two constraints which, though not normally existing in an a-cultural state, are finally impervious to meaning: force, the ultimate resort of the political, and need, the unanswerable daily argument of the economy, which in this fundamental sense must always 'determine' human life 'in the last instance'.

But the last instance, as we all remember, never comes. . . . This, the rhetorical highlight of Althusser's career, is better seen as a moment of damaging theoretical confusion. Evoking the pattern and dynamic of the October Revolution, Althusser affirmed the necessary complexity of the social whole, and excluded, in principle, the possibility of a climactic simplification of struggle to the pure terms of capital and labour – in short, he excluded a *politico-temporal* 'last instance'.[42] But the irreducible complexity of Russian revolutionary politics was based precisely on the complexity of the Tsarist socio-economic formation: a decaying feudalism interlocked with a dynamic but subaltern capitalist sector in conditions of aggressive inter-imperialist rivalry to determine the configuration of the crisis, its protagonists and its finite array of possibilities. 'The last instance' in this *structural* sense did not fail to come: it was present from the start, as the *condition* of October. Althusser's quip intended a useful but limited political caution (even if as a judgement on the general notion of a temporal 'last instance' it seems ill-considered, simply overlooking the ordinary cycles of systematized commodity production). But it mistakes and compromises the lesson of its own illustration, which – not retreating from Marx's thesis but reinforcing it – bears on the structure of the social as such, and on the differential effectivity of economic relations within it.

Modes of production are ultimately decisive in the formations and transformations of human history, and the ordering of social agency in which a mode of production humanly consists – its system of *classes* – is correspondingly central for theory and politics. The strength of this claim is perhaps better appreciated, in current conditions, through a reminder of its limitations. It does not entail the essentialist belief that the economy is the simple truth of complex appearances, or that class furnishes the exhaustive meaning of social being. No consistent historical materialist can evade the specific reality of sexual dimorphism and the relatively autonomous regimes and cultures of gender that have been constructed upon it, not to speak of other, historically more limited, forms of human bonding and antagonism such as race; and only an alchemist will maintain that these are so many base metals to be transmuted into the gold of class struggle. Concrete social beings are necessarily involved in all such forms of relationship, among which none is their 'essence'- not class *or* sex *or* race *or* nationality *or* generation. Cora Kaplan has emphasized the complex inter-coding of all these determinations in subjectivity and its representations.[43] If the problematic of class remains crucial for Marxists, this is not out of hidebound devotion to an old cause but because of the fundamental thesis that in the overdetermined totality of social life, the dominant mode of production plays a decisive structuring role, confirming or adapting or remaking the given human relations in accordance with its own logic, patterning both the necessary conditions of its own existence and the forces capable of transforming it.

It has frequently been said that this thesis is fatally dogmatic; the very assumption that social relations constitute a totality is unwarrantably speculative; 'historical materialism' is the culmination of idealist philosophy of history. The charge of dogmatism, it may be retorted, is a projection. Indeed there is no ultimate guarantee. Marxism's theoretical propositions are necessarily open to displacement by a stronger theory. But this is the normal situation of rational knowledge. The dogmatism lies rather in the ethos of the objection, which tacitly holds that uncertain knowledge is worthless. Here as so often, metaphysical yearning is greatest in the souls of the disenchanted.

The Marxist vision of socialism as an historical possibility evolved but locked within capitalism, and of labour – the exploited collective producer – as its indispensable revolutionary agency, does not affect the status of revelation. It is a rational challenge, as bold and as exposed as all genuine challenges must be. There are many on the left who would sooner say that it is a bluff that has now been called. As it was called in the 1890s? And again in the 1950s? Nothing is more suspect than the apocalyptic *Now*. 'The crisis of Marxism' has been a recurring theme of the past century, and not only for the predictable, transient reasons. Marxism is wholly involved in the crises it seeks to understand and resolve, and precisely because of this, it is the more necessary to recall another recurring phenomenon. Not a few attempts have been made to 'go beyond' Marxism; and all have entailed regression to earlier, more limited positions.[44] (Thus, for instance, the 'new' ethics and tactics of 'identity', which are nowadays urged against the old, oppressive generalities of 'class' – and 'woman' and 'black' – turn out to be a postmodern variant of a long-familiar radical liberalism.) Marxism remains what it has always been: incomplete, fallible, a tradition in process – but for all that, as Sartre once wrote, the unsurpassable horizon of thought in our time.

'*Cultural politics*' is Marxism's activist mode in this domain, and, like all lucid practice, not so much a release from the ink-horn preoccupations of theory as a tense rediscovery of them. The very idea of 'cultural politics' is monstrous, according to the liberal-humanist tradition. Culture is what hesitates before politics, resists it, in the name of values that transcend the ordinary interests and antagonisms of social life. To believe and act as though it were otherwise is morally stupid, if not criminal. The record of communism betrays the dismal truth of 'cultural politics'. Routine docketing of all art according to its 'progressive' or 'reactionary' tendency, administered creation, a repertoire of edifying kitsch – these are the images that haunt the liberal imagination (and also the collective memory of socialists) and they cannot be wished away. Yet the recent course of left cultural politics has led in the opposite direction. 'Culture', understood as the moment of meaning in social relations, is obviously not the entity enshrined in liberal tradition, but it is commonly granted a similar kind of authority. Far from being subject to external political tests, culture is in itself already political, it is said, and this in a fuller sense than the narrow conventions of parties and programmes can comprehend. The innate meta-political ambition of liberal humanism has been reborn on the left, in the reductionist analytics and practice of *culturalism*.

This is not a logically necessary outcome of cultural studies or cultural materialism; its favouring condition has been the historical situation evoked earlier in these pages. But it is facilitated also by specifically theoretical difficulties, which in practice collude with objective circumstances, and which we do well to try to resolve. The culturalist temptation is a spontaneous effect of current theoretical preferences. If the instance of culture is coextensive with sociality, it must encompass the political. Even on the closer definition of culture as the ensemble of those practices whose principal function is signification, the specificity of politics appears questionable. Culture is the necessary element of politics, whose means, moreover, are often strictly cultural. And thus, by simple elision, culture absorbs politics and assumes its titles. The attempt to affirm the political nature of culture leads, from its opposite beginnings, to a familiar conclusion: the dissolution of politics.

The conceptual germ of this confusion is, however, not so much an overweening sense of 'culture' as a deficient understanding of politics, which as a practice is always irreducible to the cultural, even when it moves wholly within its dimension. It is not that political discourse speaks of 'different' matters – let alone that culture is the province of 'higher' or 'deeper' (or 'ordinary') realities. In this respect there really is no final distinction between them. The object of politics is the totality of social relations in a given space, and this, however defined and inventoried, has also been a *topos* in important cultural traditions. But the discursive object of politics is also a practical field: more precisely defined, it is the *determination* (maintenance or alteration) of the totality. Thus, even as word and image, political practice is modally distinct from other kinds of discourse – and, finally, more than them. Political discourse is functionally specialized: it is essentially *deliberative* in character, moving always towards the question, What is to be done – and how? Its rhetoric is correspondingly distinctive: oriented towards the elaboration of contentious demands, the language of politics is in an especially strong sense performative, couched always, in effect, in the *imperative*. And the decisive resources of this deliberative-imperative practice, lacking which it is something less than itself, are no longer simply cultural at all, but *coercive*: political discourse is systemically bonded with the actual or potential sanction of force, be that exercised through the state apparatuses or through the counter-power of mass action.

Thus, it is certainly necessary to insist that all culture is shot through with political values; necessary to insist at the same time that these, as meanings, are cultural; but it is therefore all the more necessary to understand that the two are mutually irreducible, and that their relationship is most fraught when it is closest, in notions of 'cultural politics'. The co-ordination of values implied in such phrases can perfect itself only in an illusion of identity that compromises both culture and politics. Any culture is more various than its corresponding politics. It will explore and promote solidarities and differences of value according to its own spontaneous dynamics, heedless of the regular discipline of deliberative reason; and such solidarities and differences are, in this mode, quasi-absolute – as Lukács once observed, there is no peaceful coexistence in the realm of ideas.[45] Political discourse also explores and promotes solidarities and antagonisms, but while these are necessarily asserted as, if not absolute then certainly decisive, they can never simply replicate the pattern of a coexistent culture. The simplest illustration of this comes from political culture itself: party forums debate many analyses but vote only on a few programmatic conclusions. Culture and politics are thus both sectarian and ecumenical with respect to one another; each routinely makes excessive demands on the other, and that is how it must be.[46] In the field of cultural politics the only general solutions are bad ones.

The record of Marxist cultural politics itself points the moral here. Scientific positivism and artistic realism emerged as the cardinal values of the first phase. There were good reasons for this, transcending the force of cultural context. But in the historical outcome the function of these values, neither scientific nor realistic, was to orchestrate the deathly culture of bureaucratic omniscience and optimism. Realism found new defenders in the second phase, but now in the persons of such deeply anti-scientistic philosophers as Lukács and Sartre. Most 'critical' Marxism was similarly aloof from science but, contrastingly, well disposed towards modernism – again, in keeping with the ambient high culture of the time. This release from 'orthodoxy', a tonic in itself, stimulated invaluable work, but also recharged a delphic late-Romantic ethos of pessimism and abstract refusal. Neither solution was empty, neither was adequate; and both, inevitably, were deeply conditioned by politico-cultural circumstances. Today, somewhere in the history of the third phase, having seen science come again and go, having relived the realism-modernism debate as a climactic novelty, understanding at last that truth has gone the way of all modernity, we cannot delude ourselves that there is, for now, life outside the dominant culture, but we might at least learn to maintain a critical distance from its passing absolutes.[47]

In the smaller world of academic literary studies, the recurring flashpoint of cultural politics is the question of 'literary value'. I have already suggested the shortcomings of the counter-'ideological' appeal to 'literature' and 'literary value'. As a defence of *generic literariness*, it leads logically to a wider valorization of, say, storytelling or linguistic play, which works against the putative specificity of 'literature'. As a defence of *differential value*, it recedes towards a purely technical judgement unequal to its own moral pretensions. In either case, it fails in its objective purpose, which is to defend specific traditions of writing and to contain discussion of them through a disavowal of their substantive burden of meaning. We need not deny the experience of literary pleasure and unpleasure, complex and opaque as this often is, in order to maintain that value is always transitive, for given subjects in given conditions, and that it is finally moral, in the ethical or the political stress of the word. And we need not promote a meaningless equality of all texts in order to maintain that received mystifications concerning 'quality' are not a fit basis for a discipline of rational inquiry. Far from this, the academic-liberal commitment to 'great literature' is only a nuance removed from the authoritarian-deferential middlebrow cult of 'a good book' (which every literary intellectual knows how to despise). It is enough that the writings enshrined in 'the canon', along with the greater body of writings whose cultural substance is indissociable from theirs, are richly *interesting* (in the strong sense, that is: engaging actual commitments and purposes) as objects of rhetorical and other analysis, as interlocutors, as occasions of debate, as the available repertoire of writing today and tomorrow.

Expertise was Walter Benjamin's term for the cultural orientation suggested here, which implies more than skilled practice, for its contrary, in his analysis, was not 'incompetence' but *taste*.[48] 'Taste' is a relationship to culture (consumption) conditioned by estrangement from its processes of production. The inherited formations of literary study are another form of this estrangement, which tends to limit its students to the deprived accomplishment of (informed) taste. 'Expertise' might be the watchword of a cooler and not at all deferential relation to work in this field, as much for those who do not themselves aim to invent stories or song lyrics as for those who do. The distinction between 'criticism' and 'creation' has lain deep in literary studies, as it does in the wider culture, but it has no final authority. The Marxist tradition has looked, and often acted, beyond its alienated terms. We need think only of Benjamin's friend, Brecht, who gave practical meaning to the conviction that for a developed Marxist cultural politics the point is not only to interpret rhetorics in history but to change them.

1992

READING ALTHUSSER

Writing books is like sending messages in bottles, Louis Althusser was once heard to remark, in sorrowful reaction to the international phenomenon of 'Althusserianism': you can never tell who will come upon your words or what they will make of them. In literary studies, which were neither first nor last among Althusser's interests, these messages were soon found and read. The experience (a newly fateful word) was a daunting one, but there was also elation; it felt, for many, like the definitive moment of liberation. However, like all such moments, it was only a beginning, and, after more than three decades of commentary and elaboration, its meaning has come to seem more ambiguous and elusive, nothing so simple as the revelation it once appeared to be.[1]

Althusser's theoretical intervention 'for Marx' bore upon both the substance and the status of historical materialism.[2] Marx's revolution had entailed more than a materialist inversion of Hegel's dialectic, he maintained. The new theory abandoned the supposed expressivism of the old philosophy, substituting the idea of an inherently complex social whole whose political and ideological instances were 'relatively autonomous', 'specifically effective', determined only 'in the last instance' by the economic. Determination, in this conceptual scheme, was likewise complex: not singular yet not merely plural, it was, so to say, typically exceptional in its workings. Any contradiction was as a rule internally marked by the contradictions that formed its conditions of existence, in irreducible states and processes of 'overdetermination'. A complex whole and thus complex time: history so conceived could not move according to a single, regular beat; rather, it must be seen as possessing a 'differential' temporality, yielding an arhythmic succession of unique conjunctures.

These, for Althusser, were the elements of historical materialism proper, after its critical disengagement from historicism and humanism. Against the first, it proposed a decentred, non-expressive process; against the second, it asserted the primacy of structures and practices over the concrete individuals who were, rigorously conceived, their bearers; and in both respects it broke decisively with the problematic of 'the subject' as author or source of history. 'The subject' was the pivotal category in Althusser's main specific undertaking in historical materialism, the exploration of the concept of 'ideology'. This term and its associated meanings had led an irregular, mercurial life in Marxist tradition; in Althusser's thought, it assumed a constant and overwhelming role. Ideology here was a relatively autonomous practice whose principal function was to secure the reproduction of the relations of production; yet received notions of illusion, mystification, false consciousness and spiritualized interest conveyed little of its existential sway. Not the work of subjects, ideology worked them, 'interpellating' the social singularities called individuals 'as subjects', into the identities that qualified them as social agents. These identities sustained an 'imaginary' relation to real conditions, and yet were indispensable, now and in any human future. To live at all was to live in ideology. Knowledge, properly speaking, was *scientific knowledge*, the fruit of a non-subjectivist theoretical labour upon the heterogeneous data of experience, that is, ideology. Here was Althusser's complementary claim – the second aspect of his intervention – concerning the status of Marx's innovation. As a science, historical materialism founded itself in a 'break' with ideology, constructing its theoretical objects, and elaborating analyses that would be governed by the protocols of theoretical practice itself, not by the (ideological) indications of the empirical world.

Althusser's prospectus for theoretical practice must seem overweening, and in important respects it really was. Like Karl Popper, whose fallibilism is not the most distant of comparisons, Althusser accorded unique cognitive privilege to science and, furthermore, invested it with the pathos of heroism. It was not surprising that suspicions of neo-positivism and Stalinist dogmatism should so readily have arisen. Yet notwithstanding the leitmotiv of Marxist triumphalism in his writing, Althusser's 'return to Marx' was not an intellectual reversion to party type. His insistence on the integrity of science did not entail a claim of exclusivity for historical materialism. The theoretical field within which he situated Marx's science was not the old 'dialectical materialism' but the human sciences – specifically, the new 'quadrivium' of history, ethnology, psychoanalysis and linguistics, and their lingua franca, 'structuralism'.3 The pursuit of scientificity here meant the repudiation of intellectual autarky.

The general themes and orientations of Althusser's Marxism were in themselves sufficient to establish his appeal for the left in English literary studies, among whom a sense of intellectual illegitimacy was deep and persistent. From the classics, they inherited the synopsis of a general theory, and a few famous fragments concerning Ancient art or Balzac's politics or realism in the novel and drama. The great systematizers of the Second International, irrespective of their individual cultural complexions, tended to see art mainly as a prestigious test case for their general explanatory claims; they brought it down to earth, but then left it there. The Bolshevik generation – notably Lenin and Trotsky – found occasions for ideological intervention in literary life, but wrote little that might serve more general purposes. The British Marxism of the 1930s – represented by Alick West, Ralph Fox and, above all, Christopher Caudwell – was a collective embarrassment.4 Its direct inheritors sponsored an uncompelling Communist variant of familiar literary-academic procedure. The eventual scope of Raymond Williams's long revolution was as yet undiscerned. Georg Lukács's work furnished the inescapable point of contemporary reference, with his successor Lucien Goldmann an increasingly conspicuous second. And what both thinkers offered were lines of analysis that, though strong and sophisticated, were incorrigibly schematic in their treatment of history and texts, and – notoriously in Lukács's case – prone to aesthetic dogmatism. The Frankfurt School, or what was known of it in Britain at that time, offered a richer and crucially more modern intellectual culture, but was not exempt from the general suspicion of summary totalizing constructions. Thoroughly as such Marxist styles might be learned, scrupulously though they might be practised, the internalized reproach of the dominant tradition, with its watchwords of fidelity to the empirical record and the detailed life of the text, would not be stilled.[5]

Then came Althusser ('Contradiction and Overdetermination' appeared in English in 1967, the entire For Marx in 1969; Reading Capital followed in 1970) and the prospect of a new departure. Thanks to the new historical concepts, the determinist and schematizing tendencies apparently ingrained in Marxist literary studies could be criticized and overcome in uncompromisingly Marxist terms. The new understanding of ideology, with its crucial revaluation of 'experience', discomposed the first principle of conduct in the dominant critical tradition. Beyond the complementary errors of Marxist 'historicism' and liberal-humanist 'empiricism', it was possible and necessary to broach the scientific, historical-materialist concept of art as an irreducible social practice, to imagine a properly Marxist theory of an unambiguously specified object.

Althusser's personal interest in this project inspired two compelling occasional essays, one on Strehler's Paris production of El Nost Milan, the other on the paintings of Cremonini.[6] Beyond their engagement with particular cases, these texts displayed keen awareness of general questions of theory and method. Both accorded analytic primacy to the material events (the play, the canvas) and the practices they instantiated. The 'subjects' of these practices (author, director, painter, spectator) were registered but displaced: the reading of Cremonini's canvases was not controlled by the evidence of the painter's intentional project; the Brechtian reflection on empathetic theatre explored a non-psychologistic understanding of audience response. And both essays were framed as polemics against critical 'gastronomy', the established obstacle to criticism as knowledge. Yet they could not simply be taken as pilots of such a criticism. Althusser seized upon Strehler's Bertolazzi because its strange dual tempo dramatized something like his own understanding of the ideological. Cremonini's verticals and circles excited him because he saw in them a figuration of his own anti-humanism. Both texts were, so to speak, moments of counter-ideological 'recognition' (the indispensable word), the more euphorically articulate for that, but the less instructive as adumbrations of a new theory and practice.

However, Althusser's only programmatic declaration concerning aesthetics, the letter to André Daspre, appeared to underwrite this conflation of theoretical specification and aesthetic preference. Althusser's goal was 'a real knowledge of art'; his means – 'there is no other way' – a 'rigorous reflection on the basic concepts of Marxism'. For now, he would elaborate 'a first idea'. Art is categorially distinct from science; it does not produce knowledge in the strict sense. Yet it is not an indifferent mode of the ideological. For art sustains a differential relation to knowledge; it can 'make us see' the 'reality' to which it 'alludes', and this by virtue of the 'internal distance' it establishes within ideology. He was, of course, talking here about 'authentic art, not works of an average or mediocre level.'[7] . . . If this was a call to a new theoretical quest, it seemed that the likely route would be circular. 'First ideas' are always awkward (Althusser wrote movingly about the unequal struggle to innovate in received idioms), but this one seemed all too settled. Art as the special counterpart of science, working in everyday language yet capable of privileged insight; aesthetics as, in effect, the elucidation of artistic greatness, not the knowledge of a specific practice but an elaborated protocol of discrimination – these were the commonplaces of the literary academy. It was not easy, at this point, to see how Marxist self-reflection (which was not encouraged, on this occasion, to communicate with other critical knowledges) would transmute them into science.

The declared context of the letter to Daspre was the work of Althusser's young collaborator Pierre Macherey, whose *Pour une théorie de la production littéraire*, appearing in the same year, 1966, was the inaugural statement of Marxist theoretical practice in the field of the literary.[8] Macherey's book was, in two senses, a study in morphology. Its first concern was to determine the characteristic shape of received literary criticism – the forms of its attention – and to assert the contrasting protocols of a scientific alternative; its emerging theme, elaborating the founding thesis of this science, was the action of literary form in ideology. Received criticism acted as if to regulate writing and reading in the 'domain' of literature, Macherey argued. As a 'normative' practice, it judged comparative achievement; as 'interpretation' it offered to resolve and mediate meaning; and in both modes it proceeded fallaciously, actually 'replacing' what it claimed to analyse with ideal others – the work as it might have been or in its 'full' meaning. A scientific criticism, in contrast, would be a discourse of knowledge, a systematic inquiry into the 'laws' of a theoretically specified object: literary 'production' as a determinate material practice in ideology. The results of literary production, Macherey went on to claim, were the opposite of those affirmed in critical tradition: not composure and fullness but incompleteness, discrepancy and absence. These were the effects of literary form. For although literature was not science, it 'naturally scorn[ed] the credulous view of the world'; held within ideology, its 'determinate insufficiency' nevertheless parodied and caricatured ideology, thus offering an 'implicit critique' of it.[9] The task of a Marxist criticism was to trace the workings of this productive disorder and to explain it.

Macherey's theoretical excursion was in all relevant senses Althusserian but it was not in any ordinary sense Marxist. The official inspiration of the

book was Lenin – who was invoked here as elsewhere with particular ceremony – but its more substantial, though tacit, intellectual debt was to a
thinker whose example had become canonical in Althusser's circle: Freud.
The imago of text and critic in Macherey's discourse was the symptom and its
(psycho)analyst. Literary works could be understood as the dreams, jokes and
parapraxes of a divided collective subjectivity. The analogy is a powerful one
(indeed, a little further meditation upon it might have refined Macherey's
undiscriminating critique of interpretation), but it does not license the further
assumption concerning the differential critical value of the literary. Freud's
symptomatic texts are valuable as evidence for analysis; in themselves they are
modes of unknowing, denial, confusion. But according to Macherey, cognitive
privilege belonged to the literary as such, and not only to the theory that
could explain its figurations. Like Althusser, he conceded literature a place of
co-primacy with science in the hierarchy of culture.

Macherey would subsequently take quite different bearings,[10] but, for
now, a distinctive Althusserian problematic remained in force: the object
proper to Marxist theoretical investigation was 'ideology and literary form'.
This was the title of the first English-language initiative under Althusser's general aegis, Terry Eagleton's pilot essay for his Criticism and Ideology.[11] The
model of theoretical practice was evident in the shape of Eagleton's inquiry. A
probing review of the received critical culture in its liberal and socialist forms
(Leavis and Williams respectively) led to a general theoretical construction of
the place of the literary in the social whole, and thence towards the summit,
a 'science of the text'. The central propositions of the book were in the main
familiar: 'materialist criticism' as an anti-humanist, anti-historicist practice
forwarded in a break with ideology; literature as ideology 'raised to the second power'; Freud as the exemplary theorist and reader of self-divided textual production. Yet as well as elaborating and varying these themes, Eagleton
lodged punctual criticisms of Althusser and Macherey. He noted the tendentious reservation in the letter to Daspre, and insisted, in opposition to
Macherey, that the literature-ideology relationship was not necessarily subversive. It was, he observed, as if literature must be spared 'the shame of the
sheerly ideological', as if 'the aesthetic must still be granted mysteriously privileged status, but now in embarrassedly oblique style'.[12] Exactly so – but
Althusser and Macherey were not alone in the hour of their temptation. What
Eagleton feared in their texts he was in the end unable to banish from his
own. The central chapter of Criticism and Ideology recorded a struggle in
process, here assigning special powers to literature, there reserving them to
the (duly rigorous) reader, and never surrendering the conviction, which was
also secure in Althusser and Macherey, that there existed a stable entity named
'literature' (or 'form') to be known, a real object awaiting its adequate concept.

This undischarged essentialism found its counterpart in the closing chapter of the book, an attempt without precedent in Althusser or Macherey to
theorize differential literary value. Eagleton was right to affirm the need for

such a theory (while differential judgement is for many strictly analytic purposes irrelevant or even diversionary, in the ordinary world of culture it is ineluctable), but his reasoning was self-divided. His thesis was that a Marxist account of value would be relational or transitive: a text is valuable, that is, not in itself, but for certain users in specific conditions. (The presiding spirit here was Brecht.) Yet his discussion gravitated towards the opposite conclusion, seeking value in the historical conditions of production of the text, and so suggesting an originary and lasting endowment of distinction or banality; literary value was, after all, the immanent variation of an essential category.[13]

In these texts, the project of an Althusserian Marxist theory of the aesthetic was boldly launched and as surely frustrated. Their governing problematic was, as Althusser might have said, 'amphibological': an old category refigured as a new concept, an attempt to furnish a scientific answer to an unsurmounted philosophical question.[14] Macherey himself went on to reject the question 'what is literature?' as an unwarrantable intrusion into sovereign theoretical space. His later work at once redrew the theoretical image of literature to emphasize its role in the production of ideological compromise, and, more radically, turned from literature as text to literary culture as an institutionalized ideological practice – to 'the literary effect' as it is deployed in the educational apparatus of the class-divided nation.[15] Eagleton noted the possibility of such modified lines of analysis, but chose not to pursue them; his subsequent work turned away from the architectonic prospectus of *Criticism and Ideology* in favour of an interventionist 'political' criticism that, though not less theoretically engaged and still emphatically Marxist, could not be called 'Althusserian'.[16]

Meanwhile, another initiative had sprung into vigorous life. Taking early shape in the years of Althusser's greatest productivity, the collaborative work of the *Tel Quel* circle centred on Phillipe Sollers and Julia Kristeva developed rapidly, reaching a critical moment of self-definition – so history was pleased to have it – a few months after the events of May-June 1968.[17] Althusser's affiliates maintained a pointed distance from *Tel Quel*, as if in awkward consciousness of eager but unsought company.[18] Althusser was a canonical reference in the journal – like Lacan, an acknowledged *levier*, lever or influence, in its work.[19] But its closer mentors were Barthes, Derrida and Foucault, who led off the collective volume, *Théorie d'ensemble*.[20] Above all other things a resumption of French avant-garde traditions in the arts, and at this time devoted to an anarcho-Maoist programme of cultural revolution, *Tel Quel* set its theoretical bearings in an intellectual network (*réseau* was a favoured metaphor) that included Althusser and partly sustained him, but with very different intellectual and political priorities. Althusserian Marxism was thus at once valorized and displaced, functioning here as a privileged citation in a context at once familiar and alien.

The more sanguine, less defensive evaluation of this development was that *Tel Quel* offered a possible realization of Althusser's vision of a non-autarkic Marxism developing as a science among others, in the space of cultural theory. This, indeed, was the spirit animating a kindred project that took shape in Britain, in the work of *Screen*. 'The *Screen* project' is a familiar way of evoking a collaborative enterprise that eludes simple summary. The magazine never was intellectually homogeneous, in large part because of the discrepant interests in play in its parent organization, the Society for Education in Film and Television. Its dominant intellectual tendency, in the critical passage of the 1970s, was itself unstable, in part because of the quick tempos and syncopated rhythms characteristic of an import-dependent vanguard culture, and in part also because there was no pre-established harmony among the theoretical interests that now came to the fore. 'The *Screen* project' is not a true singular, and there is no definitive version of it. However, with such qualifications made, there was no mistaking the difference between this and the other, more strictly canonical reading of Althusserian possibilities.

There was, to begin with, a weighty difference of circumstance. It cannot have been unimportant that *Screen's* given field of activity was cinema rather than literature. The sheer materiality of cinema as industry, technical practice and experience was less easily spiritualized than that of the literary institution – whose conservative devotees, indeed, would affirm just so much, knowing full well the difference between a conventicle and a crowd. The strategic *topoi* of modern critical culture were not settled truths here: auteurism may have reiterated traditionalist notions of composition and reading, but it also helped to undo the disciplinary segregation of 'art' and 'entertainment'; and while essentialist theories of 'film' were advanced, they encountered stubborn resistance in the objective complexity of the developed filmic repertoire, with its multiple and variably ordered matters of expression. Furthermore, the availability of a diverse oppositional film-making culture, in which some of the journal's editors were directly involved, was bound to inflect all theoretical considerations – as Benjamin was aware, any object appears differently in the perspective of production.

Althusser's demand for the analysis of specific, relatively autonomous practices and his construction of ideology as institutionalized material practice furnished the general terms legitimating an unconstrained exploration of cinema in its full historical and structural complexity; at the same time, the whole history of both dominant and critical cinema acted against the kind of conceptual inertia that patterned the letter to Daspre. *Screen's* inquiry into the formation, functioning and tendential effects of cinematic practices was pursued along lines at first parallel and soon convergent with that of *Tel Quel*, in an inter-theoretical discourse on ideology, subject and text. Semiotics, developing through a critical ingathering of modern scientific initiatives in poetics and linguistics – formalist, structuralist and other – offered concepts and taxonomies that bore the promise of a post-aesthetic, materialist analysis of textual forms and functions. Psychoanalysis appeared not merely as a potent analogy but as a decisive contributor to the understanding of subjectivity. Marxism furnished terms of historical understanding and defined the politics of text and subject.

There was more than one summary of this theoretical conjunction. Peter Wollen identified a meta-theoretical unity of purpose: 'each concerns itself with an area of human activity that articulates natural with social history' – signs, labour and sexuality. Stephen Heath, more tentative, spoke of 'the encounter of Marxism with psychoanalysis on the terrain of semiotics'.[21] There was, equally, no regularity of proportion in the work produced under its aegis. Wollen's work did not (and does not) take the totalizing course that his general formulation might be taken to indicate, rather moving from topic to topic with unruffled flexibility of emphasis and theoretical reference. Heath was, in practice, the more concerned to probe the sense of the general strategy in particular settings of analysis. In the *Screen* circle generally, variations multiplied. Consistent with its own critical themes, this was an 'impure' project, lacking an essence.[22] The yield was very impressive, but it provided the evidence that this second version of Althusserian initiative – all at once broader, bolder and more modest – was scarcely better insured than the first. The renunciation of Marxist autarky in favour of a dialogic theoretical discourse enhanced productivity, but not, therefore, predictable analytic output. This was not a story of scientific progress from incompleteness into notional sufficiency. Marxist cultural theory had need of that critical contact, but, dialogue being what it is when not a pious simulation, theories have a way of talking back – and with results that owe something to rational debate but rather more to force of circumstance.

Throughout the 1970s, Althusser remained an inspirational reference. The intensifying and increasingly influential work of the Birmingham Centre for Contemporary Cultural Studies was indebted to him. The names of Eagleton and Macherey identified a whole critical tendency. Marxist-feminist writers – Cora Kaplan and Penny Boumelha, for example – looked to Althusser's historical concepts as a means of articulating class and gender determinations in textual analysis.[23] Tony Bennett set out to liquidate Marxism's deep dependence on essentialist notions of literature and value in a line of investigation that, though inevitably divergent from the prior analyses of Macherey and Eagleton and critical of them, was nevertheless plainly Althusserian in spirit.[24] It was easy to believe, looking around, that the outlook for theoretical practice was good.

In retrospect, however, the 1970s may be seen as the years of the great Althusserian inflation, a *trompe l'oeil* sequence in which ever-greater discursive circulation concealed a draining of conceptual value. There were at least three agencies at work in this. One was the banalizing process to which any influential idea is vulnerable. Another, more substantial, was the progress of Althusser's leading British exponents, whose quest for rigour led them to press one after another of their mentor's philosophical proposals to the point of self-destruction.[25] The third, and much the weightiest, was more general and strictly political: a relative decline of all Marxisms, attendant upon the frustration, reversal or decomposition of the historical tendencies that had seemed to vindicate them. Marxism commanded the attention of a whole gallery of intellectual and political interests because, irrespective of its theoretical or programmatic cogency in any given area (which, indeed, might not impress at all), it seemed the inescapable context of radical thought and activity. As the ideological banner of a practical movement, it had a record of achievement (however mixed), a social constituency actual or potential (the labour movement), and immediate prospects in every global theatre. Given such historical endowments, Marxist theory could survive any particular challenge. The corollary – that without these practical supports, the theory would have far less intuitive appeal – was not much dwelt upon, but there was no evading the force of the eventual demonstration.

The course of the 1980s, in every part of the world, mocked all conventional socialist expectation. Social democracy, Communism, anti-imperialism and revolutionary socialism – all were visited by counter-finalities that could be said to falsify them as general formats of political advance. The very name of socialism, long the site of fierce discursive rivalry, now seemed too monologic for some left-wing sensibilities. Historical materialism – the appropriately general theory of historical processes as dynamic wholes – fared no better. Appearing no longer to answer to common-sense estimates of the probable or the practical, it suffered a co-ordinate loss of critical authority. The stronger radical political trends of the eighties were particularist; and in the radical academy, above all in its departments of literary and cultural studies, matching styles of analysis appeared – perspectivist, and agnostic or hostile towards totalizing thought. It was this great ecological shift, rather than any newly discovered problem or any pre-given outcome of intellectual arbitration, that redrew the pattern of selection pressures, to the disadvantage of Marxism and in favour of the counter-enlightenment thematics that now proliferated as post-structuralism, or postmodernism, or – a hybrid for the times – post-Marxism.[26]

But even now, in a milieu increasingly indifferent to Marxism and ever more ignorant of it, the name of Althusser continued to be invoked. For he it was whose concept of relative autonomy had cautiously opened the transition to a social theory no longer inhibited by the dogma of a closed totality with a determining economic ground. He it was whose theory of ideology, once relieved of its functionalist embarrassment, had recentred cultural analysis on the question of the subject and its constructions. He it was who had helped to nurture the inter-theoretical dialogue that was now entering its maturity. In truth, or so some theorists persuaded themselves, Althusser really was a post-structuralist, the Monsieur Jourdain of the avant-garde. One veteran of the theory wars, Antony Easthope, discerned in the whole sequence a grand narrative of anti-humanism. Easthope's *British Post-structuralism*, a serial review of the seventies and eighties, is generous, pleasingly worldly, and firmly socialist in spirit. Yet as a construction of theoretical history it is shaped by a Whiggish evolutionism that assimilates all pre-existing virtue to Althusser, and then forwards it to the culminating moment of post-structuralism. *New Left Review's* Gramscian theses on Britain are glossed in the light of the journal's later interest in Althusser, who is now accredited with sole authorship of a theme (relative autonomy) as old as Engels. 'Althusser', we are told, 'imported into Britain at least three lines of thought . . . which can be validly regarded as post-structuralist: the account of the historical formation as decentred; the assertion that knowledge as proceeding from theoretical practice is discursively constructed; the account of the subject as effect rather than cause.' So much, then, for Darwin (the first 'line') or Popper (the second), or Freud (the third). And so much for Althusser, whose work, for all its self-interpellation as Marxist, 'is best regarded now as a structuralism passing over into post-structuralism'.[27] Excess of hindsight, teleological reversion, rationalization: Easthope's rendering provokes any or all of these objections. However motivated, it is untenable as a summation of the left theoretical culture of the past thirty-odd years. But it does, in its way, confirm the poignant impression that, by the end of the eighties, Althusser's name, enfolding certain vestiges of his ideas, survived as little more than a souvenir in a culture that had largely forgotten his intellectual and political projects.

The transition to post-structuralism, in the sense of a generalized thematics now current in a post-Marxist academic left, was not so much an autonomous critical process, more the effect of manifold political disenchantment – not a working out, however unforeseen, of Althusser's logic but an abandonment of it. To say so is not to deliver a summary judgement on the diverse founders of the post-structuralist canon, or on the varied work now proceeding in their joint and several names: the new culture of subversion is a whole far less than the sum of its parts. Neither is it to claim that there exists a pristine theoretical practice, obscured but not annihilated by years of misappropriation, to which, like Althusser to Marx, we must now return. The matter is more difficult and the prospect far less clear. In conclusion – though that is not the ideal word – it may be worthwhile to dwell a little on some of Althusser's key ideas, and to offer a provisional latter-day assessment of them.

Ideology was the theme for which Althusser became celebrated in radical literary and cultural studies; and the course of his thinking marked it as his most ambiguous theoretical venture. Althusser's view was in one respect familiar: the concept of ideology implied a determinate relationship between cognitive deficiency and social interest; it was, in the authorized words of his English translator, a mode in which 'the practico-social predominates . . . over the theoretical, over knowledge'.[28] But the discrepancy between knowledge and the practico-social had never been so insisted upon. Ideology was pervasive, the spontaneous knowing-unknowing of human experience in this and all possible societies.[29] Without relinquishing the first, more familiar sense of the concept, Althusser then pursued his elaboration of the second. The 'imaginary relation' of ideology was the mode in which the ideo-affective life of humans assumed its socially viable form as identity: ideology 'interpellates the individual as a subject.' In arguing thus, Althusser effected a drastic and damaging conflation of two distinct problems: the functioning of ideology in its more familiar sense, as a socially motivated differential relation to knowledge, and the general mechanism of human subject-formation. How, in this perspective, could ideology be known or displaced? Althusser's established response was: by science and art. But if ideology was now identical with the anthropological constant of identity-formation, how could these be conceptualized as ordinary historical practices? And if, contrariwise, they could be retained only as quasi-miraculous interventions in the imaginary – if, that is, they could not be retained at all, but must rather be discarded as rationalist and romantic mystifications – what would remain of ideology as a critical concept? These and kindred objections came from sympathetic and hostile commentators alike, and most influentially from post-structuralist quarters, where a counter-construction had already taken shape. Althusserian 'science' was apparently implicated in the disavowal characteristic of meta-discourse, which exempted itself from the conditions of existence that it stipulated for its objects. The account of subject-formation was either false, and hence unusable, or valid, and therefore subversive of its own pretensions to final rationality. In either case, the ideal of scientificity was unfounded, as also was its putative other, the supporting fiction of ideology. 'Science' was a gambit in 'the politics of truth', a power-play in the contention of discourses and their subjects.

This destructive response has proved most attractive to contemporary taste, but there were others, including at least one of Althusserian inspiration. Göran Therborn proposed a mechanism internal to ideology, such that the fatalistic unity subjectification-subjection could pass into self-contradiction, generating crises of identity and belief with uncertain outcomes – in other words, a material 'dialectic of consciousness' of the kind that Althusser tended to resist.[30] The limitation of Therborn's analysis, taken over from Althusser, was its bracketing of science (along with art) as a special case. Just as Althusser's formalist analysis of subjectification occluded the fact that all ideology advances truth-claims, so Therborn encouraged the specular inference that knowledge-bearing discourse is somehow not implicated in the formation of subjects. There is no such division of labour in the real world of discourse, where logics and rhetorics act indissociably, and seldom according to a rule of inverse proportions. If the theory of subject-formation holds at all, it must hold for all discursive practice. Yet Althusserian reason seemed unable to secure its legitimate philosophical defence of scientificity without abstractions of this kind, so provoking agnostic and irrationalist counter-attack. This predicament had a strictly epistemological ground in an anti-realist account of science, which discredited any appeal to evidence as 'empiricist' and found self-destructive confirmation in a false reduction of culture to ideology.

Raymond Williams has been pictured as the humanist antithesis of the Althusserian sensibility, but his developed theory of culture, far from incompatible with the science/ideology distinction, may prove its safer setting. Culture, in Williams's sense, is the integrally historical making of sense and of subjects, always both.[31] Its substance is the work of material practices – rhetorics, institutions. Culture does not constitute an expressive totality: its antagonisms are complex, its times differential, and its meanings discrepant and changeable. Ideology (restored to a stricter sense as socially determined mystification) and science (understood, less heroically, as fallible rational inquiry into the real) are present, but as contingent faculties of cultural practice, not its primordial essences. Literature is present too, of course, but now in a role more evident to the later Macherey than to Althusser, as an ideological formation in the history of writing and reading. However, Macherey's analytic shift from text to institution, though productive in itself, was less a resolution of his earlier theoretical difficulty than an escape from it. Inquiry into the forms and functions of textuality, however formalist it must often appear, will remain central to any literary theory deserving its name, and it is worth noting, in retrospect, that Williams's understanding of literary form was from earliest days free from the essentialism that hobbled Althusser and Macherey, as indeed it has frustrated most Marxist aesthetic theorizing.

Ideology enjoys *relative autonomy* within a complex whole determined only in the last instance by the economic. This was probably the most immediately appealing of Althusser's messages, legitimating as it did the elaboration of 'regional' theories and analyses uninhibited by the snap totalizations for which mechanistic and Hegelian styles of Marxism had become notorious. The rich yield of work done under its sign is a tribute to its intellectual worth. But as a concept, it too displayed a propensity to develop by its bad side. 'Relative autonomy' soon came under suspicion as a compromise formation mediating the antagonism between a dogmatic philosophy of history and a properly critical and materialist concept of practice. Proposed as a resolution of Marx's social topology, it was increasingly exploited as a passage into alternative theoretical space. Here again this unsought outcome was facilitated by problems in Althusser's theoretical formulations, though these were not nearly so grave as those besetting the concept of ideology. It is true that the term 'relative' often serves as an ad hoc lubricant of inter-propositional friction. But the objection, delivered with an air of unsparing materialist rigour, that ideology is either determined or autonomous – no third way – was ill-founded.[32] Conditional autonomy (a more precise designation) is the typical status of complex systems; only the humanist assumption that social life is utterly distinct from the rest of reality lent credence to the confident disjunctions of Althusser's progeny. It is also true, or so I would maintain, that Althusser's formulation of 'the last instance' was deficient, conflating the temporal and structural meanings of the concept with unfortunate results.[33] But there is no great difficulty in amending this aspect of the analysis, in a plainly Marxist sense. Indeed, it seems odd that 'relative autonomy' and 'the last instance' should have attracted so much attention when, arguably, the more original contention of Althusser's discussion lay elsewhere. The titular concept of his classic essay was neither of these, after all, but 'overdetermination'. Althusser's purpose was not – or not merely – to loosen the bad wholes of mechanist or expressivist reasoning, redistributing causal resources upwards from base to superstructure, but to substitute an alternative conception of the social *as a whole*. The concept of overdetermination did not merely designate the resultant of relatively autonomous effectivities; it offered to specify the typical form of unity of the social process, to show how any practice was internally marked by the other practices that constituted its conditions of existence, and thus – 'Hegelian' though it must seem – to rethink, not to discard, the notion of the presence of the whole in all its parts.

If 'relative autonomy' was the licence Althusser granted to radical literary and cultural studies, 'overdetermination' was the corresponding obligation or challenge. It was scarcely limiting, in an operational sense: this was a conceptual instrument suited equally to localized textual analysis and to large-scale historical constructions of period and genre. It legitimated productive working relations with psychoanalysis (the source of the term, indeed) and semiotics, where such concepts as Kristeva's 'intertextuality' provided support and specification; and it cleared a conceptual space within which key social determinations other than class could be explored in a non-reductionist manner. But it was the distinctively Marxist element in Althusser's scheme – unlike its associated concepts, which might be accommodated within any laodicean sociology of culture – and was not spared the general devaluation of the times. 'Overdetermination' was the first word of many of Althusser's English-speaking offspring; its meaning remains under-explored.

This short story of a concept and its fortunes may serve as a parable concerning the status of historical materialism in a wider theoretical culture. Althusser's restrictive definition of dialectical materialism and his revised account of Marx's concept of history were complementary aspects of a single, fundamental decision to renounce the vision of Marxism as a cosmology in the making, and therewith to renounce theoretical autarky. The return to Marx would be rational only if practised as a turning out into critical solidarity with scientific inquiry in general. Althusser's defence of Lacan – theoretically, against the Zhdanovist traditions of his own party and, practically, against psychoanalytic officialdom – furnished the strongest imaginable warrant of his commitment to this revised ethics and politics of culture. (It is now common knowledge that experience had granted him a terrible cognitive advantage in the understanding of 'differential temporality' and 'specific effectivity' in psychic life.) His great theme of 'reading' as work on the materiality of texts, which drew inspiration from psychoanalysis and also from the structuralism of the day, was the appropriate practical form of a critical and self-critical mode of intellectual conduct.

This was Althusser's most important single contribution to a Marxist culture, but because it was not merely pious it was not merely a gift. There was here a difficult – and increasingly unwelcome – demand. It was possible to believe, in more euphoric moments, that a new theoretical synthesis was in prospect: an anti-humanist materialism. But this favoured locution was actually so weak ('materialism' specifies nothing about the material world, 'anti-humanism' is a crude polemical theme) that in practice it sponsored the opposite of synthesis: a new, or not so new, perspectivism. It has always seemed to me that Althusser's orientation was less than the first but more than the second of these.

A project of synthesis can hardly help but rekindle the old cosmological dream, and in doing so, inhibit rather than assist theoretical inquiry. Historical materialism claims that human formations of sense and subjectivity are organized by determinate modes of production and their associated class relations. Psychoanalysis claims that these formations register the enduring effects of the primal entry into sociality, in patterns that are at once less and more variable than economic systems. Neither can fully account for the textual evidence; yet it seems difficult to take these claims seriously and at the same time to believe that some higher resolution awaits them. A small illustration may concretize the issue. It is true, let us grant, that L'Education sentimentale dramatizes and validates the process of a certain bourgeois political disappointment, after the failure of the 1848 revolutions. It seems true, too, that Flaubert's figuration of persons and their relations is governed by the imago of the mother. The novel condenses these distinct matters in such a way that they can be neither separated nor coordinated in a relationship of essence and expression, one or the other being the 'deeper' reality. Flaubert's textual space is, as it were, occupied twice over, saturated at once by the social meanings of French history in a certain period and by a certain pattern of unconscious desire. In this, we might say, it epitomizes the condition of all culture, where social and psychodynamic meanings are always jointly active, not only in their shared semiotic space but within each other, and according to logics that neither exclude patterns of coordination nor depend on them.

To reason so is not, however, to offer simple support for a notion of 'pluralism', a word in which a damaging ambiguity has flourished for too long. As an institutional principle affirming the rights of all intellectual tendencies, pluralism is a necessary condition of fruitful inquiry. But this meaning of the term is often used, wittingly or not, to valorize a second meaning, which is more clearly registered as relativist or perspectivist. These too have their rights, but they derive no privilege, as intellectual positions, from their simulation of institutional virtue: collective pluralism does not vindicate, let alone enjoin, individual eclecticism. And they are validated least of all by appeal to the name of Althusser. To say that no theory can claim a monopoly on knowledge of the social is not to claim that truth is relative, or parcellized. Althusser affirmed the first proposition but would have rebutted its fallacious sequel. Marxism cannot, in heroic isolation, harvest the yield of our possible social knowledge. Yet in so far as it lodges claims concerning the general structure of the social, it not only opposes alternative conjectures of the same scope, but also exercises a critical check on claims of more limited application. This is a logical entailment, by which Marxism survives or fails as a self-consistent rational theory.[34] Reduced to tending 'class factors' in a perspectivist schedule of analysis, the theory would become precisely the kind of thing against which Lenin famously defined it: a 'trade-union consciousness' in cultural studies.

Renouncing the old cosmology (though his tone sometimes belied the gesture) and resisting the false alternative of perspectivism, Louis Althusser drafted a bold, vulnerable proposal: in his own words, here transposed, an overdetermined unity of theoretical activity, endlessly novel in its configurations but determined in the last instance by Marx's science of history. Just how suggestive that proposal was, and how vulnerable to reduction or rewriting, the past thirty years have shown. Today, it remains, much worn by time and handling but still legible, a message to read, think about and act upon.

1994

INTELLIGENTSIAS
AND THEIR HISTORIES

A contemporary cartoon from Turkey depicts a man hacking at the wooden projection on which he is sitting. It is a commonplace image of self-defeating activity, though in this case the man is clearly a bourgeois and the branch-equivalent, drawn to a far larger scale, is a pencil.[1] Another cartoon from the same political context shows an imprisoned pen – but the enclosure is a bird-cage, only the nib is confined, the body, again massively drawn, lying outside the open door, like a giant unaware of its own strength. In a third image, a man sits reading. His spectacles, absorbed air and slightness of build leave no room to mistake his social type: he is a man of the pencil and pen – an *aydin* or 'enlightened one'. In this scenario too conditions are bad, but in a different sense. The pages before him can hardly be readable; the print is obscured by something like a large blot, which, however, is not the ink-as-blood that features in other drawings of this kind, but the shadow cast by the object that blocks the electric light – his own head.

Such images rehearse – the more strikingly for the extremity of their polit-ical situation – a persistent crux in all post-Enlightenment culture, that is, in the modal culture of 'intellectuals'. On the one hand, there is the hereditary conviction of the transcendent power and responsibility of the disinterested critical word; but on the other, the suspicion that the word is not, in the end, disinterested (the pencil does, after all, support the bourgeois), and that its practitioners are self-deluded weaklings. The conviction has motivated a whole tradition of intellectual self-declaration, from Zola to Chomsky, from Arnold to Said. The counterpart suspicion found some of its most notable sponsors in the Marxists of the Bolshevik generation, for whom professions of intellectual honour typically signified illusion, nuisance, even danger. Appar-ently binary opposites, the conviction and the suspicion are perhaps better seen as inseparable elements of a general discursive ambivalence. The leitmo-tiv of the affirmative tradition has been, after all, not honour but betrayal – in the phrase that Julien Benda gave to the common parlance of the educated West, *la trahison des clercs*, 'the treason of the intellectuals'. The brusque moral sociology of Bolshevik polemical tradition, itself rather 'intellectual', was to be developed, in Antonio Gramsci's thought, in a way that accorded critical strategic value to a politics of intellectual life. The energy and and variousness of intellectuals' discourse upon their own kind are the deceptive appearances of inertia.

The special interest of Régis Debray's *Teachers, Writers, Celebrities* is that it attempts to move beyond the received terms of understanding.[2] Debray's purpose is to situate *les clercs* in their constitutive material relations, but without dissolving the category into a generic logic of classes, instead analysing the specificities of intellectual life as a determinate social practice, in the historical type-site of the phenomenon, twentieth-century France. These notes will attempt first to situate the book in the history of French writing about intellectuals, and in relation to other relevant traditions; then to examine the historical specificity of the French intelligentsia and suggest some pertinent comparisons and contrasts with Britain and the United States. My object in this is to sketch the outline of a contingent historical formation I call intellectual corporatism.[3]

1

'Le clerc ne trahit jamais.' Debray's studied declaration at once invokes and challenges a whole tradition of intellectual self-reflection. The homeland of this tradition is France, and its inception, in its modern form at least, may be dated from the appearance of *La Trahison des clercs* in 1927. The cultural matrix of Benda's book was a variety of liberal humanism, its politics, amidst the crisis of post-war Europe, an unworldly rejection of all national particularism or social partisanship in the name of the disinterested service of humanity as a whole. *La Trahison des clercs* is internationally significant as a classic statement of this outlook; its added significance in France is that it laid down the protocols of a distinctive cultural occasion that was to recur in subsequent crises and under the auspices of radically contrasting positions.

Benda's symbolic counterpart between the wars was Paul Nizan, whose *Les Chiens de garde* (1932) was one Communist intellectual's 'great-minded harangue' (Debray) against the political quietism of academic philosophy. Some fifteen years later, after the Liberation, Nizan's friend Sartre launched *Les Temps Modernes* with a declaration of intellectual commitment, and wrote *Qu'est-ce que la littérature?* to demonstrate that the writer was, *qua* writer, necessarily on the left. The anti-type, in the Cold War fifties, was Raymond Aron's *L'Opium des intellectuels* (1955). May 1968 and its aftermath saw a great proliferation of such documents, of which Sartre's 1970 interview 'Ami du peuple' and the Godard-Gorin film *Tout va bien* (1972) are among the better-known instances. The confusions and disappointments, the reversals and the desertions of the later seventies – the season of the self-styled New Philosophers – proved no less conducive to this traditional activity than the antithetical conditions of ten years before. The bad objects of the Parisian high intelligentsia might vary (approximately, from Power to the Gulag to the Devil – and back) but an unassimilable plebeian stance continued to be advocated as appropriate to the age.

This tradition, then, is not confined to any particular political or intellectual position; it has been a prominent and constant theme in the national culture of twentieth-century France. Moreover, through all its changes of affiliation, it has retained a marked discursive coherence. It has characteristically been an ethics (or, in the twin classical sense, a politics) of intellectual life. Benda's text was patently and proudly a work of moral prescription founded on an ontology of the intellectual as social being. Nizan's was structurally similar, even if the imperatives were now political and the ground of being was history as class struggle. The socialist politics of *Qu'est-ce que la littérature?* were premissed on the existentialist ethics of Sartre's technical philosophy, the intermediary being an aesthetic conception of the novel as a 'pact of freedoms'.[4] Rationalist, phenomenological or dialectical-materialist, liberal or socialist, these and kindred writings sustained a common discourse whose basic character was always (not only or even principally in the pejorative sense) moralist.

Teachers, Writers, Celebrities lies uneasily among its predecessors, for the main novelty of the book is precisely its practical challenge to moralism and the analytic options and occlusions characteristic of it. It represents, in fact, a break in the tradition. Ethics is displaced here by politics, ontology by history and sociology. Benda invoked the changeless truth of a calling and prescribed its functions accordingly; Debray seeks to analyse the formation and re-formation of a determinate occupational bloc. Sartre's investigation of the relations between intellectuals and their audience concluded that writing was constitutionally leftist, that the vocation of writer was a political fatality; Debray's object, by contrast, is to discover the structured tendencies of intellectual behaviour in successive cultural production-systems and to show how these dictate the posture of the intelligentsia in given political situations. The 'mediological' discourse so initiated is markedly more historical, markedly more materialist than anything in its parent tradition.

Indeed, the novelty of the book remains clear in international comparison. When Debray complains that France is the 'political paradise' of the intelligentsia but the 'purgatory' of its analysts, he does too much justice to the implied national contrasts. More precisely, he underestimates the extent to which the selfsame or similar, essentially philosophico-literary discourse on 'the clerisy' permeates the cultures of the advanced capitalist world, not excepting the younger, scientific disciplines that claim to have superseded it.[5] Whether Debray himself has entirely settled accounts with this 'erstwhile philosophical consciousness' is a consideration that will be taken up. But the main emphasis should fall on the originality of his book. Few analysts have made so concerted an attempt to analyse what might be called, in Marx's terms, the 'social being' of 'social consciousness', the intelligentsia as a social category at work, in one of its major modern incarnations.

2

That is one context in which to read *Teachers, Writers, Celebrities*. But certain others, two in particular, probably hold greater significance for an English-language audience.

The first of these is Frankfurt Marxism. Debray's history of the French intelligentsia is conceived in the form of a study of the development of the national cultural apparatuses – the schools and universities, publishing, the press, radio and television. It is an exercise in 'mediology', and much of its argumentation pertains not so much to intellectuals as to the laws of motion of the institutions in and by which they are deployed. Two processes are given analytic priority. The first, *economic* process is that of the absorption of cultural production into general commodity production, in an era when the capitalist economy is said itself to be undergoing an inner transformation, the relative determining powers of production and distribution being switched to the advantage of the latter. The second, *technical* process involves the development of the forces of cultural production and the institutional rearrangements induced by it. The analytic object so constituted is akin to what the Frankfurt tradition called 'the culture industry'; and the substance of the analysis is no less redolent of Critical Theory, above all in its historical pessimism.[6] Debray may not altogether suppress the distinction between the technical resources of the media and the social relations within which they are utilized, but he denies that it underwrites the possibility of cultural emancipation. The electronic media are bringing forth a culture in keeping with their own unalterable nature, he argues. The modern culture industry falls under one historical law and one only: the law of increasing symbolic immiseration, in obedience to which the criterion of intrinsic worth is displaced by that of 'mediatic surface', the complexity of the message is sacrificed to the volume of its reception, cultural labour is deskilled and its products quality-controlled to ensure the optimal incidence of sensation. A society whose 'high intellectuals' reserve their main energies for appearances on Friday-night television, Debray maintains, is in truth a 'mediocracy'. 'The darkest spot in modern society is a small luminous screen.'

These echoes of the Frankfurt School are notable enough in a writer of Althusserian and Leninist formation. But such arguments stir stronger, more familiar and far more improbable associations. For many of the topics and themes of his book, and even, in places, its tones and cultural accents, were anticipated more than half a century ago in the early writings of F. R. and Q. D. Leavis. The former's *Mass Civilization and Minority Culture* (1930) and the latter's *Fiction and the Reading Public* (1932) showed the same preoccupation with the contemporary economic reorganization of culture that now motivates Debray (though he naturally thinks of the economy as capitalist, a specification that the Leavises thought secondary in the essentially monolithic conditions of 'industrialism').[7] 'Standardization and levelling down' was their conventional shorthand for the same tendencies that Debray now describes as inherent in 'mediocratic' culture. His acid accounts of intellectual life in the Latin Quarter and Montparnasse recall the Leavises' attacks on the 'coteries' of metropolitan London. His analysis of the circuits of influence and advantage in reviewing and promotion is parallel to theirs. For Bernard-Henri Lévy, actor-manager of the New Philosophy, read (say) Michael Roberts, the

strategist of the *New Signatures* and *New Country* anthologies in the early thirties. For Pivot, the tele-journalist with the power of life and death over the
season's new titles, read Arnold Bennett, the star reviewer of the London
Evening Standard. In temper too there is a striking similarity. Cool and concentrated, but then suddenly mocking, indignant or openly angry, both the
Leavises and Debray here display a tense combination of fatalism and defiance. Debray might well cite Gramsci's famous borrowing, 'pessimism of the
intelligence, optimism of the will', for this motto registers the stress at the
heart of his book, the same stress that was defined in the perhaps more lucid
Leavisian phrase, 'desperate optimism': the stress of a cultural voluntarism
armed only with its conscience and always-already-defeated, if its own strategic estimates are really to be believed.

This is not to say that Debray's mediology is in fact a belated, stray variant of *Kulturkritik*. The theoretical constitution of the book will prompt many
questions, but these are best posed in the light of prior and more widely
applicable historical questions. How should we regard this improbable confluence of English cultural criticism and French Marxism, and what does it
suggest about Debray's relationship with the national history that he dis-
cusses? But first, is there anything further to be said about the specificity of
the French case, or by way of pertinent contrast, about the differing cases of
England and the United States?

3

Debray distinguishes three 'cycles' in the past century of French intellectual
history: the academic, which he dates from 1880 to 1930; that of publishing
(1920–1960); and the mediatic, initiated in 1968 and still in its ascendant
phase. These chronological periods delimit not life-spans but hegemonies.
Just as the university displaced the Church in the last years of the nineteenth
century, so, in the inter-war years, publishing and its culture displaced the
university milieu, reorganizing the latter in a subaltern position. Then, in the
1960s, the press and broadcasting apparatuses restructured both, creating a
pyramidal culture in which a mediatic élite became paramount over a subordinate publishing sector and an abject educational system. There was a symbolic succession from Alain to Gide to Glucksmann. However, this was not
the common destiny of the West, and to the extent that it was rather a distinctive French experience, general theses concerning the development of
capitalist commerce and of communications technology cannot fully explain
it: by definition blind to national variation, they are at once too much and too
little. Other elements besides these were involved in shaping this distinctive
historical passage.

The so-called second industrial revolution came very late in France, and when
it did arrive was correspondingly intensified in its rhythms and effects. The

concentration and technical rationalization of industry, the introduction of scientific 'research and development', the production of machines by means of machines and the opening up of the mass market had begun in the United States at the end of the 1890s, and by the end of the First World War had already largely transformed the American urban economy – the baptism of Ford's assembly-line in 1915 symbolized the start of the new era. Over the same period, the multiple conjunctions of commercial pressure and opportunity with technological innovation were responsible for a whole complex of culturally decisive changes: the transformation in the status of advertising and the financial reorganization of the press, the growth of publishing of all kinds, the ascent of Hollywood and the consolidation of a nationwide broadcasting network. By 1930 the cultural format of 'mass', 'consumer' capitalism had been designed and patented. In Britain, it was the war itself and the ensuing depression that triggered the process already known as Americanization. The results, in an economy weakened by technical senescence and over-reliant on the stored fat of Empire, were naturally unequal. Yet within twenty years the economy had been considerably remodelled (most evidently in the sphere of distribution) and the national culture had been transformed – by the promotional revolution, the huge expansion of publishing and the cinema, and the creation of the British Broadcasting Corporation. The American motif was prominent among the attractions of Weimar Berlin for young English writers at that time; Paris, in contrast, was the gathering-place of American intellectuals drawn to an older Bohemian style. It was not surprising, for no comparable transformation was experienced in interwar France. The component processes of the second industrial revolution unfolded slowly and piecemeal, each in its own space and according to its own tempo, in a society that remained archaic overall. A further twenty years and a full constitutional cycle passed before le défi américain finally forced a quickened and coordinated pace of modernization on Gaullist France, the breakneck pace that led to the social collision of 1968.

Higher education forms a second plane of comparison. All three countries laid the foundations of their modern university systems around the same time: roughly, in the last quarter of the nineteenth century and first ten years of the twentieth. The great university reforms of the Third Republic date mainly from the 1880s. In England, where the foundation of London University had already weakened the hegemony of Oxford and Cambridge, the next decade saw the first 'redbrick' institutions of learning chartered as independent universities. Across the Atlantic, in the same years, the first public universities emerged from the old system of Land Grant Colleges. However, the French case stood apart from the British and the American in two decisive respects. The emergent systems in the latter cases were based on recent foundations – Liverpool or Sheffield, Wisconsin or California. The old institutions, Oxford and Cambridge in England, and in the United States the Ivy League colleges – were bypassed, so to speak, in an ambiguous gesture that signified both supersession and untouchability. But the French reforms concerned precisely the old foundations, the Sorbonne and the *grandes écoles* of the Latin Quarter. Beneath this contrast lay a fundamental difference. The late-nineteenth-century innovations in England and the United States belonged to waves of educational expansion that were themselves part of broader processes of economic and cultural change. The innovations of the Third Republic were in this sense socially blank, as the next half-century revealed. By 1930, the national academic corps had grown by under a quarter to 1,405, less than half that of slightly less populous Britain. At the same date, the United States, little more than three times the size of either country, possessed more institutions of higher education than France did academic personnel, and could claim a university and college student population ten times greater than that of France's secondary schools.[8] In sum, the reforms of the 1880s had not been expansionist or even, in any sense that Britain or the United States might have echoed, modernist. The French 'multiversity' lay very far ahead still — as far ahead as the second industrial revolution. The university remained the exclusive, hierarchical institution it had long been. Yet, as Debray explains, it had indeed been reformed: not so much in what it was or how it functioned as in what it represented.[9] The consequences for French culture were decisive.

The purpose of the reforms was directly, expressly political: it was to win the university to the role of a secular, democratic successor to the Church, to create in it the loyal and effective ideological custodian of the new, third Republic. The teaching community, with the Sorbonne and the École Normale at its head, was to be invested as a republican clergy — in the words of the Charter of the Union for Moral Action, as 'a militant lay order based on private and public duty'. The collective initiation of the new order in the struggle over Dreyfus — the very moment when the noun *intellectuel* was added to the language — is powerfully recounted here, but its lasting significance is insufficiently stressed. 'The primal scene of politics', Debray observes elsewhere in the book, is the prince with his scribes. If that is so, then the 'screening memory', in the collective psyche of the French intelligentsia, is of Conscience in the company of the Republic.

The entente between the University and the Third Republic was the formative experience of the intellectuals, the mould of a dual posture that could seem at times the defining attribute of intellectuality as such. In its 'negative' moment, the posture was factional, one of permanent readiness in the defence of threatened allegiances; but there was also the inseparable 'positive' moment that claimed generality, in cultural terms (transcendent values) and often also politically (popular-democratic 'typicality'). *La Trahison des clercs* at once exemplified and depended upon the paradigmatic authority of this dual posture, the posture of a 'republican clergy'. When the old Dreyfusard attacked the 'organizers of political passions', he cited only the extremist opponents of the Republic, like Sorel or Maurras. Durkheim, conceivably the most effective intellectual-politican of the pre-war era, was scarcely mentioned. The Third Republic was more than a party allegiance; it was the *république des professeurs*, the constitutional ground of Reason itself.

This was not a doctrine or a programme; it was rather an objectively constituted repertoire of postures and occasions, a part of the cultural inheritance of generation after generation of French intellectuals and of the audiences to and for whom they spoke. As such it persisted into the publishing and mediatic cycles of the middle and later decades of this century, as a necessary support of the milieux and the practices that Debray describes. True enough, a phenomenon like the New Philosophy presupposed late-capitalist distribution and promotion and the electronic media; and the French apparatuses, being of relatively recent date, are advanced of their kind. It also presupposed the unique degree of centralization that makes Paris the political, academic and lay cultural capital of the country (a fusion of roles elsewhere distributed among, say, Washington, Boston and New York, or London and Oxbridge). But it was quite unimaginable in the absence of the cultural syndrome that ensured that the road to Damascus would be lined with editors and paved with contracts, outside a culture in which the Pauline style was known, expected and prized.

Underlying Debray's tricyclical history there is a continuous tradition whose forcing-house was the reconstitution of the republican state after 1871. Its epitome is the career of Jean-Paul Sartre – brilliant *normalien*, privileged stipendiary of the house of Gallimard, regular focus of controversy in the media and, in the end, petitioner at the Elysée Palace. Merleau-Ponty once charged that Sartre's dramatic style of socialist 'commitment' was dictated by his unreconstructed philosophical individualism, by a 'conception of freedom that allows only for sudden interventions into the world, for camera shots and flash-bulbs.'[10] But if Sartrean commitment was a distinctively existentialist creation, the press cameras that sensationalized its public moments plainly were not. Sartre inherited not only a philosophical tradition that went back to Descartes, but the established morality, the spontaneous ideology of a corporation. His great personal distinction was that he accepted the role of 'intellectual' with the utmost self-consciousness and passion, and reached its limits in the rarest and most creditable of ways – by pressing its possibilities to the point of exhaustion.

The legendary contrast that is the British intelligentsia was shaped by a radically different political history. No one could take the Third Republic for granted: the opposite of a historical fatality, it was a project to further or to thwart, a point of controversy in its own right. But in Britain a remarkably continuous state history had the effect of largely withholding basic constitutional questions from political debate; the great issues of nation and state remained, in local parlance, 'above party politics'. The inevitable beneficiary of this history has been the Conservative Party, since the First World War the

'natural party of government' in Britain. The real hegemonic strength of Conservatism may be judged not by its celebrated pragmatism but by the fact that
it alone of the parliamentary parties in the last seventy years has a proven
capacity for disruptive confrontation – from the break-up of the Lloyd George
coalition to the onslaught on social provision. That the power of political initiative has been monopolized by the oldest and most continuist of the parties
is both cause and consequence of the exceptional constitutional quietism of
the polity.

The culture and the intelligentsia formed in this matrix were correspondingly distinctive. The institutional sequence university-publishing-media was
repeated, but within a shorter time-span and accordingly to a different principle of combination. Here, the older would characteristically *license* the
newer, ceding this specialized function or permitting the extension or dupli-
cation of that, or it would encroach upon the newer, after an initial recoil perhaps, to secure its own advantage in the new territory. In neither case was
there a decisive transfer of hegemony. The university expansion around the
turn of the century was part of a far-reaching process of cultural change, but
it scarcely dimmed the radiation of Oxford and Cambridge: if by the middle
twenties these institutions taught only one in every three university students,[11] their traditions weighed just as heavily on the other two – whose
Oxbridge counterpart, now the élite of an élite, in fact enjoyed the old prestige to the second power. At the beginning of the twenties, relations between
the university and the lay culture based on publishing were close only among
the most archaic and reactionary circles of both, the scholar-gentlemen and
the bellettrists (the Bloomsbury Group was an exceptional case, ideologically
though not socially). For the rest, the contemporary reciprocal hostility of
specialized teachers and writers made glib by commissions and deadlines was
already quasi-institutional.

Yet within twenty-five years the old guards had been dislodged, each by
new generations below them, and a new relationship was instituted in which
the power of the university was manifest. The end of the forties saw the closure of England's last successful literary magazine of extra-academic provenance, *Horizon*. Throughout the fifties, the eclipse of 'creation' by 'criticism'
and of the freelance writer by the academic was widely but unavailingly complained of. By the end of the decade, the major reviewing spaces in the
weekly journals and supplements and the prime literary-ideological occasions were largely reserved by a corps of professor-journalists, many, perhaps
a majority of them, from Oxford and Cambridge. The experience of the electronic media has been in important respects similar. The BBC, as befitted a
national broadcasting service, was apparently born venerable. What it lacked
in years was made up in the funereal propriety that Reith prescribed as its
institutional style. Yet a long time passed before radio, and far longer before
television, won the assent of British intellectuals and their established institutions. The politico-cultural innovations of the wartime service, the incep-

tion of the Third Programme and, ultimately, the creation of the Open University (complete with Vice-Chancellor 'and all the trimmings', lest any misunderstand[12]) were among the crucial steps in the acceptance-colonization of broadcasting.

It would be perverse to argue that the electronic media are the least powerful of cultural institutions. But it would be equally perverse to infer that when Oxford dons pronounce on prime-time television, truth's last citadel has fallen to mediatic barbarism. British continuism has the effect of rejuvenating the older institutions by means of the newer. The rejuvenation of the old, seen from the other side, is the legitimation and regulation of the new, and this is the real strategic value of cultural continuism. The university in effect acts as a licensing authority for other cultural institutions, recognizing and/or regulating the extent and demarcation of their various claims to knowledge and endowing them with something of its own accumulated prestige. The resulting institutional configuration is perhaps unique in its conservative adaptability.

The people whose work was in these institutions were not accustomed to think of themselves as 'intellectuals'. No form of corporate consciousness either drew them together or defined a social role for them as individuals. If the French intelligentsia formed a republican clergy, their English counterparts were decidedly Anglican in temper: aware of higher things but careful not to become tedious on that account, and not really in much doubt of the basic good sense of the nation and those who governed it. It is not that they simply constituted a kind of collective 'happy consciousness' willingly allied with the dominant classes. But two contrasting political histories produced two distinct types of intellectual formation. 'Independence' here signified not a self-defining corporate invigilation of a transcendent general interest but the freedom to pursue one's particular (usually occupational) interest without ideological distraction or politico-juridical interference, in conditions where the Constitution was not a redoubt to be defended or stormed, not even an arena of free civic activity, but a half-noticed, hardly changing country landscape.

The sectoral distribution of political allegiances also differed from one country to the other. In France, according to Debray, academics and teachers have traditionally inclined to the left, writers to the right. This was so during the Dreyfus affair, in the political crisis of the mid-thirties, and is the case again today. But in Britain, it is probably true to say, the intellectual radicalization of the thirties was more marked in the lay culture dominated by writers than in the universities. Other, not directly political motifs of intra-cultural antagonism recurred here, but again in variant forms. The struggle between Paris and the provinces, between privilege and merit, between the versatile amateur and the specialized professional, was epitomized in the hostility between the university and the Academy, between the schools of the Latin Quarter and the salons of the Right Bank. A similar deployment of values was apparent in England between the wars, but here the lines of battle were drawn *inside* the universities, dividing the scholar-gentlemen from the young professionals whose only resource was talent. The main issue in the struggle was the cultural authority of the new discipline of English, whose cause was championed by the Leavises and the writers based on the quarterly *Scrutiny*. The campaign was in one central sense successful. By the end of the Second World War the new generation had effectively displaced the old guard on their own terrain, and within a further ten to fifteen years they had extended their influence over much of the lay literary culture outside the universities. But the profession of English, as it took shape in England, was both an occupation and a claim, the one quite inseparable from the other. The claim was, in effect, that English could and must become the organizing centre of an intellectual élite capable of interpreting the general interest to a society structurally incapable of self-direction – the centre, that is, of an intelligentsia of the 'classic', 'French' type. The fortunes of this cultural effort were complex, but to the Leavises it came to seem like an unending defeat. French intellectuals could claim to represent a general interest as if by public statute; the Leavises' attempt to win the same prerogative for their discipline was met with scorn. The underlying paradox of the French intelligentsia was that its corporate independence was seen as a positive warrant of constitutional stability; it was much the same paradox that appeared, greatly exacerbated, in F. R. Leavis's increasingly wilful, subjectivist insistence that he, more or less alone, defended the 'real' world of English culture against its actual, degraded simulacrum. Every assertion of intellectual corporatism served only to emphasis the irreducible difference between the two national cultures and their respective types.

The Leavises would occasionally couple the United States with France in favourable contrast with England. There too, in the vast American public education system, careers were open to talent. At other times, they would represent the USA as England's future. It was the historic model of all the changes that were remaking traditional patterns of consumption and recreation between the wars, yet its traditions of intellectual independence were such that it seemed also to offer the most advanced paradigms of opposition to the march of 'industrial civilization'. There was demonstrable point in both suggestions, but neither really registered the historical uniqueness of the US social formation, which fostered a distinctive intellectual stratum and a remarkable national variation on the phenomenon of intellectual corporatism.

The United States, on the morrow of the Armistice, contrasted with France and Britain not only in the degree of its economic development (it was now the world's premier capitalist economy); it was also an exceptionally decentralized and, in important respects, fragmented society. Federal institutions and activity had developed rapidly in the first twenty years of the century, and would acquire unprecedented centrality in the course of the thirties, yet there was no commensurate evolution towards a national system of political parties or media along familiar European lines. Regional and other particularisms (religious and/or ethnic) remained proportionately strong in US politics and culture.

However, if in this sense US national institutions appeared underdeveloped, in another sense their politico-juridical ground-plan, the Constitution itself, enjoyed a corresponding prominence. The genesis of the modern United States might be said to have inverted the normal historical relationships of nation-state formation, a small and compact settlement achieving a basic state-form which it then 'filled' with populations and territories many times its own size. The state created the nation, as it were, in a process that continued right into the 1920s. (As late as 1920, fully one-third of US citizens were first- or second-generation settlers.) But the nationalism that arose in these conditions was necessarily different equally from the separatist and the unificationist nationalisms of Europe. Lacking – by definition – that popular prehistory of kinship and custom from which to fashion an effective 'national consciousness', an inclusive US nationalism could look no further back than the Constitution, before which there was, mythically, nothing but a wilderness and a latter-day project of Creation. Thus the founding texts of the US polity and the themes that cluster around them were internalized, in a kind of para-nationalist constitutional fetishism, as one of the true *longues durées* of American culture.

The US intelligentsia, as it took shape in the early decades of this century, reproduced this para-nationalist thematic in its own dominant collective ideology. This was, in effect, the dominant ideology of its main institutional emplacement, the national educational system, and, in its most elaborated version, the intellectual achievement of one profoundly influential thinker: John Dewey. Dewey's educational thought was radically and expressly functionalist: it envisaged a school system that would produce adequate numbers of young adults trained in the skills and attitudes required to sustain the American economic and political order. It was, in this respect, a creed of active national conformism, and in conditions where the weight of pre-bourgeois educational and other cultural values was virtually nil, its hegemony over the intelligentsia was assured. Yet pragmatism as a whole was more than this, and even in its applied forms could plausibly claim to be more than a policy-maker's schema. For the underlying warrant of its conformism was not some ancient *Volksgeist* but a body of postulate and argument, a constitutional rationalism that in principle transcended particular interests. The Deweyan watchword 'education for citizenship' was not only functionalist; it also evoked notions of an order based always and everywhere on free, reasoned participation and valuing critical independence as a cultural norm. Dewey's later career itself showed that these notions were not always and everywhere mere pieties – but only very special cultural conditions could so enhance their power that they became dominant in the ideological formation of a whole segment of the intelligentsia – as was in fact to happen in the milieu of *Partisan Review* and the 'New York intellectuals'.[13]

The nucleus of this intellectual formation was triply marginalized within its cultural environment in the thirties. First, many of its members had come out of the East European Jewish immigration, at a time when that community was only partly assimilated and discriminatory practices – most relevantly, restrictive quotas in higher education – oppressed their children. Second, the dominant political influence in the group was Trotskyism, here as elsewhere a controversial minority current within the intellectual left. Third, their cultural orientation was defiantly internationalist and avant-garde at a time when the popular-frontist literary intelligentsia had joined with an older generation of nativist ideologues in an intolerant cult of 'Americanism'. These were not auspicious circumstances for any new, independent magazine starting out in 1937. But the writers around *Partisan Review* embraced their individual and collective vulnerabilities and made them the substance of a programme, an ethos and a style. The 'New York intellectuals' were anti-academic, and even where (as increasingly) they drew their main income from university teaching, they practised a versatile, generalist mode of writing that was at odds with the prevailing 'Germanic' emphasis on specialized scholarship. Their cultural stance entailed outright opposition to the emergent 'mass culture' of the American city, but they were equally firm in their rejection of conservative nostalgia, whether populist or elitist. Their political disinterestedness was the opposite of quietist; only a minority was ever directly politically engaged, but politics was always a central reference for them, and furnished the occasions of their most vigorous polemical sorties. Bohemians in the academy, moralists in the market-place, intimates of a literature beyond factions yet veterans of the politics of culture: such were the members of what was arguably the 'alienated intelligentsia' par excellence.

Or such, rather, was what Lionel Trilling – the Arnoldian of the circle – might have called their collective 'best self'. For the historical record of the New York intellectuals was one of increasing incorporation and dependence. They may have been 'alienated' from the dominant culture but they belonged to it nonetheless. As Stalinism and the run-up to war drove their politics into crisis, the editors of *Partisan Review* came increasingly to define this alienation as the characteristic state of the displaced, propertyless intellectual. In doing so, they both mistook the real determinations of their original isolation – which had been their minoritarian politics and aesthetics – and misread the cultural affinities of the ideal of 'intellectual' in the American context. This ideal had first emerged in the writings of Van Wyck Brooks and his Westport school as part of an explicitly nationalist cultural programme; and the evolution of the New York intellectuals showed that the association would be a lasting one.[14] *Partisan Review* entered the 1950s utterly transformed. Its political poise had been badly shaken by the war against the Axis and shattered by the Cold War that followed. The journal now supported the US State Department's global effort to contain the spread of Communism. At home, it favoured a preemptive ideological strike that would deal with the political menace while averting the risk of an over-vigorous right-wing assault on civil liberties – the political proclivities of America's 'liberal' intelligentsia were the target of Trilling's major post-war intervention, *The Liberal Imagination*. In the outcome, the journal's solicitude did nothing to avert the McCarthy repression or – Philip Rahv's solitary and heavily qualified disquiet notwithstanding – to resist it when it was unleashed. By 1952, alienation was sufficiently assuaged for the *Review* to run a symposium on 'Our Country and Our Culture'.

Thus, a rhetoric of independence coexisted with a record of conformity. 'The intellectual' and the free play of 'mind' became cultic objects in a milieu that, in keeping with the surrounding culture, was conservative in the fifties, liberal and even radical in the sixties and early seventies, only to swerve rightwards again thereafter. Prominent writers were sharing drinks and ideas at the White House before the Elysée Palace was added to the social map of the high intelligentsia; and Parisian Gulag chic had its tougher-minded equivalent in the New York-Washington 'military-intellectual complex'.

The post-war history of the New York intellectuals is perhaps most starkly illuminated by the career of one of their younger representatives, Norman Podhoretz. Podhoretz studied with Trilling at Columbia (and then Leavis at Cambridge) in the immediate post-war period. Having completed his academic studies, he joined the prestigious New York magazine *Commentary*, of which he became editor in 1960. Formed in the *Partisan Review's* 'liberal anti-Communism', he later embraced an idiosyncratic 'radicalism' based on Norman Mailer, Paul Goodman and Norman O. Brown. But by the later sixties this amalgam had disintegrated, and Podhoretz became a clamorous publicist for neo-conservatism. The main purpose of his memoir *Breaking Ranks* was to recapitulate and defend these successive allegiances, but its most powerful demonstration is of a whole tradition quite radically blocked. The 'alienation', or what remains of it, is of a wayward society from the quintessential American standard represented by the 'intellectual'. And that appellation, claimed compulsively on page after page, is no longer primarily important as a reference – to a milieu, say, or a programme. It is now above all the symptom of a measureless self-regard.[15]

4

The purpose of these comparative notes is not to set the scene for general theoretical conclusions – that would presuppose more exacting historical scholarship and finer analytic tools than any utilized here. But it is difficult, as one considers these divergent yet oddly echoing histories, not to feel curious about the sources of Debray's polemical energy, not to inquire what exactly it is that underwrites his freelance oppositionism.

The main impulse in *Teachers, Writers, Celebrities* is undoubtedly political. It is political first of all in the general sense that its inquiry into the development of the French cultural apparatuses is shaped by a strong strategic preoccupation with the forms of bourgeois power. But Debray's more intimate concern here is with the political fate of a whole intellectual generation. The strength of this motivation can be measured by its very persistence. In 1967, in the first of what was to have been thirty years in a Bolivian jail, he wrote 'In Settlement of All Accounts', a vivid memoir of his student days at the École Normale.[16] He was already conscious then of a certain unreality in the political attachments of his milieu, and of the rising pressure of careerism and competition inside it. Within a decade his fears had been borne out. His *Modeste contribution aux discours et cérémonies officielles du dixième anniversaire*, published in 1978, depicted the May explosion as a functional crisis of development for consumer capitalism in France, and attacked its intellectual notables for their regression to irrationalism and political reaction.[17] The present work is a more ambitious attempt to lay bare the specifically cultural structural mechanisms that led to the all but total collapse of the Parisian left intelligentsia in the later seventies.

However, Debray's political intransigence is not his only resource. His mediology produces a quasi-Frankfurtian analysis that explicitly denies the presence of politically sufficient contradictions within the cultural order. How, then, is his own position sustained? This is the function of a second level of his text. From time to time Debray pauses to meditate on the transgenerational continuities of the old *lycées*, or to demand 'total support' for the few surviving literary reviews of the old kind, or to brood on the possibility of a world without *Le Monde*. These passages are intermittent and brief, but they are more than flourishes. They are outcrops of a discourse that underlies the expanse of *Teachers, Writers, Celebrities*: the classic discourse of the French intellectual tradition. The undeclared activity of this discourse is responsible for certain anomalous features of the text, very notably the systematic recourse to anatomical and zoological metaphor, as if in compensation for a forbidden ontology. External circumstances also suggest the ambiguities of the association. The fact that a Marxist reflecting on the involution of the French intellectual tradition can spontaneously reproduce the themes of its minoritarian English counterpart of fifty years ago is a sign that strong cultural currents are running in channels that remain to be opened for investigation. One can know only what one refuses, says Debray, paraphrasing Goethe. Mediology, with its commitment to the primacy of explanation, suggests the necessary correction. The maxim is a half-truth whose necessary complement is its inverse: one can refuse only what one knows.

1981

INTELLECTUAL CORPORATISM AND SOCIALISM
The Twenties and After

My topic is the phenomenon of intellectual corporatism, by which I mean a cultural formation in which ideologies of collective unity and independence take hold in a given intelligentsia, or in a given segment of an intelligentsia. To propose this idea is to deny that intellectuals are constituted as such by their ideological dispositions or affiliations, and, specifically, to reject the classic self-definition of 'the intellectual' as an adequate account of the category and the cultural practice so named. At the same time, however, this formulation implies a limiting judgement on the kind of sociological reductionism – whether it issues from my own theoretical tradition, Marxism, or from another quarter – that simply burns off an illusion to disclose a blackened field of class relations. Conceived in the spirit of Gramsci, the idea of intellectual corporatism implies a critical displacement of the received notion of 'the intellectual' but also an attempt to describe and explain its specific historical reality and efficacy. For what has to be reckoned with is the fierceness and resourcefulness with which the corporatist claim – be it scholarly or activist in manner, literary, philosophical or sociological in substance – has persisted down to the present – and with what confusing effects. On this occasion, I attempt, very briefly, to reconstruct something of the history of intellectual corporatism in this century, both as an objective trend and as a topic of discourse in its own right, and to show how, at a certain juncture, it became associated with socialism, mostly in the culture of the left, though the idea of this association became a commonplace on the right as well. My account covers approximately fifty years from the end of the First World War; its turning point comes in the later 1930s.

Humanistic social criticism was a familiar genre, especially in Germany and England. But the political and cultural upheavals of the 1920s renewed its energy and sense of purpose, provoking a Europe-wide rally of the traditional humanist intelligentsia. In Germany, as the First World War neared its end, the conservative anti-bourgeois tradition of *Kulturkritik* was renewed by Thomas Mann, whose *Reflections of an Unpolitical Man*, published in 1918, described and lamented the coming defeat of (German) culture by (French) civilization, the onset of a spiritless modernity given over to politics, rationalism and prose, the obsolescence of traditional 'inwardness' and the hegemony of 'civilization's literary man'.[1] In 1925 the Italian philosopher Benedetto Croce, repenting of his early attraction to Mussolini, published his response to the *Manifesto of the Fascist Intellectuals* and embarked on a course of cultural opposition centred on 'the religion of liberty' and a 'true aristocracy' of intellect.[2] Kindred themes ran through Julien Benda's *La Trahison des clercs* (1927), the legendary statement of intellectual commitment, which deplored the misalliance of mind with politics in contemporary mass movements and recalled *les clercs* to their sacred duty in the service of perennial values.[3] Then, at the turn of the decade, came F. R. Leavis's *Mass Civilization and Minority Culture* and José Ortega y Gasset's *The Revolt of the Masses* (both 1930): an English literary critic and a Spanish philosopher united in rejecting instrumental reason and the 'democratic' Babel of the modern market in values, in the name of cultural wholeness and authority.[4]

Now, these works form a historical cluster, not a faction. Their philosophical divergences were, at their extremes, irreconcilable. Leavis's cultural diagnosis associated him with Ortega and the Mann of 1918, but his episodic political sympathies, in the anti-fascist alert of the 1930s, lay rather with Benda, Croce and the later, the official Mann.[5] Croce's vision of history, contrasting with that of his English, German and Spanish contemporaries, was essentially progressivist, while Benda's quasi-platonic vision of 'the eternal' reduced history to so much degrading circumstance. Yet their affinities were crucial. All of them wrote from and for the presumptive commitments of a received humane culture. Their respective understandings of this culture revealed a shared idealism. For Mann, Leavis and Ortega, all drawing on the German romantic tradition, it was the integral human negative of commercial-industrial 'civilization'; Benda's realm of perennial values was set above and against the to-and-fro of social struggle; for Croce, modern history was in essence the self-realization of liberty, temporary appearances notwithstanding. Politically, they were rather elusive, for, in effect, their political options were emergency measures dictated finally by a commitment that was meta-political in character. Their common basic inclination was towards an authoritarian liberalism disengaged from the clashing social interests whose true moral measure it claimed exclusively to be. Croce was directly active in politics, yet his philosophy of practical reason left no space to theorize this option, distinguishing only economics and ethics. Like the others, he dwelt upon the critical intimations of culture, reason or spirit, and this led not to a politics of any ordinary kind but to an *ethics of intellectuality*. Spiritual 'treason' was Benda's theme, and the others echoed the charge; together they assembled a gallery of treachery and default. Croce and Leavis attacked patronage and academicism, Ortega deplored the proliferation of technical specialisms, and Benda condemned the pamphleteering 'organizers of political passions', right or left. The positive counterparts were Croce's 'poet militant', Leavis's 'disinterested minority', Ortega's 'man of culture', Benda's *clerc*: so many redemptive images of the genuinely autonomous and hence genuinely committed intellectual.

Here, then, we have intellectual corporatism as a subject-position, a self-affirming cultural and political identity. In the same period, it began to be focused as an *object* of analysis. The 1920s witnessed not only this late rally of the humanist intelligentsia; it also saw the beginning of a sociology of intellectuals.

Karl Mannheim was one of the legendary founders of this branch of sociology. (He also became, in later years, a target of conservative-humanist criticism, drawing fire from T. S. Eliot and from Leavis's *Scrutiny*, among others.[6]) His consideration of 'the sociological problem of the intelligentsia', in *Ideology and Utopia* – published in 1929, at the height of this cultural episode – is one of the best-known documents of its kind.[7] Its starting point, in Alfred Weber's famous phrase, was 'the free-floating intelligentsia'. How, Mannheim asked, was this phenomenon to be understood and evaluated? Mannheim dismissed all class-ascriptive analyses of the intelligentsia. In his view, neither provenance nor location nor orientation determined them as a part of any fundamental social class. The only thing that unified intellectuals was their high level of education: unified *and separated* them, for while members of fundamental social classes tended to reproduce 'directly and exclusively' the modal outlook of their peers, intellectuals were formed through an educational experience that brought the whole of society and its opposing forces into view. As a result, they acquired a special bent for 'synopsis', for 'synthesis' and 'dynamic mediation'; they were uniquely aware of society as a whole, and correspondingly less prone to sectional partisanship. Two courses were available to them, then. The more common course was to affiliate to a fundamental social class and to serve it by spiritualizing its struggle for advantage, by transmuting 'interests' into 'ideas'. This was not a satisfactory option, Mannheim believed: intellectuals were trained into a highly deliberative frame of mind that made them dubious allies, and in straining to repress this quality in themselves, they usually lapsed into an equally unserviceable fanaticism. The other and preferable course was to exploit the potential of their distinctive training; to organize *as* intellectuals in an educational 'forum' that would transcend the particularism of 'the party schools'. In such forums they would seek to fulfil 'their mission as the predestined advocate of the intellectual interests of the whole'.

Mannheim's analysis, with its social-scientific air and peaceably reformist politics, was in obvious ways a departure from the humanist tradition. Yet it surely begins to sound familiar. Indeed its continuities were fundamental. Mannheim's sociology of knowledge was led by its own relativist logic into a familiar dualism: on the one hand a driven world of 'ideology' and 'interest', on the other, the deliberative exploration of the social whole – or, in terms that he might just as well have chosen, 'mass civilization' and 'minority culture'. The outlines of his social policy are equally recognizable. His personal democratic convictions do not cancel the fact that in proposing a social peace whose cultural foundations were by definition inaccessible to the great majority – workers and capitalists alike – he was simply updating the claims of a pseudo-aristocratic authoritarian liberalism. Mannheim's sociology was thus a transposition of cultural criticism, not, in theory or in political implication, a break with it. The passage from humanistic to scientific reason occurred within the received discursive convention. However, this convention really was now nearing the point of an important mutation, the decisive condition of which was political.

The victory of fascism in Germany quickly altered the diplomatic posture of the Soviet Union and, as a consequence, the respective national orientations of the European Communist parties. Within two years, the ultra-left course of the Third Period was abandoned in favour of the militant moderation of the Popular Front. Opposition to fascism and war, organized in the widest obtainable political alliances, now took precedence over specifically anti-capitalist initiatives. The critical tests of the new orientation were political and military, but its most ostentatious novelty was an altered and intensified *cultural* practice. The late twenties and early thirties had been devoted to the assertion of 'class against class' in culture as in politics. Calls for an authentically proletarian or revolutionary literature were flanked with broadside denunciations of bourgeois culture and its representatives. Associations of worker-writers were set up, with journals to serve them: the German *Linkskurve*, or *Anvil* in the United States. Communist intellectuals drew unsparing portraits of the 'decadent', 'social-fascist' culture they had left behind: Dmitri Mirsky's *The Intelligentsia of Great Britain* and Paul Nizan's *Les Chiens de garde* (both 1932) are classics of this phase.[8] Now, the logic of popular-frontism entailed a depolarization of cultural life. 'Proletarian' activity continued, but with reduced or no official encouragement; the cultural apparatuses of the Comintern parties were henceforward devoted to mobilizing the forces of the 'democratic bourgeoisie'; the symbolic vanguard of the struggle against fascism was to be the 'critical intelligentsia'. The organizations, journals and events that incarnated the new course were typically national or universalist in address: the League of American Writers, *Das Wort*, the International Writers Congress for the Defence of Culture. Marxism and working-class struggle, where they were still urged, were refigured as the most consistent and committed inheritors of shared traditions. So, old hostilities were curbed and new allies courted. In France, for example, Henri Barbusse, the awkward notable who, exploiting the prestige he enjoyed as the author of the pacifist classic *Le Feu*, had hampered the implementation of a sectarian cultural line in French Communism, was now exalted as the very type of the 'progressive writer'; while Paul Nizan, the leftist scourge of philosophical 'buffoonery', found himself reviewing the works of Julien Benda in articles that were models of forbearance and cordiality.[9] Such were the means and circumstances of the Communist attempt to rally intellectuals in a militant humanist crusade, a 'popular front of the mind'.

Popular-Frontism was in its own most urgent terms a failure: the Spanish revolution was crushed, and within two years fascist armies had taken control of most of bourgeois Europe and were moving east against the Soviet Union. In a longer perspective, however, its impact was felt in the politics of war and reconstruction in every affected country. The cultural forces assembled in this period had many destinies. In the best of cases, that of Italy, they were consolidated in a strong, naturalized Communist tradition; in the worst, that of the USA, they were dispersed by repression. But in every case they bore witness to the necessary, even though unsought, implication of popular-front discourse. Out of these years came a potent tradition (or legend) of 'the intellectuals and the left'. In a dreamlike condensation of orthodox Leninism and high-humanist disaffection, the intellectual *as such* was figured as a critical agency of political opposition and advance, and even of revolution. This was more than a sentimental inheritance of the left. It was rather the commonplace within which both socialist and conservative reflection on intellectuals was conducted in the succeeding decades.

In 1942, after years of meditation in his native Austria and then in American exile, the economist Joseph Schumpeter published his analysis of the social order in the west.[10] His theses were stark. Unlike Mannheim, he spoke plainly of capitalism and socialism, of the inevitable defeat of the former by the latter, and of the conspicuous revolutionary role of a social group that capitalism had fostered but could not repress unless by fascist means: not, as might be thought, the working class but the intelligentsia. Capitalism was inherently self-destructive, Schumpeter believed, and this in significant measure because it tended to generate a climate of 'almost universal hostility' to itself. Capitalism created a critical habit of mind which, once formed, would stop at nothing: 'the bourgeois finds to his amazement that the rationalist attitude does not stop at the credentials of kings and popes but goes on to attack private property and bourgeois values.' The whole social order was at the mercy of intellectuals, in whose interest it supposedly was to 'work up and organize resentment, to nurse it, to voice it and to lead it'.

Although intellectuals were drawn from among the highly educated, Schumpeter wrote, their hallmark was the subjectivity of discontent: there is no such thing as a happy intellectual. He went on to detail the cultural and social developments that in his view had formed this social group. These were, he said, structural to capitalism and their upshot was inevitable. The intellectuals, searching for a social mass capable of lending force to their compulsive 'nibbling' and 'biting', would 'invade' the labour movement, flatter the workers as once they had flattered princes, and prepare them for the culminating assault on capital.

Conceived in post-Hapsburg Vienna and completed in wartime America, Schumpeter's work spanned two centres and two generations of discourse on intellectuals. The inherited theme of intellectual corporatism was refashioned in his hands. The old humanistic criticism had posited a transcendent social interest and a kind of social being who bore witness to it: Benda, Leavis and Mannheim were all devoted to a vocational ethics of intellectuality. Schumpeter dealt roughly with this project; the problem of the day was, so to speak, not 'society' but 'culture' – the intellectuals and their irrepressible socialist leanings.

Schumpeter's theses were among the opening statements in a discussion that engaged American culture for more than twenty years. The variety of this discussion is too great to be summarized in a sentence or two. But its overarching context was the Pax Americana: a long boom and a long counter-revolution. Anti-communism was the keynote of US politics and culture. At home, the left was hammered; and meanwhile the US state moved outwards, creating the financial, politico-military and cultural institutions through which it implemented its hegemony over the capitalist world: Bretton Woods, NATO and (in ironic tribute to the intellectual crusades of the thirties) the Congress for Cultural Freedom. Schumpeter's economic pessimism was controversial in these conditions, but his cultural diagnosis seemed apt. In the *film noir* lighting of the Cold War, the shadow cast by intellectuals was socialism. Lionel Trilling, a literary critic working in self-conscious descent from Matthew Arnold, went so far as to claim that the left movements of the 1930s had 'created' the US intelligentsia.[11] His own solution was a feline liberalism committed to 'variousness, possibility, complexity, and difficulty'; and there were many who agreed. But to another kind of liberal – Schumpeter's compatriot and fellow-economist Friedrich von Hayek – the Arnoldian play of mind was precisely the endemic favouring condition of anti-capitalism.[12] Little more than a measure of fastidiousness distinguished Trilling's cultural politics from official ideology. But in a world of loyalty oaths and passionate conformism, even that could seem subversive.

The theme of socialism as the new 'treason of the intellectuals' was a commonplace of North Atlantic culture in the 1950s. The Cold War bound the old and the new discursive conventions in a phobic discourse on the irresponsibility of intellectuals. However, the opposite evaluation was possible too. The idea of an essential affinity between intellectuals and socialism had first been promoted by the left, most dramatically in France, where it was a virtual cliché. Julien Benda – Nizan's *clerc de gauche*, who conceded when the time came that it was 'permissible' to support the Popular Front – was the mannered epitome of this tradition. In post-Liberation France it found a new symbol and a definitive theorist in another philosopher: Nizan's old friend, Jean-Paul Sartre.

'What is literature?' was the opening question of Sartre's post-war career.[13] His answer was: *committed* literature. And what he meant by this was that there was an *identity* between commitment to literature and commitment to socialism. Literature presupposed free inter-subjectivity, a 'pact of freedoms' between writer and reader. But capitalist class relations negated this condition. To write at all, then, was to oppose the norms of capitalist culture and to prefigure the unalienated order of socialism. An authentic commitment to literature was, logically and morally, a commitment to socialism. The writer *as such* was of the left. Or, as he later put it, in his 'Plaidoyer pour les intellectuels' (1965), the writer was necessarily an 'intellectual'.[14]

So 'what is an intellectual?' Intellectuals emerge from among what Sartre called 'the technicians of practical knowledge', under the pressure of an irresolvable contradiction. The conditions of formation of these technicians are in every way functionally associated with capitalism, yet they are educated in an official humanism (Mannheim's 'synoptic' vision). Their special skills are implicitly universalist, yet they are deployed according to the particular logics of capital and the state. Structurally defined by this situation, the technicians of practical knowledge can do one of two things: they can submit in bad faith, or they can become 'meddlers', systematic minders of other people's business – 'intellectuals'. Intellectuals are 'monsters', Sartre maintained, a 'lived impossibility'. That is the one and only principle of their social being. 'False' intellectuals try to escape their contradiction by escaping into a bogus universalism devoted to 'constructive' social criticism – like the poet Lamartine in the revolution of 1848, they cannot reason beyond the proposition that social conflict arises from 'a terrible misunderstanding'.[15] 'True' intellectuals, in contrast, embrace their contradiction. They are 'singular universals', embodiments of as-yet-unrealized human values, and as such they find common cause with the other singular universals of capitalism, above all the working class. The true intellectual is a true humanist, and the true humanist is the revolutionary socialist intellectual, the 'guardian of fundamental ends'.

Sartre's political values were in every way opposed to Schumpeter's. He wrote as a decided Marxist, with express debts to Gramsci. But whereas the main Marxist tradition had always seen the question of the intellectuals as an aspect of the larger strategic problem of political organization, Sartre made it primary. At the centre of his cultural landscape was a figure at once new and old: the independent, the intellectual as revolutionary witness. The negative historical condition of this departure was the decomposition of Stalinism, but it was fuelled from deeper-lying sources, in older cultural formations. So it was that Marxist philosophy could meet conservative sociology in a common idiom. For the parallels in these two analyses are equally strongly marked, and can be pursued in detail. They are the signs of a shared convention and a shared history. Schumpeter's sociology and Sartre's ethics were oppositely but equally interpretations of a single compelling historical image: *le clerc de gauche*, the autonomous intellectual as the herald of socialism.

There is no simple lesson to be drawn from this history; it provokes too many questions to be usable in that way. Some of these questions bear directly on social and cultural theory, and as such must be set aside for now. My closing remarks do no more than point to the terms of an ethico-political crux. What I have been trying to describe is the persistence in twentieth-century culture and politics of what might be called a 'romance of mind' – a whole set of ideas and images that have not only persisted but actually flourished, becoming as much a part of socialist cultural tradition as of more powerful liberal traditions, with results that are, to say the least, ambiguous. Humanism and its distinctive guardian – the intellectual, the Arnoldian 'best self' of an 'ordinary' world – are living, more vigorously and more variously than many of us like to think.

So where is the alternative? Michel Foucault took the view that the culture of the 'classic intellectual' had passed away in the late 1960s: that humanism had been criticized to death, that kind of intellectual posture was an anachronism. Although the cultural and political circumstances – those of Paris in the 1970s – that prompted this generalization were real enough, they are too parochial, as evidence, to validate it. Foucault's thesis was no doubt the easier to pronounce because of the other things he felt able to dispense with: the idea of society as an intelligible whole, the idea of a directed or directable historical process – ideas which, in one mode or another, have been fundamental not only to humanist traditions but also to revolutionary socialism. The anti-humanisms of the past thirty years have been either too little or too much: too little, if all they really intend is a consistent anti-essentialism, which can scarcely pretend to deal with historical humanism as a whole; too much, if they are pursued to the point where they undermine the notion of a general human emancipation, which is the ultimate goal of any socialism worthy of the name. We have to pause to ask whether there actually is an alternative in the clear, expected sense. Sartre used to say that Marxism was the unsurpassable horizon of all thought in our time: one could think against it, certainly, but not beyond it. Perhaps socialist intellectuals are similarly placed in relation to humanism: scarcely the faithful heirs of an old tradition, as the lulling tones of Popular-Front culture suggested, and scarcely the heroic consciences of Sartre's vision; struggling towards a kind of self-understanding that is consistently historical and materialist, no doubt – but a humanism all the same.

1988

TOWARDS 2000, OR NEWS FROM
YOU KNOW WHERE

Contemporary metropolitan culture is pervaded by what Raymond Williams has come to call 'the sense of the loss of the future'[1] – the future not as a continuation of recognizable forms of social existence but as a locus of realizable alternatives. The stronger probabilities of the years ahead appear dispiriting and dangerous, and, more gravely, it is increasingly widely feared that the reservoir of historical possibility is in fact a mirage. It is ironic that capitalism should at length have advanced to this. As spontaneous interpreter of the most dynamic mode of production in history, capitalist culture valorized the attainable earthly future as no prior culture could have done. The theme of 'modernity' was and is just this: an endless serial presentation, *making present*, of the future. The ambition was not empty: capitalism has remade and continues to remake the earth and its populations. But the accumulation of tomorrows is self-depleting. The physical landscapes of advanced capitalism are now littered with stalled and abandoned futures, things and people alike; much metropolitan culture is an aimless circulation of retro-chic; and apocalypse itself is just the last word.

But socialism too has seen its futures come and go. Capitalism has survived longer, and with far greater material and social successes, than most nineteenth-century socialists would have forecast. Social democracy, in spite of governmental opportunities extending over as much as half a century, has nowhere prevailed against the rule of capital, and in many cases is unable even to sustain its limited achievements. The Communist tradition has more to show, having abolished capitalism across one-third of the planet; but, for all their social gains, the bureaucratic regimes of the East one after another dissipated their original power of example and attraction for socialists elsewhere; and the Communist parties in the West are caught in a political latitude whose climate varies only between Stalinist freeze-up and the treacherous thaw of social democracy. Revolutionary tendencies have continued to assert themselves against this virtual system of political frustration, but none has yet summoned the force necessary to break through its cyclical present into a hopeful socialist future.

This is the context in which to retrace the fortunes of 'projective' and 'prospective' discourse on the left. The rhetoric of social dissent has traditionally included projections of the desired alternative. However important the main critical modes of analysis and polemic, there was obvious, perhaps even special, utility in the attempt to give body to the values that animated them.

This was the work of the 'utopia', a fictional mode in which the optative assumes the forms of the indicative, the goals of the struggle appearing as if already fully and securely achieved. The utopia was a powerful inspirational device, and was valued as such in the diverse radical culture of the nineteenth century. But its defining operation was wish-fulfilment; it dealt in idealities whose earthly home was, admittedly, 'nowhere'. By the end of the century this fiction, together with other forms of discourse to which the generic term 'utopian' was now applied, had been depreciated, as a radically different conception of intellectual priorities won hegemony over the socialist movement.

The theory inaugurated by Marx and Engels was distinctively 'scientific'. Communism was possible because of the real movement of material history, and would come about not through the redemptive human incarnation of an ideal scheme but by the overthrow of capitalism at the hands of its own social creation, the proletariat. Utopianism was now obsolete. The primary responsibilities of 'scientific socialism' were the analysis of capitalism and the states that defended it, and the development of organizations and programmes capable of mobilizing the working class against them. The projection of desirable futures now gave way to the analysis of historical prospects. Utopian and romantic writing did not wholly disappear from Marxist culture: William Morris produced the classic *News From Nowhere* (1890); Engels's *Dialectics of Nature* (1876) veered at times towards a kind of evolutionary romance; revolutionary Russia stimulated Kollontai's fiction and the rhapsodic finale of Trotsky's *Literature and Revolution* (1923); and socialist realism itself bore a heavy charge of official romance. But the main prospective mode was the strategic forecast. Works such as Trotsky's *Results and Prospects* (1906), Luxemburg's *Accumulation of Capital* (1913) and Lenin's *Imperialism* (1916) addressed themselves to the existing systemic trends of capital and its political and military apparatuses. Their analyses were in one sense bleak, predicting the impossibility of 'normal' political development in Russia, an inbuilt capitalist drive towards barbarism, a century of inter-imperialist warfare. Yet they were motivated by a powerful historical optimism. They prepared for the worst because only in that way could they prepare to forestall it, turning the contradictions of capitalist development to revolutionary account. The socialist future was not in doubt, but it depended on the strategy and tactics of the socialist revolution.

This definition of priorities remains valid, but it no longer possesses a monopoly of realism. 'Socialism' has been official fact for many hundreds of millions in Europe, Asia and the Caribbean. That ambiguous record, interlocking with the history of social-democratic management of capital, has deformed and discredited socialist politics throughout the world. In such conditions, some kinds of projection are no longer idle, and strategy risks abandonment as the last utopia.

Anything but novel, considerations of this kind have already run to practical results in the politics and culture of the left. The putative instrumentalism of traditional strategic thought has been widely challenged by an expressive politics whose key references are feminism and ecology. The cultural capacity of 'the new social movements' is widely acclaimed – and is nowhere more telling than in its rediscovery of the fictional modes of romance (Alice Walker's *The Color Purple*, from 1982) and utopia (Ursula Le Guin's *The Dispossessed*, 1975, Marge Piercy's *Woman on the Edge of Time*, 1976). Developments like these, however we evaluate them case by case, signal a deep and probably permanent change in the conditions of socialist strategic thinking.

Towards 2000

This recognition has long been a force in the work of Raymond Williams. It has governed the development of his central concept of 'culture', which, while gaining in specificity as an object of materialist analysis, has remained a criterion of moral judgement; and it has supported his steady criticism of any too-peremptory dismissal of romanticism. His writings have repeatedly questioned the meanings of 'nature' in bourgeois (and, by inheritance, socialist) culture. He has written about utopianism in Morris and Le Guin, and has made his own contribution to the fiction of the future in his 'hypothetical' novel, *The Volunteers* (1978).[2] At the same time, Williams's work has always been distinctive for the radically historical, anti-essentialist stress of its analyses, and its tough-minded wariness in political response. He has never accepted the analytic and the moral, the indicative and the optative, as truly sustainable alternatives. Constructive, if tense, argument between them is a necessary condition for the creation of an informed, authoritative and capable socialist movement.

All such positions must find their support in the evidence of the past; but their point concerns the future. In *Towards 2000*, Williams turns forward in time, to assess the probabilities of the remaining years of the century.[3] The title of the book is an argument in itself. Invoking old and non-rational traditions of discourse on the future, it signifies the decision to venture beyond strategic minimalism into the possible reality of a socialist order – and this as a condition of renewing social 'hope'. But Williams is equally concerned to avoid the typical prolepses of utopianism. His objective is to understand the future historically, in a 'prospective analysis' that seeks to interpret 'the underlying problems, forces and ideas' of capitalism and its probable future, and to 'indicate some possible ways through them' towards a decidedly non-millenarian socialism.

Towards 2000 is a difficult book to write about, in the first place because of its form, which emerges from the special circumstances of Williams's own work. It is written as a review and extension of an earlier prospective analysis entitled 'Britain in the Sixties' and first published as that decade opened, in *The Long Revolution* (1961).[4] Williams reprints his analysis here, and resumes its discussions of economic, cultural and political structures and ideologies, and of the labour movement; then takes his argument into new territories, with chapters on 'the culture of nations', the world economic and political order, and the arms race; and finally moves to a reflection on the available theoretical and political 'resources for a journey of hope'. Demanding in range, the book is also variable in analytic focus, moving from the abstract (capitalist production as such) to the concrete (the international economic system), the general (bourgeois-democratic representative practices) to the particular (the British Labour Party), sometimes without notice. *Towards 2000* can then be described as 'open' in a sense that is not merely polite: it is amenable to several quite distinct kinds of assessment, and demands not summary but elaborated responses. The scope, proportion and nuance of Williams's analyses will not be represented adequately, much less emulated, in what follows here: a brief account of his main theses, and some thoughts on their theoretical and political implications.

Old Horizons: Economy, Culture and Politics

Williams's argument is centrally a critical analysis of the dominant culture in its most practical, even functional, aspect. The real objects of this culture (economic, political and, of course, cultural too) are discussed directly, but in a selective mode whose priorities are dictated by a strategy of ideological displacement and counter-formulation. The field of analysis is Britain and its international relations, in the perspective of a reachable and sustainable socialism.

Analysing the mystifications of consumer capitalism on the eve of the 1960s, Williams queried the expectation of 'a steadily rising standard of living in this economically exposed and crowded island. Both the rapid rate of economic growth elsewhere, and the certainty of steady industrialization of many areas now undeveloped, seem ominous signs for a country so dependent on trade and in fact given its prosperity by its early industrial start (now being overtaken) and its empire (now either disappearing or changing its character).'[5] The signs were not deceptive, and now the balance of Williams's attention shifts towards production, to the fateful realities invoked in such terms as 'post-industrialism', 'de-industrialization' and 'employment'. Arguing through and against the assumptions clustered around these words, Williams maintains that the current crisis must be understood and tackled as that of the *international capitalist social order*. The closures and redundancies of recent decades are attributable not to a new phase of technical innovation *per se*, but to technologies designed and deployed in accordance with the ordinary logic of capitalist production and marketing. To construe the present restructuring of manufacturing capital as 'de-industrialization' is to misrecognize capitalism, which is now a synthetically international system, and industry itself, which will continue its uneven transformation of economic activity well into the future. In the face of this reality, such policy nostrums as reflation and protection are utterly inadequate. They fail to confront the social implications of continuing technical development and assume an impossible national autarky; they preserve the socially null value of aggregate production and – the ultimate economic irrationality – remain trapped in the bourgeois fantasy of 'infinite production' in a 'finite world'.

Yet more ominously, the crisis has begun to dissociate a trinity whose substantial unity has long been a tenet of capitalist faith and of Labour's alternative accountancy: that of 'work', 'employment' and 'income'. In effect, Williams argues, capitalism can understand work only as industrialized wage-labour. This can be seen in the conventional tripartition of economic activity, which models all social labour as a factory process, and is then obliged to classify most of it in the absurd category of 'services'; in a classification of skill that bears no relation to any rational assessment of expertise; in the occlusion of household labour and the devaluation of its socialized extensions and equivalents. The economic crisis is, among other, more familiar things, a crisis of this world view. For given the probable course of world demand for manufactured goods and the technical transformation of production processes, unemployment can be ended only by a major development of the labour-intensive activities of 'nurture and care' – kinds of work that attract low (or no) income because they do not, and cannot, reward capitalist investment. 'Welfare capitalism' has always been a contradiction in terms, Williams argues. Only if welfare is generalized as the shaping principle of all economic activity can technical innovation become 'labour-saving' in a positive sense. But this entails the institution of a planned and socialized economy, and, as a necessary practical and moral corollary, a break with capitalism's accounting of labour and income, in conditions that will demand the sharing of abundance but also of want. To propose less or to promise more is merely to echo 'the death-cry of an old social democracy'.[6]

The imagined and real bearings of technology are again to the fore in Williams's discussion of contemporary culture. Here too a new phase of technical innovation has begun, and, with it, a new round of controversy. Cultural conservatives resist cable and satellite broadcasting systems, discerning in them (as in so many earlier developments) the final onset of barbarism. They are joined in their opposition by many on the left, who see the new systems as the instruments of an increasingly powerful apparatus of cultural domination. This reaction is understandable but dangerous, for 'all that follows from so undeveloped a position is a series of disparaging remarks and defensive campaigns, leading in so many cases to tacit alliance with the defenders of old privileged and paternalist institutions, or, worse, with the fading ideas of the old cultural argument: a high culture to be preserved and by education and access extended to a whole people.'[7] Williams's response is to analyse the actual significance of contemporary developments in communications, and to assess the position of that 'old cultural argument' and its defenders. Again he insists on the fundamental distinction between *techniques* and their variable social elaborations in specific *technologies*: the former are subject to physical necessity but the latter are crucially shaped by economic, political and cultural forces. The new technologies are menacing because they are being deployed in the service of a very few 'paranational' corporations and metropolitan power-centres; the culture they relay is correspondingly homogenized, and will tend to weaken and marginalize significant alternative practice. The traditional 'minority culture' cannot resist this trend, for the simple reason that it has already succumbed. The evolution of its means of support furnishes material evidence of its loss of independence, passing from private patronage through state subsidy to commercial sponsorship – from Harriet Weaver to the Arts Council to Booker-McConnell. Where this culture survives, it is increasingly given over to a stylish, fey nostalgia financed by the 'paranational godfathers' and diffused world-wide by grace of their technologies. Modernism has meanwhile adapted itself to the conditions of commodity-exchange, its 'originally precarious and often desperate images' now routinized as a bleak social ontology whose assumptions and idioms not only persist in minority art but have entered much 'popular' culture. This convergence, impossible according to the axioms of modernist ideology, was in fact programmed by the historical conditions of modernist practice. For the processes that brought modernism into being – the new concentrations of economic and political power, the remaking of old societies and cultures – also created new systems of production and distribution, which have taken over the 'once liberating' alienations of that art and projected them as the truth of a human condition. 'The monopolizing corporations and the élite metropolitan intellectuals', apparently timeless antagonists, were in fact accomplices. 'One practised the homogenization, the other theorized it . . . The real forces which produced both, not only in culture but in the widest areas of social, economic and political life, belonged to the dominant capitalist order in its paranational phase.'[8]

'The new technologies' have of course been the instruments of this development, and much 'popular taste' has been shaped by them. But the realities to which these stereotypes are fastened retain the potential of a quite different culture. Outside the dominant order, though never safe from incorporation in it, there exist oppositional, intentionally 'popular' forms and practices; and more widely and fundamentally, there are forms of comedy, music and even 'popular "domestic" drama and fiction' that are simply irrepressible. An alternative deployment of the emerging technical systems could sustain and develop this now subordinate culture, just as it could decisively alter the conditions of many economic, social and political processes. These systems are the 'indispensable means of a new social order'.

The political forms of such an order are the subject of Williams's chapter on 'democracy old and new'. In *The Long Revolution*, Williams highlighted the autocratic strain in British parliamentary government and its reductive, 'liberal' version of democracy, and stressed that even a fully democratized parliament was not a sufficient condition of a self-determining society. *Towards 2000* renews this analysis and extends it to query prevailing norms of representation and the received political conceptions of the Labour left. 'Parliamentary democracy as we know it' is plainly not fully democratic: sovereignty resides not with the people but with 'the Crown in Parliament', a threefold entity of which only one component is elected – irregularly, according to the limited but effective discretion of the prime minister, and by means of a voting system that actively misproportions the recorded distribution of electoral options. A further limitation is the prevailing notion and practice of 'representation', which condenses two crucially distinct senses: 'making present' and 'symbolization'. The first is the democratic sense, and, fully understood, entails the principles of delegation, mandate and revocability. The second, a pre-democratic, Burkean conception derived from the metaphor of 'the body politic', describes current practice. It provides ideological support for political careerism – for the presumption that an individual can be a representative by vocation, in advance of (and often in defiance of) any specific warrant of democratic acceptability. It is part of a system of values that betrays the existence within 'parliamentary democracy as we know it' of an effective counter-ideology and counter-polity: 'the institution of a temporarily absolutist body within the carefully preserved contradictions of the electoral process and the monarchical state.' 9 Even after reform of all these undemocratic structures, Westminster's claim to embody democratic government would remain spurious. Parliamentary decisions are taken in an environment dominated by the social powers of capital: the finance houses, industry and the press. An internally reformed Westminster system would therefore remain bourgeois-democratic, its effective powers subject to the overarching will of capital.

Socialists project a 'higher' or 'fuller' democracy, Williams continues, but have yet to clarify its necessary and feasible forms. The familiar principles of 'a left government and self-management' are not self-evidently compatible. The tension between 'fully adequate general powers' and 'deeply organized and participating popular forces' must be regulated through suitably designed democratic institutions. The critique of 'representation' must extend to individuals and forums alike, 'all-purpose' mandates and assemblies giving way to decision-making processes of 'specific and varying' scale. And all such processes, including the most general and central, must be governed by 'the distinctive principle of *maximum self-management*, paired only with considerations of economic viability and reasonable equity between communities'.10 The elaboration of such socialist-democratic perspectives is now 'our central historic challenge'.

Communities, Societies and States

The economy and culture of capitalism have never readily yielded to any existing boundary, traditional or revolutionary. Structurally 'paranational' in their advanced forms, they work against all local resistances, coordinating social relations – *societies*, in the effective sense – ever more widely across the earth. Yet the bourgeois polity is entrenched in the nation-state, and its dominant ideology reserves a correspondingly prominent place for the values of nationality and patriotism. This political form is not an inert survival, Williams argues. Persisting against universalist ideals and amid the real universalizing tendencies of contemporary economic and military systems, it is centrally functional to capitalism, and an obstacle to the elaboration of a socialist alternative.

Official 'communities' such as 'the Yookay' have been raised over the bones and ashes of the human settlements whose forms they now impersonate:

> Both in its initial creation of a domestic market and in its later organization of a global market, the capitalist mode of production has always moved in on resources and then, necessarily, on people, without respect for the forms and boundaries of existing social organizations. Whole communities with settled domestic forms of production . . . were simply overridden by more developed and more centralized and concentrated capitalist and capitalist-industrial forms. Communities which at simpler levels had relatively balanced forms of livelihood found themselves, often without notice, penetrated or made marginal, to the point where many of their own people became 'redundant' and were available for transfer to new centres of production. Capitalist textile production, iron-making, grain production and a host of other industrial processes set in train immigrations and emigrations, aggregations and depopulations, on a vast scale. Typically, moreover, people were moved in and out on short-run calculations of profit and convenience, to be left stranded later, in worked-out mining valleys or abandoned textile towns, in old dockyard and shipbuilding areas, in the inner cities themselves, as trade and production moved on in their own interests.[11]

The image of capitalist progress so familiar from *The Communist Manifesto* is here set against the damning evidence of its negative. However, the image and the negative are seldom brought together in ordinary experience. The same accumulation process is felt here as catastrophe but there as prosperity, and in the era of consumer capitalism there are usually just enough means of temporary escape for just enough people just enough of the time. 'Mobile privatization' is Williams's name for this everyday culture: 'at most active social levels people are increasingly living as private, small-family units, or, disrupting even that, as private and deliberately self-enclosed individuals, while at the same time there is a quite unprecedented mobility of such restricted privacies.'[12] Such atomism is serviceable to capital, economically and also politically. Yet the processes that generate it are vulnerable to social attack. 'Thus "law and order"; armed forces called a "defence" force even when some of their weapons are obviously aggressive: these, unambiguously, are the real functions of a state.'[13] This state seeks legitimation, then, not in actual communities but by organizing identification with a larger entity hospitable to the necessary mobility of capital yet capable of miming the values of kinship and settlement: the nation. And so 'the circle is squared' and an 'artificial order' usurps the authority of 'natural communities' even as it sanctions their destruction.[14]

The nation-state is the most functional of capitalist contradictions, Williams argues; the left must think and plan beyond it. Social democrats, with their characteristic shuttle between 'patriotism' and what they call 'internationalism', simply demonstrate their own political and cultural subordination; and socialists who try to muster support for radical-nationalist economic schemes are engaged in a hopeless contest that the right alone can win. The fact is that 'the nation-state, in its classical European forms, is at once too large and too small for the range of real social purposes.'[15] States like Britain are too small and weak to be equal to the crises of the international economic and military order. Alternative economic strategies and old-style unilateralism alike are deficient in that they misread the paranational realities of the world and grossly overestimate the independent efficacy of any independent British state, including a socialist one. Such states are at the same time too large, too 'artificial' and distant to sustain 'full social identities', to attract and hold the kind of popular commitment on which a 'substantial' socialism must depend. Social relations are now 'variable' in extent, from one level to another: the spatial conditions of 'effective self-government' cannot be specified once for all. A 'substantial socialism' must therefore be a 'variable socialism', dispensing not only with 'all-purpose' assemblies and representatives but also with 'all-purpose' societies, discovering a flexibility of institutional reach adapted equally to intercontinental networks and to local communities.

Plan X or Socialism? The Labour Movement

The commanding political formula of this paranational order Williams terms 'Plan X'.[16] As a deliberate attempt to scan and shape the future, this formula is indeed a strategy – a plan. But it differs from familiar kinds of strategic thinking in that it is ultimately goalless: its object is, precisely, X. Plan X consists in the systematic pursuit of temporary advantage in an admittedly insoluble crisis. It is recognizably the creature of capitalism, its overall thrust and effects determined blindly by the assertion of self-validating particular interests, and as such, Williams argues, it finds adherents in every kind of social situation. But, crucially, it is the now-dominant practice of capitalist ruling classes and their operational élites. Plan X thinking inspired the British Conservatives' drive to break the power and will of the working class, even at the expense of existing local capitalist interests; internationally, it has motivated the West's ceaseless efforts to penetrate and reclaim the post-capitalist economies. The prospect it offers is one of increasingly authoritarian bourgeois regimes devoted to policing social distress at home and to reckless military confrontations abroad. Plan X is the long counter-revolution.

Plan X will prevail, Williams believes, unless it is cut short by socialism. But 'it is impossible, . . . in Western Europe, to conceive of any important socialist movement which is not largely based on the industrial working class, including its most traditional formations.'[17] Attempts to estimate the chances of socialism must therefore centre on the condition and prospects of the labour movement. Williams's discussion of the British labour movement opens with a critical response to recurring arguments concerning the supposed weakening of the relationship between the working class and socialist politics, of 'the dissolution of the classical proletariat'. Williams accepts much of the evidence adduced in favour of such theses – the changing occupational and gender composition of the wage-earning population, the decline in the Labour party's electoral strength after 1966, the pressure of sectionalist tendencies in the unions – but is sceptical of the conclusions drawn from it. First, he points out, there is no single, politically decisive demarcation of 'the working class'; second, all the available sociological indices suggest that the class-politics relation has never actually known the unison now supposedly lost; and finally, the fortunes of Labour, historically 'an all-purpose radical party', are by plain definition not the same thing as the fortunes of socialist politics. The general voting pattern in Britain remains substantially class-differential; the real failure is that of the received formula of 'the labour movement'.

That movement existed as a coherent and authoritative reality only in so far as workplace and political struggles were united in the pursuit of a 'general interest'. The main ground of this interest was the fact of avoidable primary hardship and want; another was the Marxist proposition that the capitalist mode of production is intrinsically exploitative and anarchic, and therefore incompatible with any general interest. The former supported the struggles of the labour movement in its most impressive phase, but now, and largely thanks to those struggles, is less generally relevant in advanced capitalist societies; the latter has remained a minority conviction. Now lacking any forceful version of a general interest, the 'movement' has lost coherence. The party's dominant tendency, its right and left variants alike, in government or in opposition, claims to speak for 'the national interest' as such. The unions, while retaining some organizational hold and political influence on the party, have increasingly been reduced to piecemeal bargaining over wages and conditions, to the serial assertion of particular interests. This negative, 'particularist' tendency is aggravated by shortcomings in the inherited self-definition of the unions. The bonds of kinship and settlement have at times been indispensable supports to those of generic 'class' in the labour movement, sustaining its struggles and its non-particularist values. But in conducting themselves purely as organizations of wage-labourers, who are then typically figured as male breadwinners, the unions abstract themselves from the complex reality of their social relations, both external and internal. This abstraction weakens and deforms them, encouraging practical adaptation to the rationality of the capitalist market and to its perfected strategic formula, Plan X.

Socialism is the only concrete alternative to Plan X. But if its necessary historical agency, the organized working class, succumbs to the politics of temporary advantage, then socialism will be reduced to a hopeless sectarian passion. This is the bleakest of Williams's anticipations. But, he insists, it is better to say such things 'than to go on acquiescing in the limited perspectives and the outdated assumptions which now govern the movement, and above all in its now sickening self-congratulatory sense of a taken-for-granted tradition and constitution. The real struggle has broadened so much, the decisive issues have been so radically changed, that only a new kind of socialist movement, fully contemporary in its ideas and methods, bringing a wide range of needs and interests together in a new definition of the general interest, has any real future.'[18]

News From You Know Where

Williams has written the agenda for a long and difficult discussion, in which openness – that is, both a calm attention to criticism and a candid offering of it – will furnish our best chance of collective self-enlightenment. Some will seek to match the range of Williams's analysis; others will bring more intensively developed specialisms to bear on the general debate. *Towards 2000* outlines the space of an argument, not the format of individual contributions to it. My intention here is to concentrate on the summarizing theoretical and political themes of the work, on the 'resources' that Williams deems necessary for a socialist 'journey of hope'.

Materialism, Technology and Production

Towards 2000 embodies what Williams describes as 'the outlines of a unified alternative social theory'. His central proposition is that economic reason must be integrated at every level with ecology, as a necessary condition of all fruitful socialist thought and planning.[19] Capitalism (including its social-democratic subaltern) assumes a possible infinity of production in a physical world whose elements are discrete and inert, Williams maintains, and this is a fantasy that no rational socialism dare entertain. There simply cannot be infinite production in a materially finite world, and the so-called 'by-products' of modern industrial economies are so many unsightly, noisome or downright lethal reminders of the earth's physical reality as a 'dynamic' and 'interactive' *system* of 'life forms and land forms'. The study of these limitations and counter-finalities is the special province of ecology. Socialists need not accept any of the currently influential quantitative forecasts issued in the name of ecology; nor should they indulge those who call for the suspension or reversal of industrializing processes – Williams is sharply critical of these. But equally, they need more than a chastened (or tactical) awareness of 'environmental issues'. What must be recognized is that no economy shaped and run in ignorance of its own ultimate conditions of possibility can be, in a fully rational sense, *planned*. Moreover, Williams maintains, the distinctively capitalist drive to mastery over nature is the real foundation of a dominative tendency that has come to pervade all social relations, from labour to sexuality, in direct contravention of any project of human emancipation. An ecologically blind socialism is in effect utopian.

This general case is supported by two arguments bearing directly on Marxist theory. The first of these animates Williams's repeated attacks on 'technological determinism', that is, the thesis that the history of technology obeys an autonomous, 'natural' logic and is, at bottom, intractable in its social functions and effects. This assumption is active in much contemporary cultural argument, where it leads the left to an implicitly reactionary pessimism, and in debates over the arms race, where it supports the politically confusing notion of 'the military industrial complex'. Against this trend in theory and analysis, Williams insists on the constitutional inseparability of the forces and relations of production, and on the economic, political and cultural determinations of all social instruments. The second argument moves from 'forces and relations' to 'production' itself. Marx's concept of 'mode of production' was misconceived, Williams believes, in so far as it generalized the specifically capitalist value of 'production' as the basic drive of all societies. In effect, Marx relayed the material triumphalism of the Victorian bourgeoisie – its commitment to natural intervention as such – as a central value of the Communist future. This is the real reason for Marxism's weak projective capacity, Williams suggests: the new mode of production – the collective appropriation of the ever-developing productive forces – would essentially be the new society, and there was little that could or need be added. A full and consistent historical materialism must advance from the idea of a 'mode of production' to the guiding concept and value of *Towards 2000*, the 'mode of *livelihood*'.

The case for a unification of economics and ecology, as Williams states it, is surely cogent. The prospect he outlines is a difficult one: quite apart from the formidable intellectual difficulties of the enterprise, ecological thinking is open to more than one kind of cultural and political elaboration; genuinely scientific analyses will be permanently vulnerable to the lure of reborn ideologies of nature, and the local successes of green movements will do as much to restyle the postures of bourgeois politics as to develop the programmes of the socialist left. However, these considerations cannot turn the point of Williams's argument. Increasing control of the physical world remains the only conceivable basis of a socialist 'realm of freedom'. But control presupposes power and knowledge. An ecologically blind economic policy is in any long historical view incapable of such control; it is a programme of main force, which no amount of stamina and ingenuity will save from ultimate frustration.

'Technological determinism' can only confuse ecologically informed analysis and projection, as it also confuses so much cultural and political argument, and Williams is right to reaffirm the constructive power of the relations of production. But caution is necessary here. Arguments against 'technological determinism' (of which there has been no shortage) quite commonly end in the opposite error, asserting the primacy of the relations over the forces of production. This kind of reductionism (symptomatically, it lacks a label) is idealist, relativizing all knowledge and denying physical necessity, and voluntarist, rediscovering always and everywhere the banal nostrum of 'struggle'. Williams's assertion must therefore be read as a twofold corrective, and indeed his own concrete analyses suggest this: the value of his distinction between 'technology' and 'technique' is that it illuminates the truly social formation of the one while respecting the specificity of the other. But the balance of the distinction is crucial: if 'technique' is tacitly marginalized in the interests of a historicist conception of 'technology', then the real physical necessities of social life are denied, and – among other things – the case for ecology is undermined.

The argument concerning 'production' and 'livelihood' is more problematic. It would be foolish to claim that Marx's writings were – or could have been – proof against the bourgeois culture of his day. But it is questionable to assert that specifically capitalist values seeped into the core of his theory. Marx did indeed assert that any society was determined in the last instance by its prevailing mode of production; his grounds for this were in effect naturalistic and anthropological, pertaining to the human species as such. But he expressly rejected the imputation that this thesis enshrined economic production as the ruling *value* of all societies. In current theoretical terminology, he distinguished between the order of social 'determination', in which the role of the economic was constant, and that of social 'dominance', which was recomposed from one mode of production to the next.[20] The capitalist mode of production was not typical but distinctive in assigning dominance to the economic. The outstanding feature of this dominance of the economic was the impersonally dictated social objective of capital: not 'production' as such, but profitable production – *accumulation*.[21] The Communist mode of production, Marx argued, would inscribe a different objective: not profit but 'use', the freely determined correlation of 'ability' and 'need' – or simply 'livelihood'. Williams's argument against Marx is misconceived. 'Livelihood' cannot be opposed to 'production', which is, unalterably, its fundamental means. The real opposition is between a mode of production governed by the logic of accumulation, all else making shift, and one in which production is organized in the service of an optimum common livelihood. Marx underestimated the havoc of capitalist progress; Williams, surveying the evidence of a century and more, is not inclined to dwell on its achievements. But on this decisive issue – the qualitative distinction between capitalist and socialist economies – they concur.

Class and Social Movements

This theoretical reorientation will find some of its strongest practical supports in the new movements of recent decades and in actually existing or potential 'effective communities', Williams believes. Of the first he writes:

All significant social *movements* of the last thirty years have started outside the organized class interests and institutions. The peace movement, the ecology movement, the women's movement, solidarity with the third world, human rights agencies, campaigns against poverty and homelessness, campaigns against cultural poverty and distortion: all . . . sprang from needs and perceptions which the interest-based organizations had no room or time for, or which they simply failed to notice. This is the reality which is often misinterpreted as 'getting beyond class politics'. The local judgement on the narrowness of the major interest groups is just. But there is not one of these issues which, followed through, fails to lead us into the central systems of the industrial-capitalist mode of production and among others into its system of classes. These movements and the needs and feelings which nourish them are now our major positive resources, but their whole problem is how they relate or can relate to the apparently more important institutions which derive from the isolation of employment and wage-labour. At the margins of those institutions, in fact, there have been significant developments which make new kinds of linkage possible.

These include plans for workers' control and for socially useful production, to name two. None of them yet commands 'the substantial support of the labour movement as a whole, yet they show that the possible resources are there.'[22]

This argument is at once contentious and not contentious enough. Addressed to the labour movement generally, it is pertinent and largely just. If the record of support for such campaigns and initiatives has been more varied than Williams's generalization allows, the partial advances of recent years have not redeemed a history of neglect and worse. But as an intervention in current socialist opinion, it runs the risk of being accepted on the nod. Not that it comes too late: the agenda it implies has scarcely been broached. But one of the sharpest ironies of left culture at the present time is that the 'new social movements', and above all women's movements, are increasingly drawn into a ceremony of approval that inhibits, and is sometimes meant to inhibit, serious political and intellectual engagement. Purposeful discussion of the 'new social movements' must begin by disaggregating the category itself, which is a spurious one. Nothing unites them except their organizational separation from the labour movement. It is true, as Williams writes, that their demands press ultimately against the very order of capital, but too much can be made of this: the same might be said of traditional strikes, which are definitionally excluded from his inventory. Some – the peace and ecology movements, for example – are essentially elaborations of single-issue campaigns, contingent in their social bases; the awesome scale of the issues in question does not alter this fact. They are therefore structurally distinct from movements based on objective social categories – nationalities or ethnic minorities, not mentioned by Williams, or women – which test socialist politics in a different way. The few remarks that follow will be confined to feminism and the women's movement, not because this is a typical case – there is no wholly typical movement – but because it is a salient one.

Williams is right to argue that women's liberation is a necessary goal of any consistent socialist politics today. 'Necessity', here, does not mean 'happy fatality': the historical record shows the real variability of class-gender relations in socialist revolution, and illustrates the antagonisms that may arise as mutually discrepant interests are pressed in difficult situations. But the feminist upsurge of the past twenty-five years has confronted traditional socialism (and above all socialist men) with a political and moral challenge that will not be withdrawn and cannot be turned aside. It is not enough for socialists to bless women's autonomous fight against their oppression. Marxists see proletarian revolution as the means to a general human emancipation, but the temporality implied in this thesis is misleading. The strategic prerequisite of revolution, optimum unification of the working class in political opposition to capital, itself implies a struggle against any oppression that jeopardizes the cohesion and morale of the class, irrespective of its kind and provenance. In other words, socialism scants even its own self-defined class duties if it does not take up the cause of all the oppressed as its own. This is the full implication of Marx and Engels's declaration that their movement had 'no interests separate and apart from those of the proletariat *as a whole*.'[23] Thus, a socialism that does not address the specific oppressions of women workers (who constitute a significant and now rapidly growing proportion of all wage-earners) is in its own terms incompetent. And it cannot hope to understand these unless it commits itself to the fight against gender oppression as such, becoming in that generic sense feminist.

However, there is nothing generic about the reality of contemporary women's movements; there is no pan-feminist programme that socialism can simply adopt. By definition, the women's movement has aspired to be inter-class in composition, and its social horizons have been correspondingly uncertain. These necessary indeterminacies have been among the main material causes of the deepening divisions in the movement. Class, ethnic and other social or cultural antagonisms have asserted themselves within it, in the form of rival ideological and political tendencies, some of which are theoretically and practically incompatible with, or expressly hostile to, socialism. (Indeed the very term 'the women's movement' is somewhat misleading, suggesting a singular and continuous phenomenon, where the apparent reality has for years been an irregular sequence of heterogeneous coalitions or fronts.) In such conditions, even the most sincere avowals of feminist commitment are abstract, and even self-defeating. The fight for a feminized socialism must be linked with an active struggle for socialist feminism within women's movements.

The main obstacle facing this twofold effort is close at hand. Women's oppression is organized at every level of the capitalist order, which benefits from it in obvious ways. But its main beneficiaries are men, as a category and as individuals, male workers and male socialists not excepted. The inherited assumptions and practices of the socialist and labour movements have not merely 'neglected' women; they have subordinated and marginalized them, often to the advantage of their 'brothers' and male comrades. A genuine commitment to women's liberation will not, then, merely supplement these assumptions and practices with 'women's issues'; it will extensively revise them. This work of revision need not always follow the rules of a zero-sum equation (in wage-bargaining against capital, for example, that could only be damaging). But in many instances it will, and should. Demands for positive discrimination, for example, whether posed in capitalist workplaces or in trade-union and socialist institutions, are aimed against male privilege, and where they succeed, individual men will be the losers, in the short run at least. Williams is rightly critical of those who imagine that 'growth' will amortize the costs of economic reconstruction; there is no painless road to women's liberation either, and only a lucid and determined socialism will prove equal to its social and psychic stresses.

Our Major Positive Resource

What does it mean to say that the social movements 'are now our major positive resource'? I have already suggested that the term 'resource' is too comfortable a summary of the necessities, opportunities and difficulties that agitate relations between socialism and feminism. There is a second, more general and fundamental objection. To speak of all or any of these movements as our major resource is to yield precious ground to those who now dismiss the labour movement as an effective socialist agency. Williams expressly rejects this position but does not state his reasons for doing so, with the result that a generally negative verdict on the existing labour movement unites with a positive judgement on the social movements to create the contrary appearance. The working class is revolutionary, Marxists have maintained, because of its historically constituted nature as the exploited collective producer within the capitalist mode of production. As the *exploited* class, it is caught in a systematic clash of interest with capital, which cannot generally and permanently satisfy its needs. As the main *producing* class, it has the power to halt – and within limits redirect – the economic apparatus of capitalism, in pursuit of its goals. And as the *collective* producer it has the objective capacity to found a new, non-exploitative mode of production. This combination of interest, power and creative capacity distinguishes the working class from every other social or political force in capitalist society, and qualifies it as the indispensable agency of socialism. To reaffirm this proposition is not to claim that socialism is assured – it is not – or that the labour movement alone is likely to achieve it. What has to be said is that 'our major positive resource' can never be other than the organized working class, and that if it cannot regenerate itself, no outside intervention can do so. If that resource should, in some calamitous historical eventuality, be dispersed or neutralized, then socialism really will be reduced to a sectarian utopia beyond the reach of even the most inspired and combative social movement.

In fact, the structural trends of late capitalism continue to corroborate Marx's fundamental thesis. The paranational economic order itself, which appears in *Towards 2000* only in its destructive aspect, as the anarchic private appropriation of whole continents, is evidence of the reality of the 'collective labourer'. The internal development of particular economies points in the same direction. High technology industries are remaking the relationship between 'mental' and 'manual' labour in ways that facilitate newly 'organic' kinds of programmatic thinking. The quasi-industrialization of social reproduction has also encouraged developments in the forms and scope of working-class struggle. For the 'goods' produced by workers in welfare, education and other public services are not particular commodities but commonly valued services; and their conditions of work and remuneration are decisively shaped by government policy. The logic of their workplace struggles is therefore intrinsically anti-particularist. Even the narrowest dispute over wages and conditions contains a political judgement on capitalist and social priorities; and mere tactical common sense, if nothing more, impels strikers in, say, the health services towards initiatives in workers control, in response to the unignorable social demand for minimum emergency cover. Williams has himself emphasized the social creativity of working-class struggle, in an essay on the South Wales railways in the 1926 general strike.[24] The scope of working-class creativity has widened since then, and will become still wider in the new century. Creativity is a potential, not an achievement – true enough. But the potential itself is not determined by the moral and political vicissitudes of the labour movement. It is fostered by the ordinary contradictions of capitalism, whose processes of expanded reproduction have brought forth a structurally collective economic and social order and, willy-nilly, the conditions and agencies of a real 'general interest'.

Class and Community

Williams would probably be critical of these suggestions, arguing that they rely on abstract class determinations and fail to appreciate the importance of the other social bonds that, for good or for ill, shape all human allegiances. One of the most insistent themes of *Towards 2000* is that socialism must commit itself to 'lived and formed identities', actual or possible, to the struggle for 'full social identities' and 'effective communities'.[25]

'Community' is a difficult and elusive idea. Its role in the historical romances and political polemics of conservative social thought is well known, not least to Williams and any reader of his work. Yet it is also a part of the cultural bequest of popular and working-class struggle, and Williams remains convinced that it must be kept and developed in this sense, as a key resource for the future. What, then, is the meaning of 'community' here? Most simply, it is associated with what Williams defends as 'the principle of maximum self-management'. In a socialist democracy, decision-making powers should as far as possible be exercised by those directly affected, in their own enterprises and localities. 'Community' is thus a necessary counter-value to the bureaucratic gigantism of Stalinist and social-democratic traditions. However, it refers also to social relationships of a certain type and quality, distinguished from those of class and official nationality by their concrete 'fullness'. The instance to which Williams returns is that where class or specific occupational allegiances are reinforced by bonds of kinship and settlement – as in the mining villages of Yorkshire and South Wales. In its first sense, this stress on 'community' is persuasive; but its second gives cause for worry.

There can be no doubt of the potency of communal allegiances as supports of class struggle. But equally there is no room to doubt the force of the familiar objection that 'community' can act very powerfully against the interests of workers – or women or oppressed minorities. Against the villages of Britain's coalfields must be set the small towns of Northern Ireland or the embattled ghettoes and hostels of France and Germany. Kinship obligations can sustain strikes but they can break them too; and they can also enforce arranged marriages and silence battered women. Continuity of settlement can be a powerful bond, but it is merely a provocation where, as in Cyprus, the land itself is in question. The real experience of 'community' is always mixed, and the attempt to abstract a stable general value from it must be correspondingly fraught. Indeed, Williams's own arguments suggest a further inadequacy in the appeal to 'community'. The 'variable socialism' envisaged in *Towards 2000* presupposes not only more local but also more extensive decision-making systems than any now existing. But how, in Williams's terms, can there be 'community' across oceans? He is wary of 'abstract' internationalism, but what other bond can define and order the necessary interrelationships of peoples or movements a hemisphere apart?

In fact, there can be 'community' across oceans, as the history of the great world religions attests; and considerations of this kind prompt closer theoretical examination of the concept itself. The meaning of 'community', in *Towards 2000*, is evoked in such phrases as 'lived and formed identities' or 'full social identities'. These are sympathetic ideas, but the distinctions they imply are dubious. How could an identity be unlived or unformed, or – for quantitative metaphors are inappropriate here – be anything other than 'full'? Identity is a universal necessity of human existence.[26] To be human at all is, among other things, to be 'identified', by oneself and others. 'Community' is likewise universal, representing one major form of identity. It is best understood as the effect of any identification that positions individuals as members of a group of comparables or counterparts; it is the work of a process of collective identification. As a singular, identity is an abstraction, for any person or group possesses more than one. Concrete human beings are a complex of such identities, which need not be harmonious or coextensive and are often

mutually contradictory. Identities of class, ethnicity, gender, religion, generation and so on coexist in all social aggregations (households, towns, trade
unions, countries alike), implying different and often conflicting rights,
duties, capacities and positions for their members. If communities are notoriously hard to find, it is because they are everywhere – not *places* but *practices* of collective identification whose variable order largely defines the
culture of any social formation. Prevailing ideological usage denies this, spu-
riously actualizing 'identity' as empirical individuality and 'community' as a
certain kind of social formation. The appeal to 'community' is normally a conservative attempt to represent one collective identification (the family, the
nation) as the real substance of social relations. This is certainly not Williams's
purpose: 'community', as he invokes it, distinguishes a kind of social formation in which the most salient identifications are mutually supporting, for
progressive ends. But inevitably it signifies much more. As Williams himself
has observed, no one speaks of 'community' with critical intent, and this fact
alone betrays its ideological function.[27] 'Community' is not an integral social
entity, past, present or possible, but a fetish that disavows the reality in which
its sponsors are so deeply engaged: the politico-cultural clash of collective
identifications. It would be wrong to undervalue the kinds of collective identification that Williams insists upon. But it is wrong also to consecrate them
as 'community' and to suppose that they can or should be generalized. Some
of these identifications are crucial: a politics that addresses the working class
only as producers is stupidly self-limiting. But others, like the very potent
community of white male privilege, are reactionary and must be attacked,
whatever the offence to customary loyalties. Furthermore, the struggle of collective identifications is not wholly autonomous: it is subject in the last
instance to the structural (and therefore strategic) determinations of class, and
to evade this is to give credence to a dangerous and now widespread opportunism. Here, as in relation to the social movements, the 'major positive
resource' of socialism can only be its own principled theory and practice.

The National Community

The most powerful of all non-class collective identifications in modern history is nationality. Williams's analysis of 'the culture of nations' is his most
important extension of 'Britain in the Sixties' and includes a great deal that is
cogent and timely. But it is precisely here that his appeal to 'community' lets
him down. No one has done more than Williams to educate the left in a properly historical and critical understanding of the 'vocabulary of culture and
society' (the subtitle of his *Keywords*, 1976).[28] It is disturbing, then, to see
him rest his analysis on a distinction between '*natural* communities' and the
'*artificial* order' of the nation-state. While there is nothing natural about
nations and the states that enclose them, there is much that is artificial in all
'communities', and Williams concedes this. But the issue is not merely one of

balance. The romantically-derived opposition between 'natural' and 'artificial' conditions of society can only obstruct historical understanding and mislead political judgement. If official nationalism were no more than a misappropriation of 'real', more local affections, much of modern political history – in the metropoles and also in the ex-colonial world – would be incomprehensible. The nations that capitalism has everywhere fostered at the expense of smaller and larger entities are more than flag-bedecked marketplaces. They are collective identifications with strong supports in economic, cultural and political histories; they are, as much as any competing formation, 'communities'. To deny this is not to rout official nationalism, merely to misjudge its very potent everyday manifestations and weaken oneself in the face of them.

Racism is a case in point. Williams rejects the ideology of a timeless and exclusive 'English' or 'British' identity, and affirms the right of black people to defend themselves by all necessary means. But his distinction between 'natural community' and the 'artificial' state disturbs the balance of his analysis of racism in Britain. He writes:

> The real working of ideology, both ways, can be seen in that most significant of current exchanges, when an English working man (English in terms of the sustained modern integration) protests at the arrival of 'foreigners' or 'aliens', and now goes on to specify them as 'blacks', to be met by the standard liberal reply that 'they are as British as you are'. Many people notice the ideological components of the protest: the rapid movement, where no other terms are available, from the resentment of unfamiliar neighbours to the ideological specifications of 'race' and 'superiority'. But what of the ideology of the reply?[29]

Williams's point, correct in itself, is that appeals to abstract legal rights (and facile and patronizing ideas of 'assimilation') are unequal to the social strains of Britain's changing ethnic composition. But he seriously underestimates the critical value of such appeals for the people who actually suffer the strains: the ethnic minorities themselves. The Northern Irish civil rights campaign of the late 1960s, in which the traditionally nationalist Catholic minority massed under the banner of 'British standards of justice', shows just how explosive the appeal to bourgeois rights may be in the struggle against communal oppression. Moreover, he neglects to consider that the British state is itself racist, with its battery of immigration laws whose leading function is to isolate and harass black people already living here (about half of them from birth), and a police force to match. And in neglecting this, he mistakes the character of popular racism, which is not merely the xenophobia of settled neighbourhoods but part of the politico-cultural inheritance of the *British* '*national community*'. This combination of terms may be offensive to Williams (and for good reasons) but its referent is no less real for that. The racism of 'the English working man' actually pre-exists the arrival of black neighbours or workmates, who merely trigger the chauvinist presumptions of the common 'national' history of empire. This is the second misrepresentation of

Williams's small parable, and it complements his occlusion of official racism. Disputing the claims of 'artificial' state nationalism, he unwittingly makes light of its real potency; at the same time upholding the settled solidarities of 'natural communities', he flinches from the necessary judgement on their negative expressions. In the resulting confusion, it is as if Bebel's famous dictum were inverted, and not popular racism but liberal anti-racism is exposed as 'the socialism of fools'. The lesson to be learned from this political misjudgement bears on the idea of 'community'. Not an actual social reality but a polemical attribution or interpellation, 'community' is an untrustworthy category. It obscures the real object of socialist analysis, which is the existing order of collective identifications, and can seriously confuse the corresponding task of socialist politics: the effort, which may be supportive but will often be antagonistic, to create a 'community' of anti-capitalist interest.

There is a further, more general difficulty in Williams's evaluation of the nation-state. The economy, he writes at one point, is where most of the people are, most of the time, and for that reason alone economic policy must be central in any socialist programme. That is well said. But the nation-state is where all of us are all of the time – now and for the directly relevant future. Williams is right to insist that the most important unities of a socialist society will be either smaller or larger than the nation-state. But to read this future back into the capitalist present is to effect a wishful *fuite en avant*, a truly utopian dissolution of politics. The arguments of *Towards 2000* press consistently in this direction. The very structure of the book dissociates the category of politics. Parliament, the military apparatus, official nationalist culture, the general game-plan of capital: all these are discussed, but separately. Nowhere is there a unified analysis of the bourgeois political order as a whole: the state and the party system organized around it. The consequence of this dispersal of attention – for, in a book so passionate and determined, that is what occurs – is an unsteady sense of the counter-order of political struggle. The concluding chapter of *Towards 2000* offers an estimate of resources, not a *strategy*. Some key elements of a strategy are present. Williams argues convincingly that the imperative task of the years ahead is the elaboration of a new 'general interest', a socialist programme, and the struggle to win active popular forces to it. He identifies the main principles of the former and the main agencies among the latter – along with the organized working class, the social movements and the campaigns of people united in their localities. But this prospectus remains abstract in one crucial respect. A politically capable anti-capitalist bloc cannot be mustered by simple addition: there is no spontaneous harmony of the oppressed and therefore no spontaneous convergence in their struggles. The formulation of a socialist 'general interest' requires a continuing process of synthesis, and this – Williams's critique of 'all-purpose' political formations notwithstanding – is the distinctive and abiding rationale of a party . . .

1984

Postscript 1998: A Null Millennium

That suspended cadence figures the relationship between the hopes of the earlier nineteen-eighties and the arbitration of the next decade. Among the possibilities then discernible to socialists in Britain, the most creative, though perhaps least widely endorsed, was that the challenge of Labour's left wing would grow irresistible, resulting, however, not in a transformation of the party – a self-contradictory goal – but in its break-up. Left socialists inside and outside that hulking, monopolistic coalition might then come together to form the nucleus of a new, potentially mass party, in conditions where open struggle over working-class political representation would be not only realistic but, for all tendencies, unavoidable. In a wider setting, I belonged to that poignantly numerous body of opinion that took it more or less as a fact-in-waiting that the crisis of post-Stalinism, once irrevocably declared, would tend to favour emancipatory outcomes, opening the way to socialist democracy in the post-capitalist world and restoring the moral authority of the anti-capitalist left elsewhere. These hopes have come to nothing. Labour leftism was defeated by a combination of purge, media detraction and politically numbing appeals to the cardinal virtue of electability; today its tenets seem not only implausible but unspeakable, thanks to a process of discursive reconstruction that has dismayed even the traditional right of the party. In Russia and Eastern Europe, capitalism and nationalism – including the most rapacious forms of the one and the most barbarous extremes of the other – have been thus far the most conspicuous beneficiaries of Soviet perestroika and the revolutions of 1989. The failure of reform communism in the East hastened the decomposition of its sister movement in the West, but in such a way as to weaken the possibility of a political renewal in firmly socialist terms, instead favouring social-democratic and eclectically radical styles.

Even in these conditions, political tendencies do not all run one way. The refashioning of British Labour as a social-liberal party brightly contemptuous of its inherited commitments has caused deep disturbance in the trade unions, and will force a correspondingly unsentimental reconsideration of old habits by the socialist left. In this as in the more general case, the loss of illusions in the historically dominant organizational traditions of the left promotes adaptation or dispersal but also offers release into possibilities which, though hardly comfortable, at least dictate an effort at lucid appraisal. A stronger and darker reason for hope is that the revised social agendas have to do less with a bold attack on new problems than with a regressive flight from the familiar ones. The justifying achievements of post-war reformism, which once were taken as the given starting point for further advance, and then upheld as the minima of a future political restoration, have now been declared controversial. The petty-bourgeois fantasy of a low-tax society mediates the brutal ruling that in the queue for welfare, capital must come first. Measured against the objective drives of capitalism and the needs of its subject populations, these agendas signify historic defeat – or, for it comes to the same thing, the re-programming of popular desire as a modality of Williams's Plan X.

While remaining convinced that this crisis cannot be resolved without recourse to strictly political means – socialist parties mobilizing against capitalist states – I am more fully persuaded now of the need to tackle the cultural conditions of political formulation – about which this essay had not enough to say. It is not that culture, polite or popular, offers autonomous grounds on which to evaluate political options; that has been the faith of literary humanism and the abiding temptation of cultural studies. My own conviction is that cultures are intimately conditioned by their counterpart political orders – but in a way that allots a specific value to cultural politics. 'The sense of the future' continues to weaken; indeed, the defining tendencies of the present – the intensification of capitalist pressures and the retro-development of the historic left alternatives – cooperate to foreclose imagination. Opening my discussion of *Towards 2000* in 1984, I suggested, in an affirmative spirit, that the new social movements had effected a probably permanent change in the conditions of socialist strategic thinking. Today, a formally parallel thought suggests itself, in a contrasting spirit and with historically opposite implications. The inaugural realities of the new century threaten the future of socialist politics *tout court*. Working-class and other popular forces will continue to assert themselves, because capitalism will not let them rest. But without imaginative access to a possible alternative social order, their struggles can have only limited, temporary success. A crucial task of socialist thought in the new century is to thwart that foreclosure of historical imagination, which, to the extent that it succeeds, will leave only nationalism and its cognates as plausible representations of our collective existence, reducing us otherwise to the idiocy of urban life.

I reproached Williams for his abstraction from politics; but that kind of abstraction, which in fact is a condition of access to the real terms of the concrete, is now coming into its own. *Towards 2000* will soon be literally out of date, but it will remain actual and exemplary for its refusal to trim its reasoning to the measure of capitalist possibility, for its commitment to the renewal of rational historical imagination.[30]

A WELFARE CULTURE?
Hoggart and Williams in the Fifties

–It is time to think again. An older phase of capitalism has ended. A received culture of class has declined with it, disarticulated by new forms of industrial organization, a transformed information economy, and changed patterns of consumption and recreation. The right has thematized these developments and prospered from them, as successive Conservative electoral victories demonstrate. The left has been slow to respond in anything like an effective contemporary spirit; but here too, now, there is potential for change. A new generation of Labour leaders, alert to the social novelties of the period and dismissive of old nostrums, is remaking the party and its politics; communism, which twenty years ago bewitched a whole radical generation, is surely finished. The left can make a new start.

It is Britain in the 1990s. Or is it the 1950s? The comparison is of course selective, deliberately overdrawn; no one will confuse the two periods. Yet the objective resemblances are close enough to be perhaps interesting. Can the familiar terms of a certain style of left-intellectual annunciation so fully replicate that of an earlier time and yet be lucid, or even self-consistent? A second-hand apocalypse is a poor revelation. Or, if the similarities really do run deep enough to justify the echoes, may it not be that the concerns of the fifties are more actual than they are conventionally thought to be? The intellectual left, above all in those densely populated quarters where cultural analysis goes on, habitually thinks of the fifties as a cradle, a thing well remembered but hardly suited to the purposes of later years. The founding texts of socialist cultural theory in Britain are just that: enablers of a certain history, not actors in it. But there may be critical value in anachronism, in returning to the period as if without the knowledge of what followed, to remember afresh the terms of its arguments as they emerged, to consider whether they may not have retained – perhaps regained – a certain value for the present.

After 1945: Welfare Liberalism

It has been claimed that effective political victory in 1945 went not to Labour but to liberalism, in its generic post-classical form. Drawn into an early contest by an over-confident Churchill, Labour acceded to office through a slump in the Conservative vote and went on to implement a social programme that

116

had been designed largely by reformers in Westminster's senior parties.[1] A parallel claim may be pressed more strongly in respect of cultural policy after 1945.

Post-elementary state education was made available to all, and compulsory to the age of fifteen; merit rather than money determined access to the upper echelon of the new tripartite system, the grammar school. Higher education expanded rapidly in the early post-war years, though from a tiny demographic base. Radio, continuing as a public monopoly, expanded and diversified its programming, but again – like education – on strict hierarchical assumptions. Access to television viewing widened dramatically, though without prejudice to Reithian paternalism. The licensing of commercial television in the middle fifties caused widespread foreboding, but in fact the new service was subject to significant public-service constraints. A government-funded council was created, succeeding the wartime CEMA, to support the arts and promote wider interest in them. And in the bookshops, the shelves turned orange and blue, the colours of Penguin and the mark of cultural quality as bestowed by Allen Lane, a more affable, more radical Reith of the printed word.[2] Of course, pure commerce too was active in every paper shop and cinema; but in the old and new centres of cultural policy, a common formula had been set in place. A minority culture, received and continuing, would be diffused to an ever-widening audience. All the terms of this summary should be noted. The expansion was real; but there was no fundamental questioning of what counted as cultural value or of the proper forms of cultural participation. Self-confirming traditions would now be unveiled for a deserving population. Culture – 'the best that is known and thought in the world', 'sweetness and light', in Arnold's famous gloss – would now, literally, be broad-cast.

The formula governing this emerging world of policy and practice was a Victorian bequest; its classic exponent was Arnold. In its mid-century applications, it was to a great extent the achievement of the two salient tendencies in liberal minority culture between the wars: the Bloomsbury circle and the group around F. R. Leavis and *Scrutiny*. It has been usual in retrospective commentary, as it was at the time, to stress the contrasts between the two formations. Bloomsbury was an upper-middle-class bohemia, a congeries of families and friends whose unity and security in the face of commercial pressure and ancestral philistinism were sustained by private money. *Scrutiny* was proudly petty-bourgeois, hostile to all metropolitan ornament and hereditary presumption, the self-conscious vanguard of a 'critical minority' that sought nothing but – and nothing less than – the recognition due to unaided intelligence. However, these social-stylistic differences were variants of a shared liberal formula, which both formations helped to promote after the war. John Maynard Keynes was not only the pioneering theorist of the new macro-economic policy; he also founded the Arts Council. Bloomsbury's free-thinking modernism was hardly consonant with Lord Reith's cultural preferences, yet that 'civilized' manner eventually lightened his own puritan tone in the BBC, just as it also became standard in the formerly 'middlebrow' cultural and recreational pages of the polite press. *Scrutiny's* insistence on careers open to talent appeared to find some acknowledgement in the weakening of class privilege in education – where, at the same time, Leavisian accents were more and more widely heard. The new styles of cultural seriousness, in education and in the media, were essentially generalizations, named or not, from these inter-war models.

Two counterpointed sequences patterned the new period. On the one hand there were expansionary trends: a significant system of welfare, rising working-class confidence and spending-power, enhanced public cultural provision, and, together with these, intensified cultivation of consumer-goods markets, including, very prominently, strictly commercial cultural enterprise. However, these trends developed within a contrary historical tendency: Britain's long relative decline as a capitalist power continued, and was now invested with a special politico-cultural pathos by the post-war retreat from colonialism, the loss and symbolic redemption of Empire in the Commonwealth. 'Progress' was the officially favoured gloss on this configuration of change, and, in the ordinary terms of liberal politics and culture, the word was not inapt. But, looking back from beyond the seventies and eighties, we can see the decade after 1945 as the formative moment of an abiding crisis. The re-balancing of existing class relations in a caste-ridden society and a declining economy, the seeding of new black communities through reverse migration from the colonies, and, pervading all things, the scarcely articulate faltering of Anglo-Britishness as a self-evident identity and mark of precedence: these familiar pretexts of the late-twentieth-century reaction against consensual liberalism were shaped together within a short historical span.

Indeed, amid all the signs of liberal paramountcy, the liberal intelligentsia itself was not free of discontent. Cultural life had become narrower and meaner since the war, according to one Bloomsbury survivor. The twenties and thirties had been bohemian and cosmopolitan; the fifties were provincial and earnest, their tone set by 'lower-middlebrows' who approached the arts in the spirit of sanitary engineers.[3] Among a younger generation inspired by Leavis, there were those who would have smiled at this caricature of themselves, who affirmed that their kind of intellectual was now poised to take possession of the heritage.[4] But others of them were disturbed by post-war Britain (or England, as they would more typically say). *Scrutiny* itself, now closed, had recoiled from the approach of educational reform; Leavis himself could see only further deterioration, the nearing extinction of English minority culture. The official vaunting of liberal nostrums, in the heyday of *Encounter* and the Congress for Cultural Freedom, intensified the air of paradox, as the highbrow passions of the thirties became the good sense of the fifties. Assimilation as rejection, advance as continuing decline, intellectual freedom as voluntary conformism: these apprehensions were voiced by both kinds of liberal intellectual as they contemplated their given place in the unfamiliar social landscape of post-war Britain.

Among conservative intellectuals, there was unequivocal resistance to the prospect of a diffusionist welfare culture. The best-known initiative from this quarter was T. S. Eliot's *Notes Towards the Definition of Culture* (1948), a work whose mannered remoteness of style belied the topicality of its theoretical concerns.[5] The 'definition' Eliot worked towards was conceptual but also political. His point in distinguishing three levels of culture – those of the individual, the group and the whole society – and insisting on the largely unconscious character of their inter-communication was to invalidate the very idea of cultural reform. His critique of atomism was intended to entrench the claims of inherited class-cultural privilege against the meritocratic proposals of the liberal Karl Mannheim and the broad Arnoldian tradition. 'Definition', as he reminded his readers, meant 'the setting of bounds', 'limitation' – in practice, a Burkean defence of customary inequality in intellectual life and education. Appearing in 1948, the year of his Nobel Prize and Order of Merit, Eliot's intervention was widely acknowledged. Yet had it been signed by anyone other than the canonized master of the new English poetic, it might have passed more or less unnoticed. For now, and for most, liberalism was an ecumenical, not a sectarian rite, in effect, an established church – the unsaid, often enough the unthought, of intellectual initiative and exchange.

Hoggart and the Abuses of Literacy

In the middle 1940s, when *Notes Towards the Definition of Culture* was written, Eliot's sense of English popular culture was already anachronistic. His vision of the English everyday – the famous montage of boating, Elgar, cabbage and the rest – was like a reprise of his own earliest impressions, one expatriate American's version of pastoral. By the turn of the 1960s, when he reissued the book without alteration, the loss of reality was complete. Between the first and second editions of *Notes*, the cultural universe of the social majority had been extensively reordered, in part by those ominous education reforms and an associated widening of cultural opportunity, and in greater part through the ever more vigorous commercial traffic in words and images. 'Classless' was the widely promoted description of a process in which the inherited signs of cultural caste were displaced in the mock-popular interest of the commercial optimum, or were themselves commodified as style and spectacle. Converging with marketing strategies in this, public policy sponsored a vision of classlessness – through equality of opportunity – but, precisely in doing so, instated the working class as a real cultural presence and topic. Among the effects of these cooperating tendencies was the emergence of a new minority in British intellectual life, a scattering of writers and artists of working-class origin, who now moved into the approved spaces of cultural production, there to assert or explore the values and prospects of the half-known, half-acknowledged social world from which they had come and to which, more often than not, they remained committed.

One of these was Richard Hoggart. Born into the Leeds working class at the end of the First World War, Hoggart made his way through a local grammar school and thence to the university, graduating in English Literature on the eve of the Second. After wartime service, he joined the Department of Adult Education at Hull University, from which he worked as a tutor until the end of the fifties. Hoggart's first book was a conventional work of literary criticism: *W.H. Auden*. However, he was also writing short sketches of working-class life for the Labour left weekly *Tribune*, where T. R. Fyvel had succeeded George Orwell as literary editor. And by the beginning of the 1950s, he was clarifying the terms of another kind of project, 'a new and natural extension', as he later described it, of 'the true stream of English studies' into the landscape of contemporary culture.[6]

His critical point of reference was Q. D. Leavis's *Fiction and the Reading Public* (1932), the founding text of *Scrutiny*'s cultural diagnostics. Twenty years on, Hoggart proposed 'a sort of guide or textbook to aspects of popular culture' that would make good the unfulfilled promise of Leavis's title by integrating the critical study of texts within an analysis of the already-formed culture of their readers: 'one had to know very much more about how people used much of the stuff which to us might seem merely dismissible trash, before one could speak confidently about the effects it might have.'[7] The work, whose precise focus would be on the impact of mass-marketed cultural forms on the inherited ethos of the working class, was to be called *The Abuses of Literacy*.

The book eventually published in 1957 differed significantly from its early design. The title was shorn of its provocative first syllable, in an attempt to mollify a publisher fearful of crushing litigation; and for the same reason, Hoggart was oblige to pastiche much of his printed evidence rather than quote it. But the major change was structural. The original analytic scheme furnished only half of *The Uses of Literacy*, its second part, which was now preceded by a long, hybrid discourse – part autobiography and memoir, part exemplary fiction, part social phenomenology – on working-class life between the wars, offered as the necessary context for the analysis of popular culture in the fifties.

It was this reflection on 'an "older" order' that gave the book its tone, distinguishing it very clearly from its Leavisian antecedent – and also from a left-wing inspiration like Orwell. Hoggart wrote here with the assurance and feeling of one who had come from the world he described, with an unflagging consciousness of Britain's class order and his own dislocated relation to it. He was, in his own later words, 'a once-born socialist' immovably committed to the welfare of his native class.[8] The contemporary cultural materials that he went on to dissect – the glossy magazines, the pulp fiction, the popular song lyrics – did not express the traditional ethos of this class and did not (yet) define it, he argued. The populism of the cultural market was an 'approach' from the outside, exploiting inherited strengths and weaknesses alike, threatening to reduce its working-class audience to a demoralized lower caste; it was a kind of spiritual 'robbery'.

However, altered social sensibility and political alignment did not undermine discursive continuity. Hoggart's evaluative idiom was saturated with *Scrutiny*'s clinical metaphorics of health and sickness, vigour and debility. His writing was at times quite possessed by the spirit of the Leavises:

> The hedonistic but passive barbarian who rides in a fifty-horse-power bus for threepence, to see a five-million-dollar film for one-and-eightpence, is not simply a social oddity; he is a portent.[9]

His closing remarks read like an oath of allegiance: here was one individual's 'contribution to a much wider discussion, a single diagnosis offered for scrutiny'.[10]

Working-class Welfare: Culture or Civilization?

Hoggart professedly saw *The Uses of Literacy* as disjunct, and has remained unmoved by those who have read it as a single composition.[11] But it is just here, in the forms of the book seen as a whole, that his discursive affiliation is more strongly registered. The dominant mode of the work is narrative; the story it tells is of decline already far gone and perhaps unarrestable. The contrast that emerges in his account is not simply between two periods in the life of working-class Leeds. His story begins with an evocation of his country-born grandmother, with her customary knowledges and skills, then remembers two generations of native city-dwellers, and turns finally to observe the life-patterns of a fourth generation, the working-class young of the early 1950s. Hoggart was aware of the temptation to nostalgia, and tried repeatedly to check it. But his qualifications were too punctually stated, too evidently concessionary in their acknowledgement of an improved material existence, to remake what was a canonical narrative of the descent from rural tradition into urban-industrial anomie.

The two-part organization of the text recalls Orwell's *The Road to Wigan Pier*, and its suasive gesture is of the same kind, though potentially more effective. In both cases, a record of experience purports to validate a critical analysis: because I have known this life, the tacit reasoning goes, I may reliably make this judgement. Yet the truth must be otherwise. Memory is a construction of the past, and in Hoggart's descriptions (as in Orwell's) there was much that was already familiar from literary characterology. In practice, Hoggart's writing appealed to a quite different kind of moral authority, as was evident in its strategy of quotation. The text draws heavily on working-class idiom, and on the actual or mimicked words of commercial culture. These are clearly marked, by punctuation or typography, as evidence for analysis; they might be termed *object*-quotations. At the same time, the text avails itself of another kind of citation, which is granted a different status. These are the epigraphs that introduce his own words, and the many phrases that occur with little or no formal marking, woven into the syntax of his own discourse as elements of itself. They are, in contrast, *subject*-quotations. Assembled as resources for Hoggart's own prose, Locke, Tocqueville, Arnold, Gorky, Benda, Auden, Forster, Lawrence, Yeats and others form an entire chorus of wisdom and insight. Theirs is the true authority of the book, the collective voice of *culture* raised against a wayward *civilization*.

This conceptual binary, familiar from more than a century of English cultural criticism, governed the vision of *The Uses of Literacy* and accounted for its most significant absence: the record of working-class self-organization in politics, work and education. Hoggart's disarming explanation for the omission was that these were the interests of a small, 'earnest' minority untypical of their class. This, coming from an active Labour Party member and WEA tutor, was hardly compelling. A stronger, though not more sympathetic explanation would cite the spontaneous perceptual effect of the convention that framed his analysis. Cultural criticism, in the strict sense I invoke here, is not one specialism among others; it proposes a certain understanding of society as a whole. The binary culture/civilization classifies all social tissue as either quality or quantity, purpose or mechanism, end or means. And the logical effect of this construction is to render politics unintelligible as a meaningful social activity; rarefied as 'values' or banalized as practical administration, its specificity is lost. Working-class political activists are no smaller a minority than the far less class-typical bourgeois novelist. If the one seemed so obviously less meaningful than the other, it was because in Hoggart's received scheme of analysis, politics as such was a secondary moral reality.

'Labour Leavisism' would be one summary of Hoggart's distinctively bifocal cultural vision. Yet he was both politically less demonstrative and culturally less desperate than these categories suggest. A moment's reflection on his subsequent work prompts a more exact characterization. Throughout his career – in the Arts Council and UNESCO as well as in public education – Hoggart thought to serve his class of origin as a *Kulturträger*, and to serve culture through the 'practical criticism' of policy and administration. (Fifty years after the founding enactments of welfare Britain, he continues to believe that his people, as he thinks of them, are being robbed.) His model institutions, the three volumes of his memoirs confirm, were adult education, the BBC and Penguin Books. Hoggart's specific novelty was to renew, in modified social conditions, the liberal tradition of the public-service intellectual. In him, the post-war British Labour movement found its own Matthew Arnold.

After 1956: a New Left

Between the writing of *The Uses of Literacy* and its publication came 1956, a year of shocks and portents that confounded the settled imagination of British politics and culture and unveiled the shapes of domestic and international relations after reconstruction. The Suez fiasco dramatized the predicament of an imperial ruling caste that could neither check its hereditary arrogance in the face of anti-colonial revolution nor readily accept its subaltern standing in an international capitalist order now dominated by the USA. Popular revulsion from the Anglo-French adventure was one sign that, at home as much as abroad, old political nostrums were losing their potency; and the scandalous cultural successes of the year – Colin Wilson's *The Outsider*, John Osborne's *Look Back in Anger* and the film *Rock Around the Clock* – gave early warning of new collective sensibilities in the making. 1956 was also a year of crisis for the left. Opening with Khrushchev's post-mortem denunciation of Stalin's rule, it ended, in bloody irony, with the crushing of the Hungarian revolt by Red Army tanks. The effect of these revelations in word and deed was convulsive, throughout the Communist movement. The British party lost one-fifth of its members, as some 7,000 militants, including a disproportionate number of intellectuals, resigned or were driven out.

It was possible to see in this constellation the hand of liberal progress: the passing of Empire, the advent of welfare and affluence, the Cold War adversary chastened, contained and discredited. In another perspective it signified complacency and exhaustion in a time of discoverable hope and shadowing danger. Intellectual disaffection mounted in the later fifties: academics, novelists, playwrights and publishers collaborated in terse collective interventions like *Declaration* (1957), *Conviction* (1958) and *The Establishment* (1959); *The Glittering Coffin* (1960) was Dennis Potter's scabrous figure for Macmillan's Britain. In the Campaign for Nuclear Disarmament, launched shortly after the Suez affair, these and broader currents of dissent found more challenging means of expression. Within this array of dissident forces, the clearest and most radical voices were those of the intellectual tendencies now converging in what soon came to be called 'the New Left'.

Two journals, both founded in 1957, formed the intellectual nuclei of the New Left. *The New Reasoner* was edited from the North of England by two ex-Communist historians, John Saville and Edward Thompson; having begun as an irregular oppositional organ within the party in direct response to Khrushchev's revelations, the journal was dedicated to the moral renewal of communism in 'socialist humanism'. Ex-Communists also featured among the editors and collaborators of *Universities and Left Review*, and the theme of a post-Stalinist socialist humanism was reiterated there. However, the more emphatic concern of the journal, which emerged from a group of Oxford students, was to elaborate an analysis and a programme that would supersede not only orthodox communism but Labourism as well, a thoroughgoing socialist critique of contemporary, welfare-capitalist Britain.[12] A *new* left for a new historical *situation*: this was *ULR's* distinctive appreciation of the intellectual challenge facing socialists after 1956. 'The New Conservatism' and Britain's modified class relations in a period of expanding social provision and imperial decline were the subject of Stuart Hall's opening contribution to this analytic agenda. This was followed, in the second issue, by a symposium on working-class culture occasioned by the newly-published *Uses of Literacy*.

It is instructive to be reminded, nearly forty years later, just how critically Hoggart's classic was received in the New Left's leading forum. The editors' opening question was courteous but incisive:

> Would a direct account in terms of readership reaction differ from Hoggart's content-analysis of the publications themselves?[13]

John McLeish likened the book's protagonist to 'a visiting anthropologist of a behaviourist persuasion'.[14] The common, though unspoken suggestion of these remarks was reinforced *a contrario* by a Welsh contributor, Gwyn Illtyd Lewis, who shared Hoggart's apprehensions of 'commercial devitalization' in the English-speaking population.[15] *The Uses of Literacy* in practice reanimated the critical discourse it offered to supersede, inflecting but not displacing the conventions of Leavisian cultural analysis. Raymond Williams, in the opening contribution to the symposium, saluted Hoggart's 'deep loyalty to his own people', but then, the more tellingly for that, made two fundamental objections. In present conditions, he insisted, 'working-class materialism' must be defended as a 'humane' value. And Hoggart was mistaken in excluding working-class activism as a 'minority' case, in effect relegating the culture of specialized class representatives to the status of social eccentricity. This minority, as he would later maintain in a recorded conversation with Hoggart, inherited and sustained a general history of struggle for democracy, trade unions and socialism – 'the high working-class tradition'.[16] The implication of these remarks was far-reaching: in reclaiming material desire as a moral good and politics as a '*high*' tradition, Williams was not simply adjusting the balance of Hoggart's analysis; he was disorganizing its basic terms, the binaries that framed it, and so intimating the possibility of an alternative way of seeing, beyond the perceptual scheme of liberal cultural criticism.

Williams: Beyond Culture-and-Society

Williams resembled Hoggart in his origins and career trajectory. A few years younger, Williams too had been born into a working-class family, risen through a local grammar school to study English at university, served in the army during the war, then gone to work in adult education, where he combined his ordinary duties with various independent writing and publishing projects. However, the differences of formation were at least as significant. Williams's family was actively socialist. Whereas Hoggart came from an urban English working class, Williams's early years were spent in the mixed-class environment of a Welsh village. Hoggart completed his formal education in his home town, where his left-wing convictions developed without assuming definite programmatic form. Williams, in contrast, crossed the national and social border to Cambridge, where, as he later recalled, the Communist Party and the University Socialist Club provided the staples of his intellectual life. These variations on an apparently common biographical scheme formed two quite different politico-cultural sensibilities: in the one case, a congenital class-tenderness sustaining allegiance to the dominant traditions of British labourism; in the other, a more radical and more consequent political training combined with an egalitarian self-possession conceding nothing to the deep fatalism of England's culture of class.

Formed once in the confident Communist sub-culture of the late 1930s, Williams underwent a difficult, protracted re-formation in the altered conditions he found upon returning to complete his studies in 1945. Although still a Communist, he was now outside the party, distrustful of its official publicity and unimpressed by its cultural orientation.[17] The red network of his first Cambridge period had collapsed, and the student socialists with whom he now sought constructive engagement took their cultural bearings from Leavis. The immediate outcome of these new associations was the short-lived journal *Politics and Letters*, which, together with its sibling, *The Critic*, explored an alliance of independent socialist politics with literary-cultural themes familiar from *Scrutiny*. This initiative has been mourned as the lost British counterpart of Sartre's *Les Temps Modernes*, but it is difficult to imagine that unrealized future.[18] *Politics and Letters* – the broken register of the title was sign enough – was the expression of a certain intellectual crisis, not a coherent intervention in it, and would have ended in confusion had not circumstantial difficulties foreclosed its development. The ground of this crisis, as Williams began to understand it, was the meaning of 'culture' itself, and 'a long line of thinking about culture' that had been 'appropriat[ed] . . . to what were by now decisively reactionary positions'.[19]

Out of this perception, which had begun to form as a response to the Cambridge Leavisians and then been clarified with the appearance of Eliot's *Notes*, came the inquiry that led, over the next eight years, to *Culture and Society*.[20] If the primary motive of the book was political, its critical strategy was, crucially, historical. The idea of culture, as a privileged term of evaluation, had emerged during the industrial revolution, Williams argued, and must then be understood as a critical actor in the remaking of social meanings that attended it. In order to undo the moral spell of 'culture', it would be necessary to retrace the process of its formation:

> For what I see in the history of this word, in its structure of meanings, is a wide
> and general movement in thought and feeling . . . I wish to show the emergence
> of *culture* as an abstraction and an absolute . . . [21]

Or, in other words, as a separate and higher social sphere, from which final moral judgement might be given and something of a moral alternative sustained.

Organized as a long sequence of author-specific analyses, *Culture and Society* was in substance the history of a discourse, its formation, variation and transmutation. Over the 150-year span from Burke to Leavis, it analysed the progressive rarefaction of *culture*, the defence of a whole and present social order narrowing, in stages, to the lament for an irrecoverable past and the desperate self-assertion of a specialized minority as the only sure trustees of an unattainable general spiritual welfare. Williams identified fundamental breaks where there was the strongest evidence of continuity (William Morris) and continuity where there was the most vigorous proclamation of a new departure (in the Marxism of the thirties). In a long concluding chapter, he synopsized the meaning of this complex, unfinished history, and situated himself within it:

> The idea of culture is a general reaction to a general and major change in the
> condition of our common life. Its basic element is its effort at total qualitative
> assessment . . . General change, when it has worked itself clear, drives us back
> on our general designs, which we have to learn to look at again, and as a whole.

The meanings of 'culture' were not unequivocal:

> The word . . . cannot automatically be pressed into service as any kind of social
> directive. . . . The arguments which can be grouped under its heading do not
> point to any inevitable action or affiliation.

Yet they 'define . . . a common field' and subserve, apparently, a common purpose: 'The working-out of the idea of culture is a slow reach again for control.'[22]

Formulations like this, abstract in reference and seemingly inclusive in address, were themselves less than unequivocal. *Culture and Society* was evidently a statement from the left, yet it was unclear what specific intellectual and political orientations it sponsored. The most influential interpretation, at first offered affirmatively and, since the early seventies, more often stated as a charge, was that the book proposed a moral refoundation of socialism in the tradition of English cultural humanism, that it was, in a phrase that became routine, a 'left-Leavisite' alternative to the ruin of Stalinized Marxism.[23] A less-well-known interpretation agreed that constructive continuity was Williams's deep theme, but argued that his intervention was for just that reason *Communist* in character, paralleling, in its own idiom, the post-war reorientation of

Party cultural analysis, which sought to trace a 'national' lineage for Marxist thought, in keeping with the new political strategy of a 'British road to socialism'.[24] There is, in the end, little difference between these readings, and both find support in textual and contextual evidence. The substantive concepts of Williams's title were those of the tradition he discussed, but they seemed often to exert reflexive control over his own discourse, inflecting his analytic and evaluative priorities towards a typically 'humanist' derogation of political reason, with correlative intimations of a finally 'common' moral interest. It is striking too that Williams conceived his revaluation of English cultural criticism in the same years that saw the Communist Party devote itself to recovering Coleridge, the Romantics, Carlyle, Ruskin and Morris as authentically national resources for the left. Edward Thompson was prominent in this politico-cultural initiative, and cognate themes were sounded in *Politics and Letters* by another Communist historian, Christopher Hill.[25]

However, neither line of interpretation leads to a secure historical estimate of *Culture and Society*. The Communist Party's cultural initiative was predominantly nationalist in thrust, an ill-judged attempt to resist the emerging North Atlantic culture of the Cold War by marshalling an essentially 'progressive' English tradition against the 'decadence' and 'barbarism' of New York and Hollywood. The result, as evidenced in the Party's cultural quarterly, *Arena*, was a crude national-populism, often mawkish or phobic, tendentious where not self-deluding or simply dishonest. There was nothing of this in *Culture and Society*, nor anything of *Arena*'s ready identification with the British Marxism of the thirties – from which, indeed, Williams took a clear, cool distance.[26] *Arena*'s repertoire included a serviceable pastiche of the *Scrutiny* manner, defining the 'function of a literary magazine', its 'lonely' function, as 'the maintenance . . . of fundamental critical standards', the pursuit of 'critical vitality' as a condition of 'creative vitality'.[27] In such moments, as in its wholesale condemnation of (American) mass-cultural production, *Arena*'s greater affinity was with *The Uses of Literacy*. There, of course, the use of that register signified a real discursive continuity. In Williams, the marks of continuity were not even, properly speaking, residual; they were rather the scars of a specific, unfinished engagement in alien country. It seems preferable, with all qualifications entered, to view *Culture and Society* as Williams himself saw it, as 'an oppositional work – not primarily designed to found a new position' but to undermine an existing one.[28]

Three considerations support this self-description – and in fact enhance its claim. Williams's attempt 'to counter the appropriation' of cultural criticism for reactionary purposes was not, as continuist interpretations must assume, the prelude to a socialist *reappropriation* of it: on the contrary, his historical summary of the tradition was fundamentally critical, speaking of the idea of culture as 'an abstraction and an absolute'. Neither did he suggest that culture in this sense might be democratized by expansion, privilege redeeming itself in the gesture of welfare. On the contrary, he expressly rejected high-cultural diffusionism, and characterized the liberal intellectual tradition of 'service' as an adapted form of bourgeois individualism.[29] Against both forms of the dominant ideology, he set the alternative principle of 'solidarity' – and this not as an ethical abstraction and absolute, but as the historical achievement of capitalism's associated producers, the working class.[30] With this plain affirmation of working-class creativity – positive cultural values made in and by, as well as against, the social relations of modern 'civilization' – Williams marked a position beyond the imaginative range of 'culture and society'.

Working-class Welfare: From Paternalism to Democracy

Appearing in 1958, *Culture and Society* announced the possibility of 'a new general theory of culture' and looked forward to 'a full restatement of principles, taking the theory of culture as a theory of relations between elements in a whole way of life.'[31] By then, the writing of *Essays and Principles* had already begun, leading to the book eventually published three years later as *The Long Revolution*. 'We live in an expanding culture,' Williams had written, 'yet we spend much of our energy regretting the fact, rather than seeking to understand its nature and conditions.'[32] *The Long Revolution* was, for the greater part, a sustained theoretical and historical effort towards that understanding, and, throughout, was governed by the ambition to clarify a politics adequate to that 'expanding culture'. *Culture and Society* had attacked the prevailing critical conception of the epoch as that of 'the masses . . . low in taste and habit'; in a short, prospective essay also published in 1958, Williams proposed his counter-thesis: 'culture is ordinary'.

Implicit in this disarming adjective were a theoretical proposition, a corresponding social revaluation, and the germ of a cultural politics, all three brought into focus in a long opening shot:

> The bus stop was outside the cathedral. I had been looking at the Mappa Mundi, with its rivers out of Paradise, and at the chained library, where a party of clergymen had got in easily, but where I had waited an hour and cajoled a verger before I even saw the chain. Now, across the street, a cinema advertised the *Six-Five Special* and a cartoon version of *Gulliver's Travels*. The bus arrived, with a driver and a conductress deeply absorbed in each other. We went out of the city, over the old bridge, and on through the orchards and the green meadows and the fields red under the plough. Ahead were the Black Mountains, and we climbed among them, watching the steep fields end at the grey walls, beyond which the bracken and heather and whin had not yet been driven back. To the east, along the ridge, stood the line of grey Norman castles; to the west, the fortress wall of the mountains. Then, as we still climbed, the rock changed under us. Here, now, was limestone, and the line of the early iron workings along the scarp. The farming valleys, with their scattered white houses, fell

away behind. Ahead of us were the narrower valleys: the steel-rolling mill, the gasworks, the grey terraces, the pitheads. The bus stopped, and the driver and conductress got out, still absorbed. They had done this journey so often, and seen all its stages.[33]

There were reminders here of Eliot, and of Hoggart as of Leavis before him. But the framing and sequence of the narrative offered an alternative to their ways of seeing. The familiar, fatal oppositions between élite and popular, culture and commerce, town and country, past and present, continuity and change, sensibility and machinery, Arnold's 'best' and 'ordinary selves' – the entire conceptual repertoire of 'culture and society' – were disordered in this complex time-space of social meaning, the shared element of everyday existence.

Culture, as Williams now proposed to theorize it, was the mode in which all human existence defined and evaluated itself; strictly speaking, the very phrase 'culture *and* society' was confusionist. The two basic processes of culture were learning and discovery, the relay of established meanings and the probing of new ones, and neither, in a period of significant expansion, was adequately served by the prevailing dual order. The case against the capitalist market in culture was familiar (most recently, in Hoggart's version), and, although intensified in Williams's theoretical perspective, was not altered by it: the inbuilt logic of market activity was philistine, interested in any kind of expansion that might show a profit, but indifferent or hostile to all else. Yet the alternative of public provision – 'common payment, for common services' – was hobbled not only by the usual complaint of ruinous expense but by the locked imagination of minority culture, to which Williams now posed a twofold challenge. It was a commonplace belief of liberal and conservative cultural criticism that the educational reforms of the later nineteenth century had engendered the trivializing mass journalism of the twentieth; and it was a commonplace of argument that, with money as with culture, the bad tended to drive out the good. Both propositions were demonstrably false, Williams retorted, and inadmissible as valid objections to enhanced educational provision. However, this counter-insistence was not offered as reassurance; for it was implicit in his theoretical concept of culture that 'growth' enjoined something other than simple 'extension':

> We should not seek to extend a ready-made culture to the benighted masses. We should accept, frankly, that if we extend our culture, we shall change it: some that is offered will be radically criticized. . . . I would not expect the working people of England to support works which, after proper and patient preparation, they could not accept. . . . [If] we understand cultural growth, we shall know that it is a continued offering for common acceptance, that we should not, therefore, try to determine in advance what should be offered, but clear the channels and let all the offerings be made, taking care to give the difficult full space, the original full time, so that it is a real growth, and not just a wider confirmation of old rules.[34]

Fellow-socialists found much to question in a passage like this, then and in later years. 'Common', if offered as a description of existing cultural relations, appeared to deny the actual inequalities and antagonisms of capitalism as 'a whole way of life'. And, if offered as the keyword of a critical anthropology (for, as Williams believed, any culture must be in some sense common, in order to be a culture at all), it appeared to float into empty ethical space – as 'an abstraction and an absolute'. The recourse to the first-person plural strengthened suspicions on these grounds, as also, in a strategic sense, did the irenic language of 'offering' and 'growth'. It is true – whatever else may or may not be true – that Williams's writing at this time inclined too much to emollience. But it is also true, and of greater historical importance then and now, that some of the best criticism of these ambiguities coexisted with them, in the same pages. There was much still to rethink and to discover, but by the turn of the 1960s Williams had established the irreducible distance between cultural liberalism in all its variants – reactionary or reforming – and an integrally socialist politics of culture. 'Paternalism', the high-minded format of cultural growth in welfare Britain, was not only inadequate as a counter to its far more vigorous 'commercial' other; it was itself mystified, and politically objectionable as a modified version of 'authoritarian cultural organization'. The true alternative, Williams maintained, lay in *democratic* and *pluralist* participation in the institutions and practices of culture, a 'common' evaluation-in-process of an undecided future.[35]

Views From the Nineties

The general history evoked here is that of a paternalist cultural liberalism, received and now actualized as the canonical format of policy in new or expanding institutions, in a phase of legislated welfare provision and intensifying consumer-capitalist enterprise. The pattern of articulated response to post-war cultural conditions seemed itself to obey a benign logic. A conservative intervention like Eliot's was widely noticed but won little support, so manifestly reactionary did it appear, even to the later *Scrutiny* – whose epigoni were themselves a dissident rearguard within a largely sanguine or complacent intelligentsia. Although Hoggart condemned the new (ab)uses of literacy in terms that recalled Leavis's, he did so in a spirit of fealty to the ideals of the liberal (now labourist) public educator. Williams's historical review of those ideals was respectful in tone, yet radically destructive, inaugurating a distinctively socialist theory and politics of culture. Lending their impetus to the wider challenge of the New Left, in the approach to an open general election, the new critical ideas might become a material force – perhaps indeed, or so the *Sunday Times* announced after Labour's victory in 1964, the doctrines of a 'New Establishment'.[36]

That is not how it turned out, of course. The new decade saw an accentuation of all the emergent tendencies of the later fifties. The culture was restyled from top to bottom, in processes that modified every variety of cultural politics, yet without settling the fortunes of any. By the end of another, far more convulsive decade, it began to be clear that the social settlement of 1945 had not been accepted by the right, that everything remained in question.

In that sense, then, the issues of the later forties and fifties remain contemporary; and conversely, the prominent cultural cruces of today (the marketization of public service television production, the advent of cable and satellite services, and of course the Internet), while they are usually announced, in sorrow or in ecstasy, as new, go on being defined in the terms of those years – when, also, they seemed new.[37] The distance of the past forty years, as we may gauge it from these early New Left writings, is evident not so much in the articulate contentions of the times as in what went more or less without saying. The society evoked by Hoggart and Williams was one of mostly settled sex-gender relations, in which the paradigmatic narratives were those of men.[38] Both writers made reference to the specific oppressions of working-class women, but these and other local qualifications were too slight to disturb the calm of a known (hence unexamined) world. In *The Long Revolution*, Williams actually posited 'the system of generation and nurture' as a specific historical structure, but his novels, the main site of his reflection on matters of gender and sexuality, reiterated a familiar discourse on moral order and disorder.[39] A second retrospective crux is the identity of Britain itself, which was neither taken wholly as given nor consistently focused in the terms of nationality and race. Hoggart noted in his working-class subjects an anachronistic confidence in the Empire. Williams discussed imperialism as a conventional sign in the nineteenth-century novel and as a central element of the contemporary political crisis; and his first published novel indexed the objective but unacknowledged cross-racial 'community' of post-imperial Britain (the 'border country' includes London, where Matthew Price's first encounter on his journey back to Wales is with a black woman bus conductor, at once the fellow transport worker and the determinate other of his signalman father). However, there was no developed sense of the 'national' culture as an imperial formation, shaped and already disturbed by the 'internal' racist logic of an 'external' history.[40] The unself-conscious citation of 'England' meaning (or not meaning?) Britain or the United Kingdom, was a sign that in this as in matters of gender, the analysis of the culture as one of classes remained abstract, and in some ways misdirected.[41]

In that analysis too, of course, contemporary readers will not fail to note anachronism. But here the anachronism is not that of certain books that linger on in print and memory; it lies also in the facile self-accounting of present tendencies in radical cultural theory and politics as they remember their 'classics' today. This is not only a matter of the familiar critical distortion that Williams later identified in the first New Left, including himself: the unmeasured stress on the putative moment of the new in history and the misreading of what persists as delayed obsolescence. The temporal parochialism of today is more damaging than that of forty years ago. For what was evident in the left cultural analyses of the fifties, but is far less evident in the far more richly resourced cultural studies radicalism of the nineties, is committed, systematic theoretical and moral resistance to the dominant cultures of capital. The forms of this resistance were radically distinct and unequal, as I have emphasized here: there is no value in recirculating 'the myth of Raymond Hoggart'.[42] But the shared motivation of Hoggart and Williams was that the principles and forms of a cultural commonwealth would have to be thought out and imposed *against* the spontaneous logic of the capitalist market as a whole system; the quite discrepant kinds of cultural politics they envisaged converged at least in their shared reach for strategic clarification. Both were fully aware of the pseudo-democratic and populist modes of market address in contemporary conditions. What they could scarcely have foreseen is how these modes would come to be internalized and reiterated as emancipatory theory by a politico-intellectual formation that honoured them as inspirations. Hoggart thought to check the effects of the audio-visual phantasmagoria through countervailing practices of public education. Williams rejected the market but also the paternalism that thought to humanize its creatures, and argued instead for collective determination in cultural production, as part of a general socialist transformation. Where Hoggart's critical liberalism is repudiated and Williams's socialism is declined, few choices remain. The rising tendency in cultural studies gives itself to a certain *anarcho-reformism*, permanently giddy in the conviction that micro-subversion is everywhere, in a totality which, at the same time, it is theoretically passé to name, let alone seek to dismantle. It is of course true that overmastering historical forces have sapped confidence and imagination in every quarter of the left; but this does not vindicate the spreading *amor fati* that rationalizes disappointment as enlightenment and reconstructs the problem as the solution. Set invocations of pervasive change and mock-heroic calls to renounce the past, whether uttered by modernizing Labour politicians or by new-wave intellectual formations that objectively converge with them, are the tropes of a self-punishing identification with the aggressor; they merely confuse the necessary effort to think and act lucidly in the real, temporally complex conditions of capitalism today. In this situation, the politico-cultural ambitions of that old New Left are indeed anachronistic – no longer contemporary, in obvious ways, but in other ways, perhaps, on hold for a recoverable future.

1996

ENGLISH READING

'My task which I am trying to achieve is, by the power of the written word to make you hear, to make you feel – it is, before all else, to make you *see*. That – and no more, and it is everything.' Joseph Conrad

'English ought to be kept up.' John Keats

What should we read, how should we read it, and why? Such questions are staple elements of any politics of reading. But they remain less than critical if they are put without consciousness of the unavowed answer they already insinuate. Issues of selection, procedure, and purpose are often settled in advance by the meanings assigned to the collective pronoun. So there is a further question: as whom, as what do 'we' read? Asked or not, this question is always answered, and my purpose here is to consider the answer given in an especially forceful practice of reading: the English literary criticism chiefly represented by F. R. and Q. D. Leavis.

1

Pressed by René Wellek for a philosophical defence of his criticism, F. R. Leavis offered a narrative:

> The cogency I hoped to achieve was to be for other readers of poetry – readers of poetry as such. I hoped, by putting in front of them, in a criticism that should keep as close to the concrete as possible, my own developed 'coherence of response', to get them to agree (with, no doubt, critical qualifications) that the map, the essential order, of English poetry seen as a whole did, when they interrogated their experience, look like that to them also. . . . My whole effort was to work in terms of concrete judgements and particular analyses: 'This – doesn't it? – bears such a relation to that; this kind of thing – don't you find it so? – wears better than that', etc.[1]

In this way, Leavis sought to elude the very terms of Wellek's demand. There would be no 'explicit' and 'systematic' account of principles, no 'abstract' evaluation of 'choices': only reading, and dialogue with other readers.

The upshot was paradoxical. Apparently unforthcoming, Leavis's countermove was perhaps more revealing than a more compliant response would have been. The founding assumption of Leavisian criticism, it turned out, was a rigorous humanism: the experiential merging of critic and poem, and of both with the experience of 'other readers', was scarcely thinkable without the 'philosophical' guarantee of a human essence – something constant, universal, and, like the Arnoldian 'best self', potentially decisive.[2] However, there is a logical strain in the notion of an essence whose efficacy is contingent, and this is evident in Leavis's narrative of 'the common pursuit'. The imagined scene is ideal: critic and interlocutor in informal, even intimate exchange. But the very informality of the critic-narrator's questions betrays the imposture of openness: negatively phrased, they presume assent – or what is imagined at another moment as corroborative self-'interrogation'. The interlocutor, meanwhile, is silent; the expected 'critical qualifications', never uttered, remain parenthetical concessions in the discourse of the critic. Lacking this interlocutor, the situation and its justifying event are jeopardized, and Leavis seems almost resigned to the loss: 'I hoped . . . I hoped . . . my whole effort was . . .', he writes, as if telling a story of what might have been.

Leavis's half-realized character – present, presumably assenting, yet silent – embodies a compromise between two incommensurable entities: the ideal interlocutor whose active, confirming presence is the necessary ground of Leavisian criticism, and an actual, contingent readership that is neither present to the author nor predictable in the range and substance of its 'qualifications'. This, abstractly speaking, is a logical dilemma: Leavisian criticism is a long-drawn-out fallacy, endlessly bent on establishing what it already assumes to exist. But practically, it is a problem of suasion. 'My task', wrote Conrad, in a declaration uncannily close to Leavis's, 'is, before all else, to make you *see*. That – and no more, and it is everything.'[3] If so little is everything, it is because there is indeed something more. The preferred reading of the passage is clearly signalled in its syntax and typography: the goal is shared vision. But these indications of emphasis are crossed by the counter-emphasis of repetition: the task is 'to make you . . . to make you . . . to make you . . .'. In a characteristic movement of disavowal, Conrad's words admit the moment of dictation in all writing. To represent the object is, measure for measure, to position the subject, the clarity of the one depending on the stability of the other. To 'make' is at once to compel and to compose: to compel the actual reader by composing an ideal one, to pre-scribe the subjective conditions of 'seeing'. No less than of Conrad's fiction, this is the rhetorical task of Leavisian criticism.

Leavis's task is to determine the object ('the map, the essential order') and, as a necessary part of this, to position the subject. His critical writing must work to reduce the discrepancy between its ideal interlocutor and real readers, to compose the *normal* subject of Leavisian reading-writing. In other words, the writing must complete the half-sketched second character in the exemplary narrative of criticism. And it really will be a 'character', not an ontological cypher. The sponsors of humanism are, dependably, rather more than generically 'human', and so equally are the normative images of their writing.

As Perry Anderson once observed, 'the real solidarities of Leavisian humanism are quite specific in time and place.'[4] The character whose features emerge in Leavisian criticism is a fully historical being, and 'normal' in every way.

2

This normalizing drive is sometimes declared, as on those occasions when critical attention turns from the literary object to the ('qualifying'?) reader: 'Here a few illustrations [from *The Prelude*] must suffice, as indeed, to point the attention effectively, they should: that once done, the demonstration is the reading, as anyone who cares to open his Wordsworth may see; the facts, to the adverted eye, are obvious'.[5]

But conspicuous interventions of this kind are only the periodic excesses of an activity whose signs are everywhere in the ordinary workings of Leavisian 'analysis and judgement'. For in this cultural zone nearly all seasons are bad ones. The imagined time of Leavisian criticism ('I hoped . . . I hoped . . . my whole effort was . . .') is that of impending loss. The ideal interlocutor is chronically prone to distraction by the spectacle of historical change. The meaning of modern history, for Leavis, was the dissolution of 'community'. Emerging in the period of the English Revolution and gathering strength in the succeeding century, a whole array of social forces had worked to undermine a traditional, integrated way of life, and then unleashed the industrializing dynamic that shook it apart. Where once there had been an 'organic' community, there were now two mutually opposed and unequal realities: 'civilization', the world of means and quantities, which drove forward according to the autonomous logic of industrial production, and 'culture', the world of qualities and ends, the memory of a 'human norm' that could never again find general social acceptance, and the only resource of those who fought to avert a final breach in 'continuity'. By the early twentieth century, the lot of 'culture' had so worsened that language, in its most demanding literary usage, was now the only element of continuity. Out of that history and that vital 'human' need came the cultural warrant of literary judgement and the objective responsibility borne by any who thought to exercise it.

Such representations of the past are not truly historical in mode. Processes of change are described and interpreted, but only as the corrosive, demoralizing environment of something that is held to be essentially changeless, and whose value is the decisive theme of the retrospect. This is the past not as history but as 'tradition'. Its characteristic mode is, so to say, transjunctive, its valued moments 'joined across' the objective order of what has been in the service of what now exists. Tradition, as Leavis himself noted, is akin to memory. And, as he did not add, their procedures and functions are the same. Tradition, usually said to be received, is in reality made, in an unceasing activity of selection, revision, and outright invention, whose function is to defend identity against the threat of heterogeneity, discontinuity and contradiction. Its purpose is to bind (and necessarily, therefore, to exclude). Tradition is prone to represent itself as custom, as the settled fact of continuity, but its real process is shot through with anxiety, as the history of Leavis's journal itself attests. *Scrutiny's* watchword, as it evaluated the claims of writing in its own day, was 'for continuity' (the title of Leavis's first collection of essays). But its retrospects were no less wary, and the last years of the journal witnessed a restless probing of the 'organic community' itself, in its putative seventeenth-century setting. The essential strengths of that period were found to be residues of pre-Reformation culture, which in its turn was discovered to run back into a pre-Christian past. And so the deepest continuities of English literature seemed to be with a society and a culture that were not in any reasonable sense 'English'.

The poignancy of this conclusion deserves emphasis, for the sovereign *topos* of Leavisian discourse was precisely the continuity of Englishness. The basic categories of *Scrutiny's* historiography were implicitly universal in application; as is manifest in the kindred sociological line descending from Tönnies's *Gemeinschaft und Gesellschaft*, they frame a certain interpretation of the transition to capitalism as such. But in Leavis's writing, their privileged reference is to England and the doom of English culture, and his key values are not so much 'culture' or 'literature' as a language and a people.

Shakespeare, Leavis affirms, is 'the pre-eminently (in his relation to the language) English poet',[6] and the decisive nuance of the adverbial is fixed in this tribute to Donne: 'This is the Shakespearian use of English: one might say that it is the English use – the use, in the essential spirit of the language, of its characteristic resources.'[7] The attributes of this 'essential spirit' are celebrated again and again. Donne's poetry exhibits 'the sinew and living nerve', the 'strength of spoken English'.[8] Jonson evinces a 'native robustness', a 'rooted and racy Englishness'; his 'toughness is lively and English', going with his 'native good sense.'[9] In Jonson, these qualities are such as to subdue the external, 'classicizing' language of the Renaissance, his 'racy personal tone' turning 'erudition into native sinew'. Where classicism prevails, as in Milton, the outcome is 'rejection of English idiom', for which the critical penalty is exile.[10] The integrity that animates this English idiom has more than one specification. Leavis largely agrees with Gerard Manley Hopkins that Dryden's 'native English strength' is 'masculine' in its stress on 'the naked thew and sinew of the language', and compliments Crabbe on his 'generous masculine strength'.[11] The lapse from this idiom is a token of moral deficiency, as the case of Shelley shows. But Keats bears witness to the possibility of regeneration, finding at last 'a strength – a native English strength – lying beyond the scope of the poet who aimed to make English as like Italian as possible [and a] vigour such as is alien to the Tennysonian habit, and such as a Tennysonian handling of the medium cannot breed.'[12]

The steady connotative pressure of Leavis's idiom is quite remarkable. The literal emphasis on the specificities of the English language is developed, across an unvarying range of metaphor, association and (scarcely intended) pun, into a positive characterization of 'Englishness'. By the later stages of *Revaluation* an elaborate order of solidarity and antagonism has been enforced: the native, racy, vigorous, strong, masculine, and against these the classicizing, Italianate, alien, corrupt, voluptuous, effeminate, impotent. In vouching for Wordsworth as 'normally and robustly human', Leavis summarizes a whole anthropology of virtue.[13] 'The facts, to the adverted eye, are obvious.'

The Great Tradition was to do for the English novel what *Revaluation* had done for English poetry. Like the earlier work, it is concerned not to construct a history (it is expressly pitched against 'the literary histories') but to ascertain the 'tradition', the 'line' of the English novel as it comes down through the heterogeneous mass of narrative fiction in prose. The nature of the operation approaches self-consciousness in this sentence from the opening pages of the work: 'One of the supreme debts one great writer can owe another is the realization of unlikeness (there is, of course, no significant unlikeness without the common concern – and the common seriousness of concern – with essential human issues).'[14] The movement of this passage epitomizes the activity of binding and exclusion in which Leavisian criticism is involved. Heterogeneity is at first acknowledged, but is then reduced to 'significant' unlikeness, which turns out to be the deceptive sign of an inner consonance whose bearing (cognitive and ethical) is the essentially human – in short, the self-identical. And the medium of the essentially human, it turns out, is English. The nativism of *Revaluation* is equally, if less euphorically, evident in *The Great Tradition*.

Of Leavis's three chosen novelists, only one (George Eliot) was English. James was Anglophone but American; the language of Conrad's novels was his third; and both learned significantly from other literatures. A key purpose of *The Great Tradition* was to reduce these complexities of formation to biographical accident and to naturalize James and Conrad as exponents of a transcendent language that must be understood as adequate, and finally as necessary, to the novelistic exploration of 'essential human values'. The story of the book is the victory of an English tradition over the circumstances of origin and, crucially, over the latterday Renaissance, French realism. Thus, James may be located in 'a distinctively American' line, but this is as it were a ruse of tradition: Hawthorne emancipated James from the influence of Thackeray and from Flaubert, making possible an authentic, enabling connection with Eliot.[15] Conrad did indeed learn from 'the French masters': the stylism and exoticism of his weaker writing is derived from Chateaubriand, and *Nostromo* recalls Flaubert.[16] Yet Conrad's work, with its 'robust vigour of melodrama', is also 'Dickensian', 'Elizabethan' even.[17] And if he evinces that 'racy strength' it is because, his origins notwithstanding, his 'themes and interests' actually called for the English language rather than any other. He is 'unquestionably a constitutive part of the tradition, belonging in the full sense.'[18]

A second major theme of *The Great Tradition* is the novel as such. It was in the course of writing this book that Leavis substantiated his conception of the novel as linguistic art. 'The differences between a lyric, a Shakespeare play, and a novel, for some purposes essential, are not in danger of being forgotten; what needs insisting on is the community,' he wrote in the early 1930s, and the criticism that ensued was to be interested not in 'character' and 'incident' but in the 'pattern of moral significances' that novelistic art might yield, in 'the novel as dramatic poem'.[19] Much of the meaning of this conception, and the polemical force with which Leavis promoted it, must be sought in the history of academic and lay literary criticism. Leavis, like others around him, was determined to redeem the novel from its common status as a cultivated or narcotic diversion and to establish its parity with the canonical arts of language. But his manner of doing so bears an interesting relation to his critical practice generally. His terminology disrupts the received classification of verbal art and redefines the novel (epic) as a combination of the two types from which it was classically distinguished, the lyric and the dramatic. The effect of this development – which reinforced an already well-established emphasis on the 'poetic' essence of verse drama – was to reorder the field of critical perception at the expense of narrative. All wider differences set aside, it can still be said that the greatest weakness of Leavisian criticism lay just here; and part of the sense of that weakness may be glimpsed in Leavis's reading of *Typhoon*.

The 'elemental frenzy' (Leavis's phrase) that occupies most of Conrad's story is a literal event: a British merchant ship is exposed to a devastating tropical storm and only narrowly escapes destruction. But from the outset it is metaphorized as a psychic and political ordeal. The ship's captain, MacWhirr, is an obsessional. Locks and charts are the emblems of his life; his letters to his wife are phatic observances, without value as registrations of feeling or incident; his speech, which he enforces as a shipboard norm, is laconic, literal, and untouched by the smallest acquaintance with pidgin. However, the circumstances of this voyage are not wholly routine. The ship has been transferred from the British to the Siamese flag; and the cargo on this occasion is human – 200 Chinese coolies returning from periods of labour in various colonies. Sailing under 'queer' colours, its crew outnumbered by their freight of alien bodies, the *Nan-Shan* heads into 'dirty' weather. The storm attacks every established social relationship of the vessel. Masculinity is abandoned for hysteria; linguistic order fails, as speech turns figural or obscene, is blocked by superstition or swept away by the gale. MacWhirr and his first mate, Jukes, reach for each other in encounters that mingle duty and desire, resolution and bewilderment; while in the hold the Chinese have apparently gone berserk. The lowering of the British ensign brings on a storm that unfixes identity ('He started shouting aimlessly to the man he could feel near him in that fiendish blackness, "Is it you, sir? Is it you, sir?" till his temples seemed ready to burst. And he heard in answer a voice, as if crying far away, as if screaming to him fretfully from a very great distance, the one word "Yes!".'), and *Homo Britannicus* is abandoned to a chaos of effeminacy, homoeroticism, and gibberish – the terrifying counter-order of the Chinese labourers below. The ship survives. But the restoration of order is understood as a furtive improvisation, the hurried winding-up of an incident better forgotten. It is related not by the main narrator but in a chattily complacent letter from Jukes, who, in his uncertain sexual orientation (his regular correspondent is male) and openness to linguistic transgression (metaphor, pidgin), is socially perverse. Worse, the protagonist himself is fatally ambiguous: MacWhirr, as we have learned from an early narrative recollection, is not British but Irish. The chief officers of the *Nan-Shan*, ultimate guarantors of imperial order, bear the typhoon within themselves.

Leavis's account discloses virtually nothing of this. Where he quotes passages whose manifest sense discourages any other reading, he confines himself to dubious technical observations on 'a novelist's art', and his wider commentary on *Typhoon* strikes a directly contrary emphasis. It is the 'ordinariness' and 'matter-of-factness' of the ship's captain and crew that hold his attention, 'the qualities which, in a triumph of discipline – a triumph of the spirit – have enabled a handful of ordinary men to impose sanity on a frantic mob'.[20] Leavis's language reveals his ideological relationship to *Typhoon* and, at the same time, the strategy of his reading. Identifying himself with the norms of the text, he sets out to rewrite its ending and to unwrite the greater part of the narrative. *Typhoon* works through a fearsome 'return of the repressed'; Leavis's reading functions to assist repression, indeed to perfect it, simply silencing the anxieties that generated the story in the first instance.

Leavis's encounter with *Typhoon* may serve as a hyperbolic illustration of his critical relationship with narrative generally. Narratives vary, it need hardly be said; but the work of narrativity is always an opening and closing, a loosening and rebinding of sense. All but the most sedate or the most forensic narratives are in some degree unsettling, and *Typhoon* is neither. It may be ventured, then, that a criticism bent on affirming an essential human identity will be inhibited in the face of narrative, and will revise its object-texts (as the ego is said to revise dreams and memories) in that interest. It is apt that Leavis, confronted with a fictional dispersal of that identity, in a text of his own choosing by one of his canonical authors, should read with an averted eye.

3

The 'human' is a closely specified term in Leavisian discourse, as, in turn, is 'English': *Revaluation* makes this plain. They are normalizing terms that arrogate the common names of a species, a language and an ethnic formation as the honorific titles of particular social commitments and agencies. They are, in the necessary strict meaning of a slackened concept, ideological. The nature of these commitments and agencies is manifest in the social history of Leavis and his collaborators, and equally in their critical writing. The normal subject of Leavisian discourse is specified not only by nationality but also by class, gender, and sexual orientation.

The *Scrutiny* 'connection', as Leavis sometimes called it, was petty-bourgeois. Its leading members were generally such by provenance, as were its
contributors and regular readers – teachers in the main – by occupation.
The politics of the 'connection' were likewise suspended over the main
national and international conflicts of the time. The anti-industrialism of
the journal was inevitably shaded with anti-capitalism, sometimes
markedly. But *Scrutiny's* stand against Marxism is a legend; and notwithstanding social compassion and episodic political sympathy, Leavis and his
collaborators rebuffed any suggestion that the industrial working class had
the capacity to sustain or develop 'humane culture'. The class disposition of
the journal was plainest in its constant attacks on the leisured academic
rearguard of Oxford and Cambridge, and the part-rentier, part-commercial
intelligentsia of the capital. One among many needling allusions to the former can be discerned in Leavis's repeated reference, in *Revaluation*, to 'the
mob of gentlemen' who versified at the court of Charles I; and a more striking index of this academic class antagonism is the diction of Leavisian criticism, which quite characteristically qualifies the received idiom of
cultivated leisure ('taste', 'sensibility', 'fineness') with a new and challenging
idiom of effort ('strenuous', 'labour', 'collaboration', 'enactment'). The
strategic prize in *Scrutiny's* contention with the metropolitan élites was the
status of 'centrality', which Leavis and his collaborators sought to invest
with a strictly cultural rather than social meaning. Here too the polemical
idiom was telling: in a metaphorical economy of intellectual life, the
'inflated currencies' of the capital were to be regulated by authentic 'standards' and 'values', real measures of work and self-improvement.

Much of Q. D. Leavis's assault on Virginia Woolf can be read in this light.
The latter's *Three Guineas*, she charged, exemplified the conceptions of a class-
blinded 'social parasite'; Woolf's feminist critique of educational provision was
'a sort of chatty restatement of the rights and wrongs' of propertied women
intellectuals like herself, designed to 'penalize specialists' in the interests of
amateur 'boudoir scholarship'. But there was more than righteous class hostility in a passage like this, which duly places Leavis's occasional concessions
to feminism:

> 'Daughters of educated men have always done their thinking from hand to
> mouth . . . [Woolf had written]. They have thought while they stirred the pot,
> while they rocked the cradle'. I agree with someone who complained that to
> judge from the acquaintance with the realities of life displayed in this book
> there is no reason to suppose Mrs Woolf would know which end of the cradle
> to stir. . . . I feel bound to disagree with Mrs Woolf's assumption that running
> a household and a family unaided necessarily hinders or weakens thinking.
> One's own kitchen and nursery, and not the drawing-room and dinner-table
> where tired professional men relax among the ladies (thus Mrs Woolf), is the
> realm where living takes place, and I see no profit in letting our servants live
> for us. The activities Mrs Woolf wishes to free educated women from as waste-

ful not only provide a valuable discipline, they serve as a sieve for determining which values are important and genuine and which are conventional and contemptible. It is this order of experience that often makes the conversation of an uncultivated charmless woman who has merely worked hard and reared a family interesting and stimulating, while its absence renders a hypertrophied conversation piece like *Three Guineas* tiresome and worthless.[21]

That Virginia Woolf was prone to rentier myopia is undeniable, and Q. D. Leavis's attack would be sympathetic were not its terms and tone those of a far more myopic, truculently conformist femininity. Not merely a self-pampering 'victim' of class privilege, the suggestion went, Woolf was deficient as a woman. In such judgements the Leavises stood side by side. Corresponding assumptions animate the language of *Revaluation*, with its ready gendering of poetic idiom and associated imagery of virility and procreation (or their vicious substitutes). Woolf did not lack male company either: F. R. Leavis's summarizing review of E. M. Forster, in one way a moving tribute, hesitated several times before the novelist's 'spinsterish' prose; and the most-lamented poetic wastrel of the 1930s, W. H. Auden, was cast out in an article deploring his 'inverted' development.[22] There were so many tests of what was 'normally and robustly human'.

The evidence of these canonical works – the critical books and essays – is supported by that of the apocrypha: the joint autobiography that occupied the Leavises (and those around them) all their lives. This 'work' was never written, in the ordinary sense, but as Raymond Williams observed, it might as well have been: 'Most of those who have heard [the story] will know how compellingly it was told. It was a sustained structure of feeling through the only apparently random episodes. It was essentially composed, in a literary sense.'[23] Williams was referring to the institutional history of Cambridge, *Scrutiny*, the London 'literary racket', and so on. But the volume of memoirs from which his words come extends their sense to the sphere of the domestic and personal. What emerges from Denys Thompson's gathering of 'recollections and impressions' is how strongly, how theatrically, the Leavises emphasized the proprieties of gender and family, and with what impact on those who were close to them. Frank was vain to the point of boasting about his athletic prowess, as was Queenie about her domestic skills; his running and her scones are staple topics of their memoirists. Their famous intellectual 'collaboration' was subject to strict gender regulation and a corresponding division of domestic labour. This was not a trouble-free formula: Queenie, proudly a working woman intellectual but just as proudly the wife and mother who never broke a cup, suffered conflicts of identity and interest from which her husband was largely exempt, and she knew it. But, in all, it seems that the drama of Leavisian criticism was encoded also as a determined and conservative politics of 'mature', 'normal' gender and sexuality, whose ideal scene was the family. It is not merely that the Leavises lived in a certain way

– that is of purely biographical interest. What is important is that they actively represented their life together as a further specification of the 'human norm'.

The style of life, thus organized and projected, joined the critical style in a discourse of formidable appeal, as grateful pupils soon began to testify. 'Sanity and vigour and masculinity and Britishness' were the qualities that compelled one early tribute – Martin Green's. F. R. Leavis seemed

> intensely and integrally British. Not Europeanized, not of the intelligentsia, not of the upper classes, not of Bloomsbury, not of any group or set. . . . [He] comes to us from generations of decency and conscience and reasonableness and separateness, of private houses hidden behind hedges, along the road from Matthew Arnold and John Stuart Mill . . . . Alone in all Cambridge his voice has echoes of the best things in my parents' England, makes connections between all the parts of my experience.[24]

These are ingenuous words, but they are apt. Their structure of feeling is manifestly Leavisian. In such terms, the ideal interlocutor finds a social identity and begins to speak.

4

The governing values of Leavisian discourse are class-restrictive, (hetero)sexist and ethnocentric. The 'human' image is caught in a sepia print of family life in lower-middle-class England. In this composition of values, the fixing element, the guarantee of integrity, was the notion of an abiding, self-evident Englishness. Ethnocentrism did much to frame the perspective of *Scrutiny's* literary criticism – which in turn cannot fully be understood apart from its conditions of formation in mid-century England.

'Ethnocentric' need not mean stay-at-home. If *Scrutiny* was less cosmopolitan than some other literary journals of its time, it was not insular. The literature of England was always its major concern, but that was hardly an unreasonable option. French, German, and US literature were extensively discussed, and other national literatures were surveyed or sampled. Neither was the journal in any ordinary sense patriotic: on the contrary, opposition to British chauvinism was a point of honour during the Second World War. The traces of *Scrutiny's* ethnocentrism are to be found not in the range of its international coverage, which by the standards of the day was merely unremarkable, but in its characteristic manner. *Scrutiny* was most confident when dealing with native literatures: those emerging from the home ground of their respective languages – English, French, German, Italian. Inhibition and resistance became evident in the face of 'rootless' diversity. 'More and more does human life depart from the natural rhythms,' Leavis wrote, in an early, qualified reference to Spengler; 'the cultures have mingled, and the forms have dissolved into chaos.'[25] *Scrutiny's* criticism – and more pointedly his own – attempted to restore integrity and order. Thus, the Renaissance was legitimate on its own territory, but not when it threatened to 'classicize' English poetic idiom; and whatever might be said for the French novel as a moment in the cultural history of France, it could not be granted a formative role in the novelistic tradition of England.

Within Anglophone culture itself there were special problems, for imperialism had made the metropolitan tongue a lingua franca whose users were, in majority, not ethnically English. The language had won its international eminence at the cost of its native integrity. The most salient foreign literary vernaculars in English at this date were those of the United States and Ireland. America was always important, and in many ways attractive, to *Scrutiny*. But attempts to characterize its literature were unresolved. The journal's most sustained effort to describe a distinctive American literary tradition – the work of an American contributor, Marius Bewley – ran a paradoxical course. Bewley's purpose, openly opposed to Leavis's, was to establish the 'essential Americanism' of Henry James. But this critical difference was not all its principals took it to be, for Bewley's thesis ended in bathos: setting out from the example of Jane Austen and returning to England in the person of James, the American 'line' turned out to be a loop circuit of 'the great tradition'.[26] *Scrutiny's* coverage of Irish writing, in contrast, was sparse and fragmentary. But its greatest interwar representative, James Joyce, was rejected early and decisively, and in telling terms. Joyce, for Leavis, was the anti-Shakespeare, his work the destructive antithesis of an authentic, 'rooted' idiom.[27] The charge was appropriate in a way, but the historical impetus of Joyce's work was not one that Leavis, in his own pregnant word, could easily 'recognize'. What is lost in Joyce is indeed any sense of the English language as second nature. Unlike James and Conrad, as *The Great Tradition* portrays them, Joyce was not relieved of his circumstantial beginnings by the language of Shakespeare. He was a product of colonial Ireland and wrote out of that formation. His writing is, in this respect, a dramatization of the 'native' as alien, the 'mother' language as another language. (Stephen, of the Dean of Studies: 'The language in which we are speaking is his before it is mine. How different are the words *home*, *Christ*, *ale*, *master*, on his lips and on mine! I cannot speak or write these words without unrest of spirit. His language, so familiar and so foreign, will always be for me an acquired speech. I have not made or accepted its words. My voice holds them at bay. My soul frets in the shadow of his language.') It is the writing of one for whom 'English' could not be self-identical, a literary practice whose 'roots' lay in the history of colonialism.

That history sank just as deeply into the metropolitan culture, sparing none, not even the disinterested humanists of *Scrutiny*. Critical writing, like any other, proposes a subjective place of reading, but dictation is beyond its power. Many things may be written and read, but rather few are internalized, reiterated, elaborated, and applied. The ideal match of inscribed addressee and contingent reader cannot happen in the absence of favouring extra-textual conditions – whose shapes are, therefore, ultimately decisive for cultural history. The historical conditions of Leavisian discourse are those of Britain in the fifty-odd years between the Armistice and 'the end of empire'.

Scrutiny and its active audience emerged as part of a long re-formation of the dominant culture – its practices, orientation, and social equilibrium. One of the main constituent processes in this complex change was a recomposition of the intelligentsia. In the thirty years after the First World War, an established intellectual bloc was obliged to adapt or yield to an emergent formation of a quite distinct character. The old bloc was essentially Victorian. Lodged in the old universities and in the cultural centres of the capital, it cultivated a wide variety of interests without prejudice to its fundamental social unity. Even its most radical personalities tended to speak as if by right of inheritance, secure in the presumptions and licences of the class to which they directly or vicariously belonged. The postwar levies, in contrast, were not cohesive in much except their objective difference from this culture; both generational experience and typical class background estranged them. Drawn largely from the petty bourgeoisie, coming up through grammar rather than public schools and – more and more likely – the 'civic' universities rather than Oxford and Cambridge, they were perforce 'professionals', making livings and careers in a world still held by the mystique of effortless distinction. The forms and outcomes of this historical encounter were naturally various. There were stylistic accommodations on both sides, and mere generational turnover, reinforced by continuing educational reform, ensured the ultimate practical advantage of the new formation. But there were also passages of open conflict, of which the most acrimonious was the long affair of Leavis and *Scrutiny*. The new 'provincialism' of British intellectual life was widely observed, and celebrated or deplored, in the 1950s. Martin Green's sentiments are a vivid expression of it, and an index of the critical role of Leavis in its emergence.

'Provincial', as used then by both the exponents and the misfits of the new ethos, was the summary term for a whole social complex: tributary terms like 'ordinary', 'serious', and 'decent' (or 'lower-middle-class', 'earnest', and 'puritan') were seldom far away. However, Green's catalogue of virtue is a reminder of another sense of the term, and of the fact that these internal shifts in British culture occurred in the context of a fundamental alteration in its global position. Another difference between the old and the new intellectual dispensations is that they matured respectively before and after Britain's withdrawal from India. The old intellectual bloc was part of an *imperial* élite: its collective imagination, patrician and cosmopolitan in tone, was nourished by the international eminence of the British state. The successor formation came of age in a palpably shrinking country, in the years of imperial retreat and the rise of a new, American hegemony. 'Britain' and 'England', in Green's vocabulary, are exclusive terms: summarizing 'all the parts' of his experience yet surrounded by emphatic negatives, they are in effect diminutives.

In this sense Green was already 'post-Leavisian' – or, for it comes to the same thing, Leavis was not, as Green was, subjectively 'post-imperial'. There is nothing diminutive about the functioning of such terms in *Revaluation* or *The Great Tradition*. 'English', in these works, is both exclusive, socially and morally, and universalizing, systematically offered as the instance of a 'human norm'. It was not a given: the most rigorous discriminations were necessary. But these were for the sake of its unquestioned claim to moral sovereignty. Here, as in much else, Leavis was critically disaffected from a world to which, however, he could imagine no alternative. He had inherited the humanism of 'the intellectual aristocracy' but not its patrician ease; he asserted a specific and normative Englishness but was still too much a cosmopolitan to settle for the gnawing, cheated chauvinism of Little England. Leavisian discourse in its high period – the *Scrutiny* years – cannot be assimilated either to the old, imperial literary culture or to its 'provincial' successor: its distinctive shape was that of the transition between them.

But transitions prolonged beyond their time are liable to decay. F. R. Leavis's 1967 Clark Lectures read in places like a desperate last struggle against silence. Rejecting all 'chauvinism' or 'patriotic nationalism', and any suggestion of a 'compensatory nostalgia for lost imperial greatness', he persisted nevertheless in his appeal to a reality that could and should be valued as England's 'national greatness'.[28] His affirmation was almost literally hollow: so many disavowals englobing an inexpressible faith. His partner's late conclusions, on the other hand, were typically forthright. In 1980, Q. D. Leavis gave her last public lecture. Her theme, appropriately synoptic, was 'the Englishness of the English novel'; the venue was Cheltenham. As she neared the end of her presentation, she turned to reflect on the plight of 'our run-down Britain', and the deep harmonies of the occasion became audible:

> The England that bore the classical English novel has gone forever, and we can't expect a country of high-rise flat-dwellers, office workers and factory robots and unassimilated multi-racial minorities, with a suburbanized countryside, factory farming, sexual emancipation without responsibility, rising crime and violence, and the Trade Union mentality, to give rise to a literature comparable with its novel tradition of a so different past.[29]

Decadence, whose decadence? The 'humanism' that found words for that noxious elegy had decayed into simple misanthropy.

Yet Q. D. Leavis was right in this at least: the cultural bases of Leavisian discourse have weakened greatly in the forty years since *Scrutiny*'s closure. This is so above all in schools, whose young population – most of them children of the working-class and of settled minorities from the ex-colonial world – cannot often be made to adjust their intuitions to the normalizing imperative of her kind of Englishness. Most English teachers have long been aware of this, and many positively assert it as a premiss of their work. In the higher, exclusive reaches of the education system, however, old traditions are more durable. About 'the Leavisites' themselves, there is little to say: they abide. What is important is that the deepest assumptions of Leavisian (and kindred) criticism will tend to persist except where new objects and priorities of analysis are asserted against them. In this perspective, a work like Williams's *The Country and the City* remains exemplary, more than two decades after its publication, for its refusal of that familiar condensation of a nationality, a state and a language in the spellbinding notion of 'English', for its attempt to re-read English literature in its real formative conditions, and to interpret the words of the classes and populations, at home and abroad, that it marginalized or silenced. Initiatives of this kind are vulnerable, but they are indispensable for those of us who really believe that our common humanity is less a heritage than a goal, and that it will be defined, in its 'essential' diversity, by all or by none.[30]

1990

A NATION, YET AGAIN
The Field Day Anthology

Anthologies are strategic weapons in literary politics. Authored texts of all kinds – poems, novels, plays, reviews, analyses – play more or less telling parts in a theatre of shifting alliances and antagonisms, but anthologies deploy a special type of rhetorical force: the simulation of self-evidence. Here it is as it *was*: the very fact of re-presentation, flanked by equally self-attesting editorial learning, deters anyone so merely carping as a critic. And so, in principle, whole corpuses, genres, movements and periods can be 'finished' – resolved, secured, perfected or, as the case may be, killed off. Anthological initiatives may be purely antiquarian, but more often they are not. The venerable Oxford compilations of English verse functioned for many decades as the official gazette in their field; Michael Roberts's *Faber Book of Modern Verse*, published in 1936, reordered the recent past and, by suggestion, indicated the future course of English poetry. Anthology-making has played a significant role even where the main means and stake of battle are not only symbolic and not at all polite. There cannot be many nations on earth that have not affirmed the integrity of their struggles or triumphs in such rallies of the national imagination.

The Field Day Theatre Company has for more than a decade played a conspicuous role in Irish cultural politics. Formed in 1980 in Derry to produce Brian Friel's now-classic play *Translations*, it has become a constant factor in Irish theatre. The company's repertoire now includes, as well as Friel's subsequent work, Tom Kilroy's *Double Cross*, Tom Paulin's version of *Antigone* (*The Riot Act*), and Terry Eagleton's *Saint Oscar*, all touring well beyond the familiar city venues and some adapted for television. Impressive in itself, this is only one aspect of Field Day's activity. Academics, critics and poets feature largely in its membership – Seamus Deane, Seamus Heaney and Tom Paulin are all three – and a second notable Field Day project has been its pamphlet series. These productions are often more occasional in character, and correspondingly more pointed; in other cases they promote a counter-academic discourse in which familiar literary topics are boldly reframed. Paulin, speaking from a Northern Protestant background, explores the existing cultures of language in Ireland; Heaney addresses an open letter to the London anthologists who have assimilated him to the history of 'British' verse; Edward Said writes on Yeats and decolonization; Joyce is refocused by Fredric Jameson, in a synoptic discussion of modernism and imperialism.[1] Meanwhile, Chekhov's *Three Sisters*, retuned for Irish voices, plays in the school halls of provincial towns, and the Belfast actor Stephen Rea, co-founder of the company, introduces Southern audiences to their latest and least probable saint. This is a vivid, sometimes startling record of activity, and even if its cumulative meaning eludes summary, nothing so determined is likely to be merely eclectic. For any who are still inclined to make light of the company's ambition, there is now the overwhelming testimony of *The Field Day Anthology of Irish Writing*.[2]

The ambition is patent in the very scale of the anthology, which must be among the most extensive of its kind anywhere in the world. Efforts at qualitative description quickly lapse into blurbspeak; but the measurable proportions of the work are telling enough. Three large-format volumes bind some 4,000 pages of double-column print representing 1,500 years of writing and recorded speech from Saint Patrick to the present. The roll of authors numbers something like 600. A crude count gives six languages of composition (with translations where needed): Latin, Norman French, Medieval and Modern Irish, Middle English, and what may be called, in inadequate shorthand, Modern English. Twenty-three editors have collaborated to produce a selection ordered in forty-three categories, all with introductions that would themselves fill a substantial book.

Together with vastness of scope goes complexity of design. This is not a pageant of the centuries. Chronological marking is constant, but does not imply a single temporality; calendar time is cross-cut here or there by any of six parameters. Some of these are familiar: language (Early and Middle Irish Literature, Latin Writing in Ireland), period culture (Anglo-Irish Verse 1675–1825), mode (Poetry, Prose Fiction, Drama, Political Prose), or biography (Swift, Edgeworth, Joyce). Others are less so: genre (Irish Gothic) or historico-thematic (Constructing the Canon: Versions of National Identity). The effect is of an irreducibly plural history, polyphonic and differential, in which voices are echoed or answered by other voices, are heard again, and differently, in the changing acoustics of period, place and interest, in which events (the plantations, the risings, the Famine, independence) are in some ways punctual and decisive but in other ways go on happening with unabated subjective force.

Seamus Deane's general introduction gives direct expression to the editorial self-consciousness of the project. Understanding that the excuses proper to such occasions are both counter-suggestive and naive, he moves directly against critical common sense. The anthology is, as it must be, a selection, neither comprehensive nor neutral, not a transcript of 'cultural creation' in Ireland but 'one further act' in that history. Further, the selected material is not proposed as a 'canon'. The substantive term of the title is not 'literature' but 'writing': here, as in the eighteenth-century convention, 'many forms of discourse are "polite" and . . . literature is one of them', but the idea of the literary neither controls the corpus of eligible writing nor serves as an index of distinction within it. The notion of an *Irish* canon is similarly discounted. The return of the Northern crisis has exposed the lack of 'any system of cultural consent that would effectively legitimize and secure the existing political arrangements' of the island, least of all one based on the usual nationalist appeals to an originary identity. Indeed, Ireland is 'exemplary' as a real-world *mise-en-abîme*, the place where canon-making achieves little more than the exposure of its own political partiality. Nor is there salvation in the ideal of history 'as it really was', Deane continues. The anthology is, perforce, 'at the mercy of the present moment'; its governing question cannot be answered in the perspective of eternity, but it may at least be posed in the relative freedom of self-awareness: 'How, in the light of what is happening now, can we re-present what was, then and since, believed to have been the significance of what "really" happened?' And thus, the grand modesty of the editorial aim: 'to re-present a series of representations concerning the island of Ireland[,] its history, geography, political experience, social forms and economy', and to do so without appeal to the essences of art or nation, instead exploring 'the nexus of values, assumptions and beliefs in which the idea of Ireland, Irish and writing are grounded'.[3] Deane proposes a bold venture in what someone will sooner or later call 'post-anthological reason'. Avowedly situated and committed but repudiating customary foundational assumptions, it illustrates a cultural orientation that the Northern critic Edna Longley has captioned 'Derry with Derrida'. Yet Derry-as-sign is the nemesis of deconstruction, and the 'post' marks of Deane's opening statement are not unambiguous tokens of its provenance. 'There *is* a story here,' he writes, 'a meta-narrative, which is, we believe, hospitable to all the micro-narratives that, from time to time, have achieved prominence as the official version of the true history, political and literary, of the island's past and present.'[4] This cool recall of the 'micro-narratives' and their vicissitudes is in keeping with the general theme of the introduction (though the disarming appeal to the 'hospitality' of narrative echoes the manner of mid-century Anglo-American literary criticism, with its self-consciously 'civil' versions of art as reconciliation). But the main claim, registered with sudden, proleptic emphasis, remains an alien, unsupported and not even elucidated in the pages that follow. It can hardly concern the 'national story' (nationalism, Deane asserts, is 'no more than an inverted image of the colonialism it seeks to replace') and no other meta-narrative is seriously considered. Late on in his text, Deane entertains the possibility that the work as a whole may turn out to be a supersubtle gnostic compilation, within which the 'story' awaits the adept. 'If we could claim that in every corner of the anthology one could find contained, *in parvo*, the whole scheme and meaning of it, then our ambitions would be fulfilled. But if the scheme . . . is not so discovered, we have little doubt that some alternative to it will be revealed, whatever page is opened, whatever work or excerpt is read. It is the endless fecundity of such reading that gives justification to the selections with which we here attempt to define our subject.'[5] It is not the least provocative feature of this sequence that it should close on the incongruous verb *define*. Nothing could be further from the 'attempt to define' than these teasing sentences. But they are the more significant for that: and not as tokens of a familiar literary-academic coyness (Deane's characteristic style, splendidly exercised in his local introductions, is quick and biting) but as symptoms of a splitting of knowledge and belief – belief in a 'story' that, in spite of so many critical probabilities, remains compelling.

The Feminist Response

However, Deane was not mistaken in his expectation of 'alternative' meta-narratives. 'Fecundity of reading' was confirmed immediately, though not, it seems, in a spirit the editors had foreseen. The 'story' now discerned was of an all-male editorial team sponsored by an all-male company and an anthology in which women and their distinctive concerns had been swept to the margins of cultural life. This case has been elaborated in newspapers and magazines, television programmes and public meetings in Ireland, Britain and elsewhere, and it is not easily answered.[6] The selectivity of the anthology is, in an odd way, downright resourceful. Some forty of the identified authors are women – well under ten per cent of the total. They are, of course, better represented in the twentieth than in earlier centuries, but not nearly so strongly as comparative historical probabilities would indicate. If the eighteenth century can show a dozen women writers (half or more of them part of Swift's circle), the twentieth can surely muster more than sixteen, including only five poets. The representation of specifically feminist writing is bizarre. The anthology contains only two self-identified feminist texts, and both are by men: William Thompson's *Appeal of One Half of the Human Race . . .* (1825) and Francis Sheehy-Skeffington's 'Feminism and War' (1914), which, as it happens, is a polemic against the positions of Christabel Pankhurst. Thompson's friend and co-thinker Anna Wheeler appears in the biographical apparatus, but her role in the production of the *Appeal* is minimized and her literary collaboration, as 'Vlasta', with Robert Owen goes unrepresented; apart from Sheehy-Skeffington's pacifist intervention, the files of the suffragist *Irish Citizen* are left to the mice. Nell McCafferty has observed that, while the anthology rightly makes room for Ian Paisley's oratory and for the late Harold McCusker's moving Westminster speech on the Anglo-Irish Agreement, it passes over a signal moment in the modern history of the South: Senator (later President) Mary Robinson's parliamentary intervention on behalf of legalised contraception in 1970.[7] (McCafferty would not add, but others may, that her own pioneering work as an *Irish Times* columnist is also central to an understanding of Irish public life in the seventies.) The more strictly literary domain of feminist writing is, apparently, an untilled field. In 1781, 'An Irish Lady' publishes *The Triumph of Prudence Over Passion*; two centuries later, Nuala Ní Dhomhnaill writes an invective against rural machismo, a short poem in Irish with the Latin title 'Masculus Giganticus Hibernicus'. But now and in English, as the story goes, there is little or nothing. Declan Kiberd, who finds a 'sharp feminist intelligence' in *The Importance of Being Earnest*, proffers an explanation that Myles na gCopaleen would have enjoyed: 'In the south, the struggles of women against a patriarchal church and an archaic legal code are, if anything, under-represented in contemporary poetry.' He mentions, but does not represent, the 'cool elegance' of Eavan Boland's poems on middle-class suburbia, before commending her more public concerns, instanced here by a poem on emigration. (Boland, a veteran feminist, is a fierce critic of the anthology.) The 'general political reticence' that limits the range of female expression may be, he concludes, 'a measure of the privatization of all poetry . . .'[8] – and, as the whole world knows, feminism has nothing to say about private life.

After months of nearly complete silence, Field Day responded to its critics with the offer of a supplementary volume in which the shortcomings of the original trio might be made good. This was a large admission and a large gesture of reparation, but many will judge that it is inadequate if it serves to lull critical interest in the selective mechanism at work in the anthology 'proper'. Seamus Deane, in an early, individual response to critics, conceded 'a serious flaw' left by 'prejudice, which is all the worse for being unconscious.'[9] These are plain words, but not, on that account, revealing ones; further probing is called for. The inference encouraged here, as by the pattern of the controversy as a whole, is that Field Day's editorial judgement has been misled by generic sexism. However, it may be that the marginalization of women and feminism, together with a certain lightness of touch in matters of sexuality in the public sphere,[10] is more than a local instance of universal 'prejudice'; that it is the spontaneous negative effect of positive preferences – all the stronger for being, perhaps, unconscious – in the assessment of 'Irish' writing.

Identities and their Others

'Irishness' is, unsurprisingly, a constant preoccupation in the anthology, whose avowedly critical purpose is to dramatize and test the notion in its various, more or less refractory historical meanings. Perhaps not one of the numerous cultural-nationalist writers presented here would freely underwrite the work in which they now appear. Irish birth is neither a necessary nor a sufficient criterion for inclusion: Edmund Spenser is present, as having devoted much of his literary and political life to the island, while Congreve, merely born there, is not. Old English, Anglo-Irish and Ulster Protestant traditions participate on equal terms with Gaelic Ireland and its rivalrous posterity. The aporias of authenticity are traced in frequent returns to Field Day's founding theme of cultural translation. Yeats's Celticist programme for the Literary Revival makes its way against 'Irish Ireland' positions and in the face of critical fire from the universalist John Eglinton. In the ranks of militant nationalism proper, and even during the run-up to the 1916 Rising and the War of Independence, the meanings of Gaelic Irish identity continue in debate. And so on, past the Treaty and into the partitioned Ireland of the past seventy years. In a culture so marred by identitarian dogma, this foregrounding of discrepancy and difficulty, this methodic hesitation, seems an exemplary departure.

But the ulterior suggestion of the project is less novel – at least as it emerges in the contributions of Luke Gibbons, whose edited sequences on the national canon and its critics, rehearsing in parvo a principal theme of the work as a whole, convey more than the usual freight of political implication. The purpose of the earlier sequence (c. 1895–1940) is to confound the hostile stereotype of Irish nationalism as a monolithic, exclusivist or even racist cult of ethnic essence.[11] Writers like D. P. Moran, Patrick Pearse and Daniel Corkery sponsored such tendencies, and were countered by the 'radical humanists' around the magazine Dana. What is decisive for Gibbons, however, is the presence within the national movement of an unmystified, pluralist current of thought, instanced in the work of Thomas MacDonagh and Aodh de Blácam. The point is well made and must be taken, but we do well not to rush to conclusions. For it is one thing to seek an ample and diversified Irish identity, we discover, quite another to do so in the name of an alternative, non-'national' cultural sovereignty. James Connolly's proletarian humanism is the historic crux here, and Gibbons acts boldly to resolve it. Not content with reiterating the simple truth that Connolly decided, for good or ill, to fall in with the insurrectionary plans of the Irish Republican Brotherhood, Gibbons renders the question more profound, discovering a 'strategic' rejection of 'theory' in favour of 'history' and a coordinate political focus on 'nation' rather than 'state'.[12] It is worth pausing here to recall that Connolly's indifference to the encyclopaedic pursuits of Second International Kathedersozialisten did not extend to 'the materialist conception of history' (his own, orthodox phrasing), which he actively promoted as the theoretical key to social understanding, in Ireland as elsewhere; and that his last free act was, after all, a set-piece illustration of state-focused revolutionary politics. But to continue so would be literal-minded. This critical farrago is less an offering of knowledge than a defence against cultural anxiety. For 'history' and 'nation', read 'dominant local tradition'; in 'theory' and 'state', mark the presence of those others who resist that tradition and decline its authorized versions of identity.

The others are duly named. Gibbons's second sequence, running from the mid-century to the present, dramatises the struggle between 'canonical' culture and 'revisionism'.[13] Conor Cruise O'Brien, the academic historian Roy Foster, and Edna Longley are among the representatives of the 'progressive', 'modernizing', 'universalist' anti-nationalist intelligentsia that Gibbons here assembles for judgement and dispatch. Their role has been destructive, he explains: the essentialist, racist nationalism they polemicize against is an ugly stereotype of their own making, ill-founded in the complex history of Irish cultural politics. However, they are now themselves anachronistic. 'The modernization project has lost its way in Ireland.' Cosmopolitan reality has turned on its votaries, delivering not bourgeois affluence but recession, not a belated Enlightenment but, as we might say, Cultural Studies. 'Exposed to the theoretical voltage of Marxism, psychoanalysis and post-structuralism, [the revisionists] have advocated a new form of intellectual protectionism, thereby emulating the most conservative strands of cultural nationalism of the past. It is not just the rearguard but the avant-garde that threatens their critical composure, the fusion of "Derry with Derrida" . . .' And the avant-garde, of whom Gibbons is unmistakably one (and with whom he here associates his general editor), can see, as the masochistic revisionists cannot, that the discomfiture of progressive schemes in the eighties was not the handiwork of benighted peasants: for in 'an international perspective' it can be argued that the recrudescence of Irish clericalism was 'part of a general offensive in Western societies against the social-democratic advances of the post-war years' and that, far from favouring such advances, 'incorporation in the EC' and 'the Anglo-American cultural complex' left the country undefended against the 'backlash'.[14]

It is hard to say where, in all of this, opportunism sinks into sincere confusion. Marxist 'theory' must yield to Irish 'history', but, given the favouring conditions of economic deconstruction and intellectual slump, will still serve to electrocute modernizing liberals. The 'Anglo-American cultural complex' is bad when it propagates old-fashioned humanist universalism but, presumably, good when it markets textbooks on 'difference'. The public ethos of the fifties and earlier sixties, deprecated by some for its stunted welfarism and unchecked clerical arrogance, is remembered as the abandoned national 'defence' against the 'international' neo-liberal and fundamentalist *revanche* of the eighties. And then there is the category of 'revisionism' itself, through which Gibbons perpetrates his gravest misrepresentation. A liberal current generally termed 'revisionist' has been salient in Irish culture and politics over the past thirty years. It is obviously right that the anthology should represent and assess it – and right too, in my own view, that it be assessed stringently. In the career of O'Brien, the critic-turned-censor of Irish public discourse, the democratic pretensions of one kind of liberal have been tested and found wanting; and Longley's commonplace literary utopianism is well epitomized in the motto she borrows, apparently without irony, from Derek Mahon: 'A good poem is a paradigm of good politics.'[15] Yet, it is tendentious to reduce Irish cultural controversy since the forties to a drama of nationalism and its critics; and it is inexcusable to stereotype the latter in the image of bourgeois liberalism. In this phantasmagoria, nationalism is plural, revisionism monolithic. O'Brien and kindred commentators are offered as a synecdoche for those quite different critics whose language and themes may be mimicked for radical effect but not granted an autonomous presence. Gibbons is of course aware of socialist and feminist critiques of Ireland's canonical culture. He even volunteers that the nation is, in Benedict Anderson's phrase, an 'imagined community' torn by conflicts of 'class' and 'gender'.[16] But these words echo strangely in the context he has made for them. Just a few volts of psycho-analysis illuminate them as a case of negation, to be interpreted in reverse. Socialist and feminist discourse will inevitably trouble a nationalist cultural canon, because of their shared appeal to some version of 'international' or 'humanist' or 'Enlightenment' values. Yet Gibbons cannot venture the absurd claim that they are merely radical variations on patrician liberalism. Post-structuralist 'heterogeneity' legitimates Gibbons's neo-nationalism, but the rhetoric of nationality insists on closure, on the ultimate sublimation of class and gender antagonisms in the sameness of national 'difference'. And thus socialism must be domesticated and feminism silenced outright, each in its way too radically other to share in the resolution of this strictly-plotted cul-tural narrative.

'Irishness' and the Merely Irish

Gibbons's position in the anthology is less than official: he cannot be assumed to speak for those editors who abstain from intervention in the large political issues of the anthology, or who, like Bill Mc Cormack, imply a different sense of social priorities.[17] Yet no one charged with a critical task so central as his can be discounted as a maverick. He is perhaps best viewed as giving unusu-ally intense, and unguarded, expression to a wider tendency. His comment on Thomas MacDonagh is particularly revealing: '"Irishness" for him was not a genetic or racial inheritance: it was something to be achieved as part of a con-certed, cultural effort.'[18] These words reiterate the familiar theme of 'prospec-tive' nationalism: there never was an Irish nation in any of the canonical senses, but it is possible and necessary to achieve it in the future. Here, if any-where, is the motivating conviction of the anthology. No other meaning can be attached to Deane's claim that, organizing all the literary evidence of con-tradiction and discontinuity, 'there *is* a story . . .'. There is merit in this cul-tural formula: the normal generosity and frankness of the editors bear witness to it. But there is also grave limitation. The ideal of a common, consenting 'Irishness' is crucially ambiguous: open to the extent of acknowledging his-torical complexity, yet confining in that it prescribes an order of legitimate cultural initiative. Field Day takes its distance from one after another version of cultural nationalism but holds on to the axiom that founds them all: the proposition that the sovereign cultural concern of the Irish population is its national identity. To a nationalist this is self-evident truth; others, not nation-alist at all, may say that in Irish conditions it is, if not perennially valid, at least historically pertinent. But even this down-to-earth consideration can be exag-gerated. The assumption that Irish life is centrally the drama of an unresolved national question – that 'Irish writing' is, above all, writing about 'Irishness' –

undermines the very sense of cultural projects whose engagement with the country's realities, while taking all due account of a specific situation, follows bearings other than those of national identity. The result is the spontaneous pattern of misrecognition, oversight and exclusion that compromises the marvellous achievement of these volumes.

The problem may be stated topographically. The anthology is largely a Dublin production – most of the editors teach there, and half of them are present or past members of Deane's own faculty in University College. But its spiritual centre is Derry, birthplace of Field Day. Dublin is the capital of an independent – and, by the emerging standards of the late twentieth century, relatively old – nation-state. But Derry is the symbolic capital of the Northern crisis, and it is from there that all of Ireland is effectively seen. In this imaginary present – Dublin as Derry – Southern society is rendered marginal to itself. The data of its specific politico-cultural history are centred or marginalized, lit up or shadowed, cued or cut according to a vicarious monocular 'Northern' scheme. The intensified capitalist development of the past thirty years has generated antagonisms in every area of Southern life, and again and again the most formidable conservative actor has been the Catholic church. The Northern crisis has of course exerted a constant pressure in Southern politics, but the recurring issue has been that unbroken confessional ascendancy. Irish feminists have been the exposed vanguard in a prolonged struggle to end clerical usurpation of women's reproductive rights, and thus to open the way to a fully secular public domain. But this tempestuous history is all but erased from the cultural record. The 'forces of conservatism and reaction' and their opponents are noted as figures in the landscape, but neither is adequately represented. The prolific literary output of Irish clericalism – newspapers, magazines, pamphlets, pastoral letters, edifying fictions and prized legal statutes – goes unsampled; the culture of the opposition is ignored or declared nonexistent. The fiercely contested abortion and divorce referenda of the early eighties receive passing note as moments in a thwarted liberal crusade to make a constitution fit for (Northern) Protestants. It is as if the South must be forever the old Free State, caught in the terms of an unended colonial past; recent history, where not made across the border, is so much luckless modernization.[19] (In Heaney's manly metaphor, '. . . the South's been made a cuckold', and an 'impotent' one.)[20] Once 'Dublin' is overwritten as 'Derry', much latter-day Irish culture becomes hard to imagine. 'Revisionism' and 'the Anglo-American cultural complex' are the sour tropes by which alone it is possible to acknowledge critical cultural trends that do not privilege nationality as a value, that see fit to be Irish without 'being Irish'.

Field Day's proposition is that a process of critical cultural exploration can assist a new political settlement in Ireland. In so far as this goes beyond truism – after all, there is no politics without culture – it passes into question. Attempts to define an autonomous political role for culture are normally circular. High humanism and post-structuralism, the two most likely sponsors of such attempts, are indifferently prone to deny that culture gives to politics little more than it borrows to begin with (for evidence, see, respectively, Longley and Gibbons), and this because politics, in one of its defining functions, is always already a practice in culture. Field Day's intervention, as this anthology illustrates it, is adapted in advance to an unexamined hierarchy of values in which the crux of Ireland-as-unfulfilled-nation is paramount, with the consequence that culture neither civilizes nor deconstructs the national question but essentializes it as an Irish fate. This variety of cultural nationalism appears less exclusive, more sceptical and probing, precisely because it assumes *enhanced* powers of cultural validation: all are welcome to participate, on the tacit condition that their guiding theme is nationality.

An unresolved national question encourages nation-centred cultural tendencies, yet principled, democratic response towards the one does not entail indulgence towards the other: certainly not in the South, where the valorization of Irishness as the main collective identity is more often than not repressive, and not even in the stalemated North, where the colonial aftermath has fashioned a society and a pattern of interests and identities more complex than tradition willingly acknowledges. Eamonn McCann's analysis of the passage from civil rights agitation to renewed armed struggle is worth having; but his memories of the politico-cultural hierarchy of Catholic Derry in the fifties, recorded elsewhere in the book excerpted here, tell an equally important and rarer story.[21] James Simmons features only as a poet; the polemics he wrote as founding editor of *The Honest Ulsterman*, an eclectic 'handbook for a revolution' that quickened Northern literary culture in the tantalizing climate of the mid-sixties, go unremembered. And Van Morrison (not polite, granted, and an icon of the Anglo-American cultural complex, what's more) furnishes the missing evidence that Ulster Protestants know more than one way of singing about Belfast.[22] McCann registers the high tide of political class-consciousness in the Catholic North. Simmons's editorial effort, resisting all religious puritanism in the name of a moralized sexual frankness, reminds us, the more strongly because of its period quality, that 'the British presence in Northern Ireland' has been more than a matter of repression and hereditary dole. Morrison's song-writing is scarcely 'national', but anyone who thinks *Madame George* indifferently mid-Atlantic has forgotten to turn on the hi-fi. And here too, with apologies to none, are elements of actually existing Irish culture.

'A Nation, Yet Again . . .'[23]

A decade ago, in an early Field Day pamphlet, Seamus Deane wrote: 'It is about time we put aside the idea of essence – that hungry Hegelian ghost looking for a stereotype to live in. As Irishness or as Northernness [it] stimulates the provincial unhappiness we create and fly from, becoming virtuoso metropolitans to the exact degree that we have created an idea of Ireland as provincialism incarnate. These are worn oppositions. They used to be the parentheses in which the Irish destiny was isolated. That is no longer the case. Everything, including our politics and our literature, has to be rewritten – i.e. re-read. That will enable new writing, new politics, unblemished by Irishness, but securely Irish.'[24] The crux of this bold and necessary prospectus lay in its last two phrases. Everything would turn on the determination with which the distinction registered there was observed and made actual. *The Field Day Anthology* is the mixed result – in most respects a *tour de force* of critical reconstruction, but in others a further attempt to discover an appropriate ending for the long story of the nation (and, in the hands of its more 'avant-garde' contributors, an exercise in the current mid-Atlantic routines of identity politics). Politics concerns states and the social relations they secure. The peoples of Ireland face a political agenda as long and difficult as any. But nationality need not be its decisive term, and – arguably – cannot be. Deane notes that Ireland illustrates the final embarrassment of canon-making, but is then inclined to act as if believing that a super-canon may yet lift the curse of incompleteness. His undischarged assumption is that 'Irish' is a qualifier in need of a substantive 'nation'. Yet it may be that the moment of Irish self-identity, such as it could plausibly be, has already passed. Unable to make good its claims upon its putative citizens in the North or to stanch the flow of those who really were its own to every corner of the English-speaking world, confined in an autarkic economy with the Church for wisdom and the Gaelic Athletic Association for exercise, de Valera's Republic was, nevertheless, the fulfilling moment of cultural nationhood. Sovereignty remained as its great achievement, but the unravelling of the associated social-cultural formula meant, in effect, the obsolescence of 'the Irish nation' as a sustainable cardinal value – and not only the dismal narcissism of de Valera's vision but cultural nationalism *as such*. Irish culture since that time has been, in a risky phrase, 'post-national': in important respects 'Anglo-American', increasingly 'European' (whatever that may turn out to mean), still deeply and variously 'traditional'. These are the heterogeneous scripts, none of them internally coherent, in which a diverse society, torn by class, gender and other conflicts, reads its situation and prospects. The 'story' now in process is not 'national' in any sense that would satisfy the adepts of origin and destiny; nor is it simply 'international' in the schematic terms of liberal utopianism or traditionalist phobia. Irish culture, like so many late-twentieth-century cultures, is an unprogrammed hybrid, the shifting repertoire of social initiative and resistance in the island. Both Irish populations show a growing readiness to tackle old and disabling certainties. It would be a pity if their critical intelligentsia, scanning a society but dwelling mainly on the elements of a nation, failed to keep pace.

1993

POSTCOLONIAL MELANCHOLY

[My discussion of the *Field Day Anthology* provoked an immediate response from the editor most sharply criticized in it, Luke Gibbons. His text, 'Dialogue Without the Other' appeared in the same journal, *Radical Philosophy*. I replied in the following terms.[1]]

The substance of Gibbons's reply gives me little reason for self-reproach; I stand by my assessment of *The Field Day Anthology* and the controversy it aroused.[2] However, in countering my analysis, Gibbons invokes more general terms of debate – Marxism, nationalism, the postcolonial. I propose to follow him in this, believing that his article furnishes de facto evidence supporting my reading of his positions, and confirms quite fundamental differences between us. While resolution of these differences seems unlikely, an attempt to clarify them may be useful.

The first issue is theoretical-methodological, concerning the meanings of *specificity* as a norm of cultural analysis. The second is one of socialist political theory: the relationship between national *rights* and nationalism. I then pass to some closing remarks on political actualities.

The Meanings of Specificity

Gibbons charges me with 'indifference to any form of cultural specificity'; apparently I cannot accept that, in the words of another commentator, Paul Willemen, 'discourses of nationalism and those addressing national specificity are not identical.' Yet he seeks to rebut my claim concerning the monological tendency of nationalist discourse by appealing to evidence of non-closure in unspecified 'Irish contributions to the cultural canon' – that is, in texts that are in some sense 'national' but not necessarily national*ist* at all. My 'difficulty', Gibbons conjectures, seems to be 'not just with nationalism, but with "Irishness" and, indeed, with the very existence of Ireland as a nation.' This perceived difficulty, it appears to me, is the shadow cast by his own difficulty, which consists in an inability to think of Ireland except in the terms of nationality, or of nationality in other than the special terms of nationalism. 'It may indeed be necessary,' Gibbons concedes, 'to go beyond the paradigms of nationalism, but only after having absorbed their insistence on difference, and the specificity of historical time and cultural space.'[3] In other words, such paradigms are, at least for now, the indispensable conditions of access to the concrete reality of Ireland.

The bad alternative, Gibbons maintains, has been the kind of positivist developmental scheme sponsored first by bourgeois political economy and, in a Marxist derivation, by the Second International, with its naturalistic laws and iron necessities of 'progress'. Such schemes are false: 'there is no universal template for modernization or, for that matter socialism', which 'must engage dialogically with the precise cultural, historical and . . . national conjunctures in which they find themselves.' Further, 'economic necessity does not operate in the same way in the undeveloped periphery (particularly under colonialism) as it does in the metropolitan heartlands'; as James Connolly perceived, it is subject to processes of '*cultural mediation*' that produce distinctive outcomes, or specificities.

It is of course true that there is no 'universal template' of development. Paradoxically, however, Gibbons's arguments against this notion are fatally weak, and not at all a compelling illustration of the procedural specificity he insists upon. The binary opposition of modernizing economic thrust, which is putatively general or standardizing in character, and cultural mediation, which is particular ('native', 'indigenous', 'traditional'), in fact replicates the conceptual structure it purports to criticize, differing only in reversing its distribution of values. The attempt to win a cognitive advance from this theoretical stasis, to *specify* an 'actual history', leads to dualism and logical regression: 'economic necessity' works differently in metropolitan and peripheral zones, and this is so, Gibbons seems to say, because these differ in their respective coefficients of 'cultural mediation'. Why this difference should obtain we are not told, but it is a fair guess that an attempted explanation would call upon a deeper contrast, and that, in turn, upon a still more fundamental one, and so on . . . I do not believe that Gibbons actually entertains this logic, whose terminus is mysticism, but it haunts his discourse none the less. What he illustrates here is a kind of narrative that has probably been reiterated in every country that has borne the shocks of capitalist transformation, whether through internal development and free association across borders, or in the far worse conditions of colonial subjection. To inquire forensically into them is to mistake their genre: they are, as Marx wrote, the spontaneous counter-discourse of capitalism itself, a protest rather than an analysis.[4]

Particularity is central to the feeling of such narratives, because the damage and loss they record is the work of a mode of production whose innovative social norm is indifference – the ideal in-difference of commodity and contract. And it is this, I believe, that Gibbons mistakenly offers as illustrating the idea of historical specificity. The principle of specificity, as I understand it, calls for the analytic appropriation of 'the concrete' in the sense of 'the concentration of many determinations' (Marx again),[5] 'abstractions' that really exist but only in specific configurations, which are always and everywhere economic *and* political *and* cultural. It is not that 'economic necessity' (a debatable phrase) 'operates' differently, but that it is differently figured, with correspondingly distinct effects. Thus (to take an outstanding instance of contemporary Marxist cultural analysis) Roberto Schwarz discovers the specificity of modern Brazil not in the resultant of opposed 'traditional' and 'modernizing' forces, but in the formative paradox of its social order – a slave-owning latifundist agriculture structurally integrated into the 'liberal' world export market.[6] Cora Kaplan's remarks on the necessary interdetermination of class, race and gender in social subjectivities, which Gibbons cites approvingly, parallel this kind of understanding.[7] A concrete analysis of Irish culture in this sense would try to specify the place and functioning of ideas of 'the nation' within it; but this objective becomes unattainable if it is assumed in advance that 'the nation', however defined, enjoys a quasi-natural preeminence among the collective subjectivities of Irish people, if the idea of nationality is pre-constructed according to nationalist canons. I *do* accept Willemen's distinction – which, after all, matches a basic assumption in what I wrote – and return it to Luke Gibbons for his further consideration.[8]

Nationalism and National Rights

'An unresolved national question,' I wrote, 'encourages nation-centred cultural tendencies'; however, 'principled, democratic response towards the one does not entail indulgence towards the other', and 'certainly not in the South, where the valorization of Irishness as the main collective identity is more often than not repressive. . .'.[9] Gibbons quotes these words without specific, substantive comment; presumably they are self-evidently wrong-headed, the defensive rationalization of someone for whom 'the very existence of Ireland as a nation' is seemingly a 'difficulty'. Let me offer a political clarification, part theoretical and part historical.

The distinction made here is Lenin's. Like much else in his thinking it is unseasonable yet unsurpassed. Nations have a *right* to self-determination, Lenin maintained, which may be exercised either in a separate state or in free association with other national populations in a larger sovereign entity.[10] Socialists must uphold this right, even where they see fit to argue against specific implementations of it. However, the principle at stake here is not itself intrinsically nationalist in kind; national demands are legitimate in so far as they bear upon the *democratic* right of self-determination but not otherwise; nationalism as such – the privileging of national differences – is a divisive mystification born out of national oppression, which should be ended so that nationalism itself can be overcome. The criterion of self-determination is political in a strict sense: it fulfils itself in the attainment of territorial sovereignty (separate or merged), and is not gainsaid by the persistence of other oppressions and inequalities within or between states. It does not presuppose economic self-sufficiency, let alone autarky (by that measure hardly any contemporary nation-state could be deemed independent). And, as Lenin particularly insisted, it is not conditional upon a general valorization of cultural nationality. Traditional codes of identity are not intrinsically less various in their suggestions than those of so-called modernization, and neither may presume to dictate canons of affinity. Where valued continuities are threatened for no better reason than that they offend against bureaucratic convenience or commercial realism, they should be defended as a matter of principle. But the propagation of nationality as the necessary cultural warrant of political independence, or of a deeper social emancipation beyond that, is a reactionary diversion.

Luke Gibbons does not espouse a purist cultural nationalism (he would have me believe he does, but I cannot oblige him); his affinities lie closer to the 'civic' nationalisms of Scotland or Lithuania than to the ethnic particularisms of the Balkans. But Lithuania was until very recently an unwilling partner in an oppressive 'union'; the people of Scotland have not (yet) severed the Anglo-British lien on their national rights. What is Gibbons's national cause? The interpretive bent of his reply is telling. My article was written in a pragmatic present tense; its address was from and to a current situation. But Gibbons submits it to a preteritive reading, converting present into past. I described Old English, Anglo-Irish, Ulster Protestant and Gaelic traditions as participating on 'equal' terms in the ecumenical design of *The Field Day Anthology*; he reminds me that the first three represented different 'intensities of conquest'. My criticism of skewed editorial perception in respect of feminism and socialism is met with the counter-charge that I have ignored the complex pattern of ideological forces in Ireland 'at the turn of the century'. A reference to the 'dominant local tradition', meaning that of Southern Ireland since Independence, prompts a sonorous evocation of 'the might of the British Empire'. The summarizing judgement on me is that I lack sympathy with 'a culture still trying to come to terms with centuries of colonial domination'.[11] In short (the phrase is embarrassingly trite, but it applies), Gibbons is living in the past.

The supremely important fact about Irish nationalism is that it was successful, forcing the withdrawal of the imperial power from most of the island, pressing the agrarian settlement to an unambiguous popular conclusion, and securing, by the late forties, a stable, neutral republican state. To describe the culture and society thus created as 'postcolonial' is either platitudinous – what else could it be? – or, more interestingly, tendentious.[12] Had the old Gaelic order by some counter-factual miracle frustrated the purposes of its far more powerful neighbour, and also the rival purposes of continental powers equally well aware of the country's crucial strategic value, Ireland would of course be a different place today. But to represent the history that actually unfolded, the accomplished colonial fact, as the defining crux of Irish culture today – *three generations after Independence* – is tantamount to suggesting that indigenous propertied classes and their politico-cultural élites are not really responsible for the forms of exploitation and oppression they have conserved or developed in their own bourgeois state, and that radical social critics must acknowledge a continuing, mitigating 'national' ordeal. The name for this is postcolonial melancholy.[13] Its political implication, like that of any nationalism prolonged beyond its validating political occasions, is confusionist and retrograde.

Northern Exposures

No one will have overlooked the objection to my line of argument. The Irish national revolution was by its own standards *not* wholly successful, falling short of its historic ambition to reconquer the entire island. Nation-building in the South was conditioned from its traumatic outset – the Civil War – by that fact. Across the border, and also amid bloodshed, Orangeism set about subduing a Catholic population now locked in a rump Union sustained by a large Protestant majority. The history of that ugly, introverted state and of Catholic resistance to its systematic injustices has normally been told as that of a colonial residue and an unfinished national struggle to recover it.

However, the test facing Irish nationalism in the current 'peace process' is not that envisaged in the familiar narrative.[14] It is, finally, to confront the reality of Protestant Ulster. Partition came about and was consolidated above all because that regional majority refused to join the island majority in a single, separate state, and no other party to the crisis was both willing and able to overrule it. The outcome was serviceable to British interests at the time and for some decades to come, and a profound affront to the nationalist movement; the territorial scale of the partition flouted democratic mandates, encouraging still greater extremes of paranoia and abjection in a predictable future. Yet some division of political space had been made unavoidable by the whole anterior development of the island, which, by then, was home to two clearly distinct and mutually antagonistic societies.[15] A whole colonial history went into the making of partition. But to insist on that today, nearly four hundred years after the expropriations that founded the Ulster settlement, is an evasion. The Irish Protestants of north-east Ulster are no longer frontier settlers in an exposed imperial possession, but they never became part of the subject people that rallied in the nineteenth century as 'the Irish nation'. This is the historical reality, 'postcolonial' in an uncommonly prosaic and exacting sense, that shapes Northern political and cultural prospects today.

A democratic and just peace for Northern Catholics: that, the surviving rationale of historic Irish nationalism, is the first requirement in any formula deserving the name of 'solution'. But it cannot be attained except as part of an historic compromise with Ulster Protestants, and this requires a recognition that Irish nationalism has no rightful (let alone realistic) claim to their collective political allegiance. Any agreed constitutional arrangement that secures these two requirements will serve as a valid beginning of an end of Ireland's national question.

The possible forms of the end (there have always been more than the canonical two, and the development of the European Union will modify the balance of considerations in all cases) are, decisively, political. However it is already clear that struggles over constitutional and social outcomes will be overdetermined by a cultural politics of identity – this, precisely, has been the rationale of Field Day's projects – and here too the advocates of Ireland-as-nation must accept a test and a heavy responsibility. Northern Catholics are more widely practised in the complexities of identity and affiliation than their traditional champions care to believe; Ulster Protestants will be slow to venture out of the garish bunker of loyalism if the only Irishness allowed them is one entailing accession to the 'national' identity and an all-island state. Workers in both communities, whose organic leaderships are now emerging as the more creative forces in Northern politics, need to find ways of articulating their common class interests. It was such things, among others, that I had in mind in writing that 'nationality need not be . . . and – arguably – cannot be' the 'decisive term' of Irish politics today.[16] The idioms, symbols and tropisms of a reconciled Northern culture (if the favouring political conditions for it prove attainable) will grate on many a nationalist and Orange sensibility, but they will be as Irish as any others in the island. Those who cannot live with this prospect will have to resort to the Brechtian 'solution': dismiss the Irish people and recruit a proper nation.

1995

TRANSLATION
Re-writing Degree Zero

Translation should be faithful yet unconstrained, not so free as to misrepresent the original sense it must reincarnate, yet not so literal as to disturb the spontaneous movement of the host body. Its highest aspiration should be self-effacement, the attainment of a state akin to Roland Barthes's 'degree zero' of writing, an unmarked communication of an essential meaning. This is common sense, a truth both canonical and intuitively compelling, and, in just that degree, tendentious and questionable. In contemporary conditions, where the seemingly marginal process of translation has become quite central, involving not only texts and their linguistic codes but forms, practices and whole populations, this common sense has acquired conspicuous cultural-political significance. Indeed, translation practices have always borne this significance, and disputes concerning them have seldom been purely technical. Any translation, between languages or within them, effects a comparative cultural evaluation, in which only the forms are matters of special learning; the priorities that govern the volume and pattern of translating activity, and the norms that regulate its variety, relay the priorities of the host culture overall, and are wholly engaged in the antagonisms that shape it. This is the uncommon-sensical position that Lawrence Venuti has set out in his critical studies in the history of translation.[1]

All translation 'domesticates' its foreign original, and in doing so inflicts a certain 'ethnocentric violence' on culturally alien material. But the dominant Anglo-American tradition has canonized domestication as the one legitimate translation strategy, prescribing 'transparency' as the universal goal of the process and 'fluency' as its palpable textual sign. In this way, Anglo-British and US publishing cultures reinforce in their own linguistic zone what they achieve by the unequal balance of trade in the homelands of other languages. English has become the most translated language in the world, during the 1980s originating some 40 per cent of all translated titles in a range of a dozen languages, including Spanish, Russian and Arabic. At the same time, translations have accounted for no more than 2–4 per cent of Anglo-American titles since the 1950s – as against rates as high as 8–12 per cent in France, 14 per cent in Germany, and fully 25 per cent in Italy. Hegemonic abroad, the major English-language publishing centres promote uniformity at home. The relatively few foreign works that find a way into English must satisfy the rules of the dominant 'plain style', with its cardinal requirement of fluency – must be, in both senses of the word, recognizable. Specifically literary-philosophical ideas of

164

authorship, originality and interpretation make their own artless contribution to this situation: romantic and humanist conceptions of writing as the linguistic coding of autonomous personalities and their meanings, and of reading as a process of sympathetic understanding, furnish another kind of rationale for the predominance of transparency and fluency. The culture so fashioned is 'aggressively monolingual' and deeply narcissistic, discovering in apparent otherness only reassuring confirmation of the self. It is then only 'natural' – that is, obvious and necessary – that translation should be, or aim to be, 'invisible'.

Just how little nature there is in the inherited culture of translation Venuti shows in forensically-argued detail, in a sequence of theoretically-informed and scholarly case studies. These do not constitute an ordinary 'history'; they are, in Venuti's preferred Foucauldian metaphor, elements of a 'genealogy', a selective and polemical reading of the archive in the perspective of present-day interests. Distributed across three centuries, from the middle seventeenth to the present, and five translating cultures (Anglo-British, North American, German, Italian and French), and implicating source-languages ancient, medieval and modern, these episodes form a loose sequence but a strong configuration of cultural values; the recurring issue is the concrete historical meaning of domesticating, fluent translation and the possible counter-significance of the 'foreignizing', 'resistant' initiatives that have arisen to oppose it. Case by case, these analyses are historical in the strongest sense, showing that translation cannot be reduced to a skilled technical practice of inter-linguistic transfer, but must be understood and practised as a mode of cultural politics.

The norm of transparency took practical shape in English in the last decades of the Stuart regime, and was consolidated by Sir John Denham, whose *Destruction of Troy, An Essay Upon the Second Book of Virgil's Aeneis*, composed in 1636 but only published, in revised form, twenty years later, set a benchmark for subsequent commentary and practice. Denham recommended a course of faithful freedom, in which the essential spirit of the foreign original might be recreated as native meaning. The specific rhetorical entailments of this goal – the subordination of sound to sense, the canonization of the English pentameter line – became the commonplaces of the new, neo-classical decorum of Dryden and Pope and a long successor tradition. Alexander Tytler's *Essay on the Principles of Translation* (1791), one of the most influential statements in this tradition, canonized equivalence and fluency as the mutually controlling principles of a process that should in the most literal sense domesticate its material:

> I would therefore describe a good translation to be, *That, in which the merit of the original work is so completely transfused into another language, as to be as distinctly apprehended, and as strongly felt, by a native of the country to which that language belongs, as it is by those who speak the language of the original work.*[2]

The romantic turn in English literary culture reinflected but did not displace these canons. As George Lamb's *Poems of Caius Valerius Catullus* (1821) attested, the new aesthetic value of expressiveness offered equally strong support for the ideal of transparency. Naturalness, the rematerialization of necessary sense in familiar language, was the imprescriptible aim in translating Homer (and therefore all else), Matthew Arnold reminded his Oxford audience, forty years later. And thus into our own century, where the norm of fluency still holds sway. It continues to be reformulated, as in the influential writings of Eugene Nida, who sponsors a strategy of 'dynamic' or 'functional equivalence' characterized by 'complete naturalness of expression';[3] it receives everyday support from an economy that relies massively on standardized, instrumental linguistic practices; and, as Venuti shows, in a rich gathering of quotation and anecdote, it is the working wisdom of most translators, editors, reviewers and critics.

The norm of fluency is second nature – as binding as that in common intuition, but nevertheless historically contingent. The 'national' culture of the Anglo-British state was a relatively early and confident formation, and its linguistic standard appeared correspondingly well founded. The cases of nineteenth-century Germany and Italy, where no such identity of state, language and people could so easily be presumed, offer interesting, in ways exemplary, contrasts. The Prussian academic and pastor, Friedrich Schleiermacher, saw the choice between domesticating and foreignizing translation as a strategic crux, and opted for the latter. The reader he imagined and sought to cultivate, he explained in his 1813 lecture 'On the Different Methods of Translating', was an educated traveller, who through the experience of translated writing would come to be at home, 'in peace', elsewhere, with the foreign author. Schleiermacher's sense of cultural difference did not run deep (he believed that inter-subjective affinity could be released from inter-linguistic alienation) and was not sweetly cosmopolitan (hostility to the domesticating norms of French neo-classicism conditioned his contrary preferences); his politico-cultural purpose was to further the national mission of a Prussian-led Germany. In the contrasting career of Iginio Ugo Tarchetti, however, foreignizing assumed a clearly dissident meaning. Tarchetti was associated with the Milanese *scapigliatura*, a 'dishevelled' mid-nineteenth-century bohemia democratic in political temper and anti-realist in literary tendency. He wrote in the modes of melodrama, romance and fantasy, in conscious opposition to the aesthetic and social values implicit in the standard literary language, whose exemplary text was Manzoni's *I promessi sposi*; and he supplemented his original works with translations strategically chosen to further his campaign against emergent 'national' canons. Resourceful to the point of recklessness, Tarchetti confounded the intuitive simplicities of 'original' and 'translated'. His *Il mortale immortale*, qualified parenthetically as a story 'dall'inglese', was in substance a plagiarism of Mary Shelley's 'Immortal Mortal', but one that, while infiltrating the English author's feminism into Italy's official literary space, also took leave to modify the conservative class and ethnic valuations of her text, so exemplifying a practice of translation that performs a double critical operation, exploiting the disruptive value of the foreign while purposefully rewriting it.

Tarchetti, if anyone, is the hero of Venuti's account. But even in England and America, under the discouraging regime of fluency, dissident initiatives recurred. Dr John Nott's versions of Catullus, which preceded Lamb's by twenty-five years, embodied a foreignizing 'mimetic' strategy intended to conserve the cultural specificities of their originals. The difference between the translations, which extended in Nott's case to an unabashed sexual frankness and in Lamb's to the kind of bowdlerism that marked his productions of Shakespeare, was at bottom one of social affinity and perspective. Nott, whose working milieu was aristocratic, maintained a distance from the emerging norms of morality and refinement in English bourgeois culture, whereas Lamb actively sought to consolidate them. Basic politico-cultural motives – this time radical and democratic – were again manifest in the work of Francis Newman. Newman, whose *Iliad* (1856) provoked Arnold's Oxford lectures on 'natural' principles, advocated a method consisting in the search for equivalents that would signify the foreignness of the translated text.[4] Like the socialist William Morris after him, he exploited the heterogeneous deposits of local languages and forms in the attempt to render his authors present and active without first reducing them to familiarity, that is, to the dominant bourgeois code.

The early-twentieth-century modernist tradition was equivocal. As modernism, it was in some sense disruptive; yet in so far as it insisted that the translation should achieve literary autonomy in its own language, modernism took a domesticating course: although the quasi-original so created might not gratify conservative taste, it would be nevertheless a self-subsistent English work. This was T. S. Eliot's understanding – 'the work of translation is to make something foreign . . . live with our own life'[5] – and it also expressed one tendency in Ezra Pound's theory and practice of translation. In Pound's 'interpretive' versions, by contrast, a more radical tendency was at work: his translations from Provençal and Tuscan attempted by their use of archaism and other kinds of linguistic heterogeneity to figure their originals as, precisely, *un*English, as cultural strangers. The domesticating element in modernism became dominant in the mid-century, by virtue of the compromise inherent in the notion of the translation as a new original, but did not altogether stifle alternative projects. Celia and Louis Zukofsky's 'homophone' translations of Catullus (1969) attempted to rewrite the sound as well as the sense of the Latin (for example, rendering *dicere*, 'say', by the slangy, punning 'dicker'), and thus to expose ears tuned for fluency to communicative noise, the heterogeneous linguistic 'remainder' in which the unfinished business of a culture becomes articulate.

In an autobiographical case history concerning his own work on the poems of a contemporary, the Italian Milo de Angelis, and its fate at the hands of publishers' readers, Venuti assesses the force and the limitations of the commonplace notion of translation as a process of inter-subjective 'sympathy'. Ostensibly more hospitable to the evidences of cultural specificity, the appeal to a basic like-mindedness is philosophically suspect, he maintains, and, in the outcome, may simply rationalize a habit of projection that is as impatient of the foreign as any other version of the fluent style. Foreignizing, the leading mode of the 'resistance' to ethnocentric fluency, should not be banalized to a process of psychological *rapprochement*. Its aim is to signify the difference of the foreign text in the language of the translation, and this entails critical work on the language(s) and forms of the translating culture, where fluency will normally be the naturalized sign of those values that are historically dominant within it. The attempt to refigure the foreignness of an other-language text always entails an exploration or reassertion of the alien within, the symbols, dialects, registers and idioms that the prevailing decorum marks as awkward or improper, thereby marking itself not as the natural genius of the local tongue but as the social order in linguistic form. A canonical theorist like Tytler saw clearly that the boundaries of good style were social and moral – as, with opposite intent, did the guttersnipe radical Tarchetti. Translation, as Venuti encourages us to understand it, is a central cultural practice, not a supplementary aid for the relief of linguistic limitation. More than a technical practice, it is value-bearing, an intervention for good or ill in a domain where choices – a text, a register, a word – are seldom innocent. And whether it domesticates conspicuously or not, translation is always itself an internal affair; like Freud's uncanny, the unfamiliar figure is no mere foreigner, rather the stranger who has been here all along. The invisibility to which translators have been condemned, or which they have been taught to seek as their own kind of perfection, not only marks the denial of due financial, legal and moral entitlements; it also assists in rationalizing a conservative politics of culture.

Venuti's critical account of this cultural politics is plausible, as, in general terms, is his call for an alternative strategy of resistancy, not only for the kinds of inter-cultural situation he studies, but also for others rather differently structured.

Translation was a key issue in the literary politics of mid-nineteenth-century Ireland, in conditions of accelerated Anglicization and a rising national movement. For Samuel Ferguson, fluent re-presentation of the Gaelic literary record was a primary means of political-cultural diplomacy in the island: the spirit of an unriven other world, reincarnated in canonical forms of the English-language poetic, would foster an irenic Irish identity and so assist political healing. Ferguson achieved his fluency, in part by straining the historical grit from his originals, which now re-materialized in a language that, for all the otherness of its scenarios, seems strikingly English, in a restrictive sense. A less inhibited, some would say more authentic, kind of engagement with this cultural archive has been read in the work of James Clarence Mangan, whom Joyce honoured as the only Irish important poet of the century. Like a darker, more restless first version of Tarchetti, Mangan wrote across languages, neither finding peace nor making it; his translations were unconventional, cavalier, often imaginary pretexts internal to the fictions of his poetry; his tropes of place and identity were Irish but also European and Eastern. Where Ferguson designed and implemented a strategy of fluency, Mangan seems to have embodied a practice of resistancy that defeated any simple appeal to essential, recoverable sense.[6]

In England in our own century, then, Tony Harrison's poetry approaches these issues of inter-cultural translation as they occur within what is too easily accepted as a single, basically cohesive language. Foreign-language materials occur throughout his writing, but usually as signifiers of social relations in the vernacular; they belong with the forms of register and dialect as indices of authority, entitlement and belonging, and their opposites. At times drawn back to familiar humanist ground – in parts of *v.*, for example – in its more radical moments Harrison's poetry mounts a challenge to the sweet presumption of literary English, laying bare its real cultural conditions and effects. The poem sequence *The School of Eloquence*, which opens with the untranslated text of a Latin sonnet by Milton and then borrows that form as its own template, dramatizes a kind of civil war in language – a war, as we read in a poem slyly dedicated to 'Professor Richard Hoggart', between 'Them & [uz]'.[7] In Harrison as in Venuti, fluency and resistancy, awkwardness and eloquence, emerge as the stylistic poles of quite profane cultural struggles.

However, the concept of resistancy cannot claim exemption from its own critical dialectic. Venuti emphasizes the historical variability of translation norms, and his analyses observe a strict contextualizing discipline. Yet the key critical opposition between domesticating and foreignizing strategies never varies so radically as to reverse itself. This seems questionable. Venuti deprecates orientalist writing, with its stereotyping misappropriations of other cultures, but does not appear to acknowledge the most general implication of his own judgement, which is that foreignizing may assume the degraded, conservative shape of exoticism. Thus he can commend John Nott's stand against Eurocentrism and the cultural barbarism of colonizers without noticing that Nott's defence of 'the glow of Eastern dialogue' against 'our colder feelings and ideas' is, in one clear sense, orientalist.[8] Venuti contrasts Paul Blackburn's Poundian work on Provençal troubadour poetry with his fluent versions of the Argentine Julio Cortázar, and suggests that the latter style of translation, apparently incongruous with the first, indicated that Blackburn's priority here was to challenge existing novelistic canons in English.[9] But he does not pursue the general implication of the case, which is that domestication may sometimes be the more radical, dissident strategy. Such instances of selective reasoning are protected by other kinds of selectivity – in evidence and theoretical reference. The linguistic material that Venuti examines is all literary, and mostly poetic; he defends this option on the grounds that the literary furnishes the conventional standard for all writing. But this is tendentious. Literature may enjoy primary *status* in written culture, as poetry has done within the literary, but neither sets a universal rhetorical *pattern* for the field it commands. The post-structuralist theorizing which Venuti too matter-of-factly reiterates provides a rationale for this kind of elision, dwelling on the material processes of the text, the vicissitudes of communicative intention, the instability of meaning in all language use. In this perspective, poetry of a certain kind becomes if not typical then certainly exemplary, while contrasting rhetorics – and above all, literary realism – are depreciated. The primary distinguishing claims of initiatives in realism have been cognitive, positing an actually existing moral-social world that may be disclosed, interpreted, even explained, in secular terms. Their rhetorical ideal (a mirage, but that is not the point) is literalism: unadorned, univocal, quasi-veridical and at the limit para-scientific utterance. Venuti endorses the standard critique of such claims, but declines to acknowledge the crux they represent for his politics of translation. Ideal-typical realism valorizes transparency as a critical instrument, not an anodyne; its plainness is an ideological abrasive. The dissident, foreignizing ambition of realism is propositional and contextual, not oriented, in Venuti's strictly limiting sense, to conspicuous work on the signifier – and, if it is to be acknowledged at all, is surely best served by a dissident practice of fluent translation.

'Foreignizing', as it operates here, is a conceptual pun, by means of which a dissident practice of translation draws its inspiration from a particular tradition of aesthetic and philosophical affinity, which, by way of return, imposes its own narrow priorities on a putatively general strategy. The value of foreignness is so obviously an issue in any discussion of translation that its general currency as a cultural positive may be overlooked. It has been a nostrum of artistic modernism and its successor avant-gardes throughout this century. Russian Formalism, cued by Futurist poetry, promoted 'defamiliarization'; Pound endeavoured to 'make it new'; Brecht created a theatre of constructive 'alienation'; poststructuralism has privileged an aesthetic of transgression. And now, in the field of translation, Venuti resumes the old radical-modernist programme with his call to 'foreignize'. His critique is informed, incisive and committed – the word *fluency* will never again trip quite so lightly off the tongue. But resistancy must be more variable in its means than he seems to envisage, and cannot be reduced, in modernist fashion, to a matter of formal-textual preferences; it will indicate one approach to De Angelis but another, surely, to Gramsci. Foreignizing, however potent it may often be, will not serve as a general strategy; resistancy must sometimes take the form of naturalizing the alien – and this precisely for the sake of the critical possibilities that are always at issue in the culture of translation.

1995

A EUROPEAN HOME?

The political maps of the present are systematic misprojections of its real social geographies – such, in effect, was the thesis of Raymond Williams's *Towards 2000*. Indeed, he argued, the idea of the world as a patchwork of singular societies is itself an anachronism: the real spaces of human activity expand or shrink according to perspective, purpose and occasion; and – the crucial point – all *significant* societies are either larger or smaller than the nation-state. Shaped in this understanding, the political institutions of a sustainable socialist future would undo the false identification of social and territorial sovereignties, surpassing not merely the pattern of the nation-state but the very principle of all-purpose social boundaries. Societies, as the effective unities of collective life, would be variable in extent, with decision-making practices to match.[1]

This is a compelling prospectus. Tapping both classical Marxist resources and all that he intended in his critical appeal to 'community', Williams was seeking to affirm the necessarily international character of a new social order while refusing the brutalism of scale that has fixated too much practical socialist thinking, to affirm the value of local familiarities without concession to populist nostalgia, and to unite these considerations in a clarified political formula: 'variable socialism'. For now, however, his vision is compelling mainly as a negative reminder of the present, which anticipates it in the form of travesty.

We need only think of a scenario like this. In London a transnational corporation publishes a controversial novel by a celebrated writer. The event is carefully planned and primed for maximum cultural-commercial effect, but soon escapes into a magical-realist life of its own. The book causes religious offence, and is denounced and publicly burned by outraged members of a religious – and ethnic – minority community: it *must* be suppressed. Here is a problem for official Britain – for its law enforcement and community relations agencies and for its half-formulated and largely untested cultural indifferentism – and it worsens by the day. These people are black, and thus conventional objects of liberal concern; but they are book burners, and thus stock characters in the liberal nightmare. The left is divided, and fascists opportunistically join the struggle for freedom of expression. But the affair has already passed beyond the frontiers of British jurisdiction and debate. The opponents of the book express absolute commitment to the norms of an international religious faith, which in recent times has achieved a special authority within a still larger, though less quotable, community of sentiment – the once-colonized peoples of the world. Old networks of belief and solidarity combine with the new telecommunications satellites to create an audience of many millions and a struggle across frontiers. Bookshops are torched, traitors executed, while others die in riots. And then the international status of the affair is confirmed and deadlocked in the plainest and most conventional terms, as another nation-state, casting itself as the divinity's earthly executive, pronounces the author a planetary outlaw, to be put to the sword by any believer so privileged as to find the opportunity.

Improbabilities multiply. The author, in hiding, issues a public appeal on behalf of the imagination, which for now can be exercised only under the protection of the secret services. A prominent literary liberal discovers feminist reasons for judging the offended – or offending – Holy Book inferior to the locally preferred text of revelation. A year and a day go by, but without the usual release. More months pass, then the author announces his coming to terms with the divinity and returns discreetly to the world; the death sentence is not rescinded; and that is or is not that. No one is vindicated, few are convinced or even relieved, unless perhaps the Special Branch. Resolutions are not part of the format of such stories, which indeed can be far more menacing than this one. Imagine what might ensue, immediately and over the longer run, if a not dissimilar ensemble of interests, authorities and sovereignties were called into play not over a mere book but, say, over the political status of a small but oil-rich state . . .

Contemporary history does indeed seem to bear out the thesis that the significant unities of today are either larger or smaller than the nation-state – but with the critical qualification that the nation-state persists, at once too weak and too strong, as their nearly exclusive field and means of action. In this way, contemporary history gives new life to a hackneyed phrase: it is, quite simply and quite lethally, out of control.

The Logic of European (Dis)integration

Out of control, yet not chaotic, for this disorder is generated by a reality quite systematic in itself: the capitalist mode of production. The self-expansion of this system within and across national and continental boundaries has been the leading force in world history for more than two centuries now. It continues, and, with the collapse of Stalinism, has entered a critical new phase. Liberals hailed this unfolding history as one that would also be universalist in politics and culture, and socialists, with all important qualifications made, began by agreeing. But it is now clear that capitalist universalism coexists with and actually stimulates intensified particularism, in the familiar forms of national, religious and ethnic/racial chauvinisms.

The current condition of the European Community furnishes one pertinent illustration of this pattern.[2] Here, perhaps the most ambitious planned reorganization in the history of capitalism is reaching a decisive point of advance. Following long-laid schemes, but galvanized now by the need to maximize West European advantage in the newly breached markets to the

East, the EC is moving fast towards monetary and political union. At the same time, the zone is experiencing a new wave of militant chauvinism, expressed variously in a transnational upswing of racist terror and the emergence of new rightist electoral forces – Le Pen's National Front in France, the German Republicans, and, in Italy, the perhaps more equivocal *Lega Nord*. What must be emphasized here is that such developments are not merely atavistic reactions to the emergence of an assuredly more cosmopolitan European order. They are its natural counterpart. Both emerge from a single process: the active (or radioactive) decay of the European nation-state as the principal means and field of political determination.

As superintendent of an economy, the nation-state seeks to optimize the internal and external conditions of capital accumulation. But it does so specifically as representative of the *nation*, confirming its population in an identity in which the elements of territory and descent are dominant. The politico-cultural formula of the nation-state tends to compose or recompose all prevailing discourse on social being in the language of nationality, so that any disturbance of the one is rendered spontaneously as a disturbance of the other. The move towards integrated markets and political federation, for all its upsets and rivalries, is consistent with the long-established functions of the state, but disrupts its politico-cultural formula. The nation-state appears to abrogate its 'national' responsibilities, but the identitarian formula remains, and now offers a 'natural' code of discontent – to the natural advantage of the right. In the same process, the minorities who have been the oppressed others of the dominant identity are newly exposed, and frequently driven to respond in the same communitarian terms – again, to the natural advantage of their most conservative members. The regional pennants of the *Lega Nord* are indeed antique, but the alienations they dignify and mobilize are thoroughly modern. Bourgeois cosmopolitanism is the progenitor of particularist identities. Margaret Thatcher was for years the nationalistic curmudgeon of EC politics, but few things are more truly 'European' than the self-destructive ambivalence that so largely contributed to her downfall. (The other ambivalence, true to the general pattern sketched here, was a dogmatic anti-statism that worked itself out in a centralist attack on the traditional discretions of local government.)

The theme of a new, 'European' identity is, of course, increasingly current. But, in present conditions, there is little here that the left can hope to embrace. The real probabilities of such an identity are either weak or dangerous. Weak, because its main denominators are constitutional and market-based, and do little to recompose identities of descent and place, unless negatively. Dangerous, because in so far as a new Europe does begin to form, it will be as a continental bloc in the new global pattern of economic rivalry now taking shape. And either way, for the growing populations of 'non-Europeans' living and working in EC territory (as also now, for the second-class Europeans from the East) the most cosmopolitan feature of the new order will be its transnational, multi-lingual racism.

Moscow's more generous visions of a 'common European home' are hardly convincing. The *gemütlich* phrasing itself betrays the cold reality. It reminds us that in making a new 'home' in Europe, the Soviet Union would be withdrawing into a far smaller world, and probably relinquishing its traditional solidarities with a larger one. It reminds us too that the truly cosy homes of Europe are smaller still – in the West and even more so in the East. The process under way in the East of the continent is in important respects the opposite of that in the West. An interstate system has been dismantled. The East European states have been released from an oppressive overlordship, and the multinational USSR is being dismembered. But the results to date appear familiar. The political and economic perspectives so far shaped in these countries are convergent with those of the West: constitutional norms of a bourgeois-democratic type and market-led economies (led, that is, more or less briskly to capitalism). And the wider political culture of the area is more and more strongly patterned by ethnic particularism, sometimes democratic and pacific in its forms but at others bigoted and brutal. In the East as, less vividly, in the West, the past is reaching out to claim tomorrow. The new European home has already been squatted, looted and defiled by foreigners and unbelievers. Many in the old Eastern bloc see their future in a kind of Sweden; it may turn out a little more like Iran.

Postmodernism and Socialism

So, here too are some salient postmodern phenomena: some more assertions of heterogeneity, some more initiatives in identity politics, some new others intervening in defiance of the grand narrative. And with every necessary and substantial qualification made, it must be said that they compromise any plausible prospect of human emancipation. Particularism and fundamentalism suppress dissent, confuse and divide working classes, subordinate women, oppress vulnerable minorities. They are, as a whole, reactionary. But they are not merely atavistic. If they have a shared motivation, it lies in the effort to assert some kind of collective control over the common life, to establish basic securities in conditions where these things are now denied or threatened. Their common, negative precondition is the frustration of socialism.

Capitalist development may be more or less planned and supervised here or there; it may be favoured by circumstance or not; but its central dynamic is in the end uncontrollable. For that reason it can never sustain a general social interest. Some eighty years of social-democratic governmental experience suggest that capitalism cannot be transformed gradually, or even held to a stable, socially-corrected course; the Communist-governed countries suppressed capitalist economic relations only to create party dictatorships presiding voluntaristically over command economies. Both the social-democratic and Communist traditions espoused values that might have framed a general popular interest capable of respecting inherited and emergent particular identities.

But both, in effect, succumbed to official nationalism: social democracy through its strategic surrender to the bourgeois state, communism through the workings of the doctrine of 'socialism in one country'. In the one case, cultural pluralism meant indifference moderated by complacency; in the other, it was frequently repressed outright.

And now capitalism stands poised to claim the greatest single victory in its history: the reconquest of markets and spaces denied to it for a half-century and more, and the apparent elimination of its historic antagonist. The prospects for socialism seem bleak; but they can only be made bleaker if we accept the bland language of convergence in which the defeat of historical communism is rendered. A task force of strategic euphemisms and conflations has been mobilized – 'markets', 'democracy', 'freedom' and so on – to obliterate all critical knowledge of capitalism and socialism and of the qualitative difference between them. This is not the time for postmodern fascination with the postmodern scene. Even where fascination is critical, it remains contemplative, fulfilled in the timeless presence of its object. 'Difference' and 'discontinuity', valorized without regard for their specific contents and real conditions of existence, are the alibi of conformists and chastened doctrinaires. There will be a day for a Europe (and a world) of differences, lived as a history without closure, but its precondition is a general social transformation that will not come through the free proliferation of particularities. The strong alternative to a flawed grand narrative is surely a critically revised one, not a winsome anthology of (very) short stories. Similar considerations apply to the superficially quite different political value of 'realism'. 'Realism' is habitually offered as meaning a lucid appraisal of probabilities: what can be done, where, how soon, and on what scale? But it also entails a judgement of *adequacy*. A solution that fails to deal with the problem in hand is not redeemed by the mere fact of its availability; inadequate solutions are, by definition, not 'realistic'. Thus, an appeal to 'realism' implies, against the grain of its own usual motivation, an appeal to critical norms, and thence to a qualitative judgement on the existing order of things – on capitalist civilization.

This is the decisive reality of 'Europe', with its multiply-stressed politics and culture. Identities made out of 'these people in this place' belong to the romances of nationalism and imperialism. The attempt to make a European identity in such terms must prove self-defeating. In effect, the matter will be settled in other terms, by the answers given to another kind of question: what kind of social order can best sustain the general and particular interests of these changing populations in this shifting space? Capitalism as fact and socialism as concrete possibility are still the poles between which our history moves, and the task of enriching the critique of the one and the promise of the other is now more urgent than ever; for in the decades ahead, when capitalism seems likely, for the first time, to inherit the earth, the worst, the most truly hopeless of all European identities would be one in which that comfortless critical knowledge has been forgotten.

NOTES

The Present Lasts a Long Time

1. Peter Osborne, *The Politics of Time: Modernity and Avant-garde* (London: Verso, 1995).
2. See pp. 55–69.
3. See n. 38, p. 182.
4. Fernand Braudel, 'History and the Social Sciences', in his *On History*, trans. Sarah Matthews (London: Weidenfeld and Nicolson, 1980). The durations I instance here are actually short, by Braudel's standards; but the terms of his analysis apply on smaller as well as larger historical scales.
5. For Benda, see pp. 70–2 and 86 below; for Mannheim, see pp. 87–9. Edward Said, *Representations of the Intellectual*, the 1993 Reith Lectures (London: Vintage, 1994).
6. For Schumpeter, see pp. 90–1 below; and for Nizan, see pp. 72 and 89–90. Pierre Bourdieu and his collaborators in the journal and book series *Liber* offer a striking militant fusion of the two modes. The exacting social-scientific procedures for which Bourdieu is well known in cultural studies have here been mobilized to serve the wider social resistance to neo-liberalism, whose strategy, Bourdieu is prepared to say, threatens 'the destruction of a *civilization*'. The prophetic note is quite classical, though that can hardly be said of the venue in which it was sounded: a meeting of striking railway workers in Paris in 1995. See *Contre-feux* (Paris: Liber: Raisons d'agir, 1998), p. 30. Another book in this series, attacking the neo-liberal claque in the French media intelligentsia, deliberately recalls Nizan; see Serge Halimi, *Les nouveaux chiens de garde* (1977).
7. George Watson's *Politics and Literature in Modern Britain* (London: Macmillan, 1977) is a relevant specimen of this ugly genre.
8. Said, pp. 3–4.
9. 'Intelligentsias and Their Histories', pp. 71–85.
10. For example, Jacques Le Goff, *Gli intellettuali nel medioevo* (Milan: Mondadori, 1979). (The preface to this edition cites genealogies extending far back beyond the twelfth century, which is Le Goff's own starting point, to antiquity.)
11. I take this distinction from Rudolf Bahro, in preference to the more familiar distinction between 'mental' and 'manual' labour, which reduces a social-cultural relation to a simply technical one. 'General labour' is that which works on the social whole, in contrast with 'particular labour', whose sphere is always partial, and which is therefore heteronomous; see Rudolf Bahro, *The Alternative in Eastern Europe* (London: Verso, 1977), p. 104f. The cardinal instance of general labour is the state, whose given forms and functions are, for that precise reason, a decisive context for interpreting the dispositions and authority-claims of intellectual formations within its jurisdiction.
12. Jonathan Rée coined this phrase in a different context of argument: 'The Vanity of Historicism', *New Literary History*, vol. 22, no. 4 (Autumn 1991), p. 980. The point, of course, is not to cultivate anachronism, but to challenge

the common-sense philosophy of history that gives the notion its spurious judgemental force.

13. I try to show the morphological continuity between cultural criticism and cultural studies in a short book *Culture/Metaculture* (London: Routledge, forthcoming).

14. The declared position of Second International Marxism, formulated by so dour a theoretician as Karl Kautsky, was in fact more radically pluralist than cultural liberalism has ever been, calling for 'communism in material production, anarchism in the intellectual'; see *The Social Revolution* (New York: Charles H. Kerr and Company, 1903), p. 183.

15. See pp. 52–3 below. These sentences occasionally borrow the phrasings of my 'The Politics of Cultural Studies', *Monthly Review*, vol. 47, no. 3 (July-August 1995), pp. 31–40.

16. Matthew Arnold, 'The Function of Criticism at the Present Time' (1864), *Essays in Criticism* (London: Dent, 1964), p. 16. Arnold was quoting Joseph Joubert.

17. This was the case in *New Left Review*, on which I served as an editor for eleven years from 1975. It has long been conventional, on both sides of the Irish Sea, to castigate the journal for its inadequate coverage of the Northern crisis, after the early days. The long silence was the mark of repeated failed efforts to find material that most editors would feel confident about publishing. Fellow-editor Tom Nairn's 'Northern Ireland: Relic or Portent?', which first appeared in a London cultural review, was included in the New Left Books/Verso collection of his writings on nationalism and the British state, *The Break-up of Britain* (1977; 2nd enlarged ed., 1981).

18. This was the *What is to be done . . . ?* series published by Penguin Books for the Socialist Society in the early eighties.

19. *The Politics of Time*, p. xii.

20. Eamon de Valera, 'The Undeserted Village Ireland' (1943), *The Field Day Anthology of Irish Writing*, III (Derry: Field Day Publications, 1991), p. 748.

21. The sequence goes: Sinn Féin, Sinn Féin (Official), Sinn Féin the Workers' Party, Workers' Party, Democratic Left.

22. For a wider cultural-historical view, see Franco Moretti, *The Way of the World: The Bildungsroman in European Culture* (London: Verso, 1987), which perceives in the novel of youth the privileged symbolic form of modernity.

23. Roberto Schwarz, *Misplaced Ideas: Essays on Brazilian Culture*, trans. by John Gledson (London: Verso, 1992), pp. 19–32.

24. 'A dialética enveneneda de Roberto Schwarz', *Folha de S. Paulo*, 1 June 1997.

Marxist Literary Criticism: Past and Future

1. 'Socialism: Utopian and Scientific', in Karl Marx and Frederick Engels, *Selected Works* (London: Lawrence and Wishart, 1970), pp. 375–428. A mode of production, the central concept of Marxist theory, is a determinate combination of forces and relations of production. The former include the existing means of production, not only technologies and raw materials but also the developed powers of living men and women; the latter include the relations of appropriation of the means and products of economic activity and also the systemic objective of production. Thus, in contrast with the narrowly technical idea of

'the economy' that predominates in bourgeois culture, a mode of production is in itself a fully social organization. And to argue for its determining role in social life is to point to the effects of structured relationships, not – again contrary to bourgeois ideology – to some essential human acquisitiveness.

2. Karl Marx and Frederick Engels, *On Literature and Art* (Moscow: Progress Publishers, 1976); S. S. Prawer, *Karl Marx and World Literature* (Oxford: Clarendon Press, 1976).

3. See Mikhail Lifschitz, *The Philosophy of Art of Karl Marx* (1933; reprint ed., London: Pluto Press, 1973); Georg Lukács, *Record of a Life: an Autobiographical Sketch* (London: Verso, 1983), pp. 163–4; Raymond Williams, 'Marxism and Culture' and 'Lukács: a Man Without Frustration' (a review of the foregoing) in his *What I Came to Say* (London: Hutchinson Radius, 1989), pp. 195–225 and 267–74 respectively.

4. Frederick Engels, 'Ludwig Feuerbach . . . ' in Karl Marx and Frederick Engels, *Selected Works*, pp. 584–622; letter to C. Schmidt (1890), pp. 678–80, pp. 684–9; to J. Bloch (1890), pp. 682–3; to F. Mehring (1893), pp. 689–93.

5. Marx (19 April 1859) and Engels (18 May 1859) to Lassalle, *Collected Works*, vol. 40 (London: Lawrence and Wishart, 1983), pp. 419–20 and 441–6 respectively; Engels to Harkness (April 1888) in *Marx and Engels on Literature and Art*, ed. Lee Baxandall and Stefan Morawski (New York: International General, 1974), pp. 115–17.

6. Karl Marx, *Grundrisse, Foundations of the Critique of Political Economy (Rough Draft)*, trans. Martin Nicolaus (Harmondsworth: Penguin, 1973), pp. 110–11.

7. See generally Richard Jenkyns, *The Victorians and Ancient Greece* (Oxford: Basil Blackwell, 1980).

8. Georgi Plekhanov, *Unaddressed Letters and Art and Social Life* (Moscow: Progress Publishers, 1957); cf. Karl Kautsky, *The Materialist Conception of History*, ed. John H. Kautsky (New Haven and London: Yale University Press, 1988), pp. 101–2.

9. Perry Anderson's *Considerations on Western Marxism* (London: New Left Books, 1976) is the outstanding reconstruction of this history. My indebtedness to it will be evident to anyone who reads it. My main disagreement here is that whereas Anderson regards a strong orientation to contemporaneous bourgeois culture as distinctively Western Marxist, I see it as historically normal – though not therefore a matter of indifference.

10. Georg Lukács, *History and Class Consciousness* (London: Merlin Press, 1971), p. xx.

11. This is Arno Mayer's telling designation for the period 1914–45: see his *The Persistence of the Old Regime* (London: Croom Helm, 1981); see also Eric Hobsbawm, *Age of Extremes: the Short Twentieth Century 1914–1991* (London: Michael Joseph, 1994).

12. The standard account of the Frankfurt School is Martin Jay, *The Dialectical Imagination* (London: Heinemann, 1973); see also Eugene Lunn, *Marxism and Modernism* (London: Verso, 1985).

13. See, for example, Lucien Goldmann, *The Hidden God: a Study of Tragic Vision in the Pensées of Pascal and the Tragedies of Racine* (London: Routledge and Kegan Paul, 1964); idem, *Towards a Sociology of the Novel* (London: Tavistock, 1975).

14.   See Jean-Paul Sartre, *What Is Literature?*, trans. Bernard Frechtman (London: Methuen, 1950); idem *The Family Idiot: Gustave Flaubert 1821–1857*, trans. Carol Cosman (Chicago, London: University of Chicago Press, 1993).

15.   See Louis Althusser, 'Contradiction and Overdetermination' (1962) in his *For Marx* (London: New Left Books, 1977), pp. 89–128.

16.   For a fuller discussion of this passage and its sequels, see 'Reading Althusser', pp. 56–70 below.

17.   Herbert Marcuse, *Eros and Civilization* (London: Routledge and Kegan Paul, 1956).

18.   Galvano Della Volpe, *Critique of Taste*, trans. Michael Caesar (London: New Left Books, 1978).

19.   See *Signs Taken For Wonders*, trans. Susan Fischer, David Forgacs (London: Verso, 1983; 2nd ed., 1988). The contents of the first edition exemplify these interests. The essays on tragedy and on evolution added in the second initiate a new phase in which genre becomes the privileged object of analysis and Darwinian biology emerges as the analogical basis of a selectionist literary history.

20.   Fredric Jameson, *The Ideologies of Theory*, Vol. I *Situations of Theory* and Vol. II *The Syntax of History* (London: Routledge and Kegan Paul, 1988).

21.   Peter Bürger, *Theory of the Avant-garde*, trans. Michael Shaw (Manchester: Manchester University Press/Minneapolis: University of Minnesota Press, 1984).

22.   Raymond Williams, *Marxism and Literature* (Oxford: Oxford University Press, 1977) named and codified this position.

23.   Tony Bennett, *Formalism and Marxism* (London: Methuen, 1979); idem, *Outside Literature* (London: Routledge, 1990).

24.   Edward Said, *Orientalism* (New York: Pantheon, 1978); Frederic Jameson, *Postmodernism, or the Cultural Logic of Late Capitalism* (London: Verso, 1991). For critical discussion of the contextual parallax to which such globalizing constructions are prone, see Kumkum Sangari, 'The Politics of the Possible', *Cultural Critique* 7 (Fall 1987), pp. 157–86.

25.   Raymond Williams, *The Politics of Modernism: Against the New Conformists*, ed. Tony Pinkney (London: Verso, 1989); Franco Moretti, 'The Moment of Truth' (on the geography of modern tragedy in Europe), *Signs Taken For Wonders*, pp. 249–261.

26.   A passage like this one, which quotes the breeze rather than signed and dated texts, must seem indiscriminate, and even unjust in respect of particular persons. My generalizations refer not to a totality of individuals but the stronger tendencies of the milieu they currently inhabit. They focus, moreover, on a particular generation (of work and experience, not necessarily of age) and may be inapplicable to students, teachers and writers of more recent formation. Aijaz Ahmad's *In Theory: Classes, Nations, Literatures* (London: Verso, 1992) sets out a powerful, documented analysis of one salient formation of contemporary academic production in the metropolis, postcolonial theory.

27.   Here and later I use the term 'intertextuality' in the sense of Julia Kristeva's original coinage, i.e. the presence within a text of other texts of its culture. It does not mean simple influence and does not bear only on the special case of allusion, but rather is part of a redefinition of textuality as such. This sense should be distinguished from a later one, marked only by the insertion of a vulnerable hyphen (inter-textuality) and referring to the effect, in reading, of a given text's

changeable associations with other existing texts; see Tony Bennett and Janet Woollacott, *Bond and Beyond* (London: Macmillan, 1987), pp. 6–8.

28. Sigmund Freud, 'The Question of a *Weltanschauung*', *New Introductory Lectures*, Standard Edition of the Complete Psychological Works, Vol. XXII (London: The Hogarth Press, 1964), p. 158.

29. See Sebastiano Timpanaro, *On Materialism* (London: New Left Books, 1975).

30. The analysis of 'reading formations' is developed in Bennett and Woollacott, *Bond and Beyond*.

31. The Soviet/Estonian semiotician Yuri M. Lotman proposes the concept of *repertoire*, but with specific reference to 'text-oriented cultures', which he distinguishes from 'grammar-oriented' cultures governed, contrastingly, by *system*; see his *Universe of the Mind: a Semiotic Theory of Culture* (London: I. B. Tauris, 1990), and Umberto Eco's 'Introduction'. This analytic option seems to me to spare Romantic notions of culture just when it is poised to displace them. A distinction between, say, 'prescribed' and 'discretionary' repertoires might be a less tendentious way of acknowledging the historical differences he has in view.

32. See Roland Barthes, *Mythologies* (London: Paladin, 1973), especially the concluding essay, 'Myth Today', pp. 109–59.

33. Etienne Balibar and Pierre Macherey, 'On Literature as an Ideological Form', Francis Mulhern, ed., *Contemporary Marxist Literary Criticism* (London: Longman, 1992), pp. 34–54; Terry Eagleton, *Literary Theory: an Introduction* (Oxford: Blackwell, 1983); Tony Bennett, 'Marxism and Popular Fiction', Mulhern, ed., pp. 188–210; Raymond Williams, *Marxism and Literature* (Oxford: Oxford University Press, 1977) and *Writing in Society* (London: Verso, 1984).

34. Cf. Terry Eagleton, *Literary Theory* (Oxford: Blackwell, 1983), pp. 1–16.

35. Terry Eagleton, *The Ideology of the Aesthetic* (Oxford: Blackwell, 1990), pp. 13–30; Herbert Marcuse, *The Aesthetic Dimension* (London: Macmillan, 1979).

36. See Fredric Jameson, *The Political Unconscious* (Ithaca, NY: Cornell University Press, 1981), ch. 6; Sigmund Freud, *Jokes and Their Relation to the Unconscious* (Harmondsworth: Penguin, 1976); Julia Kristeva, *Desire in Language*, ed. Leon S. Roudiez (Oxford: Basil Blackwell, 1980). Perry Anderson is among those Marxists who resist the displacement of the literary/aesthetic and of canon-defined fields of study, discerning in it a well-meaning ('democratic' and 'egalitarian') but misjudged liquidation of the practice of judgement and, above all, a denial of differential technical accomplishment; see 'A Culture in Contraflow – II', *New Left Review*, 182 (1990), pp. 85–137, at pp. 85–97. His case does not convince, either as criticism or as recommendation, founded as it is on certain stock associations of ideas. Decisions concerning the *range* of inquiry do not necessarily dictate the nature of the inquiry itself; and the issue of the literary/aesthetic as a category is logically distinct from that of generic or differential textual 'value'. The recall of technical achievement is insufficient as a defence of historic canons (some traditionalists would shun it, fearing damnation by faint praise) and, more importantly, misleading as a corrective for the future: to deny differential 'skill' is simple populism, but to privilege it as an object of study is simple connoisseurism. The truly democratic and egalitarian demand for the widest possible learning of skills imagines a culture no longer deformed by the mutually confirming antipathies of populist and connoisseur.

37. For an interesting discussion see 'The "Text in Itself"', *Southern Review* (Adelaide), 17 (1984), a symposium led off by Terry Eagleton and Tony Bennett, and continuing with interventions by Noel King, Ian Hunter, Peter Hulme, Catherine Belsey and John Frow.

38. The classic statement, much debated over the years, is Quentin Skinner, 'Meaning and Understanding in the History of Ideas', *History and Theory*, 8 (1969). Skinner's polemical precedent was, aptly enough, literary-critical: the debate between F. R. Leavis and the 'contextualist' F. W. Bateson in *Essays in Criticism*, III (1953) and *Scrutiny*, XIX (1953).

39. This passage draws freely on Louis Althusser, *Reading Capital* (London: New Left Books, 1971); some historiographical themes of the *Annales* school, especially in Pierre Vilar, 'Marxist History, a History in the Making: Dialogue With Althusser', *New Left Review*, 80 (1973), pp. 65–106; and on Stephen Jay Gould's explorations of the structures and processes of natural history in, for example, *Time's Arrow, Time's Cycle: Myth and Metaphor in the Discovery of Geological Time* (Cambridge, Mass: Harvard University Press, 1987).

40. Rosalind Coward and John Ellis, *Language and Materialism* (London: Routledge and Kegan Paul, 1977) and Williams, *Marxism and Literature*, are in their different ways influential statements of this general tendency; see also Terry Eagleton's critical assessment, 'Base and Superstructure in Raymond Williams', in Eagleton, ed., *Raymond Williams: Critical Perspectives* (Oxford: Polity, 1989), pp. 165–75.

41. Lucio Colletti, 'Marxism as a Sociology' (1958), in his *From Rousseau to Lenin* (London: New Left Books, 1972), p. 5.

42. Althusser, 'Contradiction and Overdetermination', *For Marx*, pp. 95–8, 113.

43. Cora Kaplan, 'Pandora's Box: Subjectivity, Class and Sexuality in Socialist Feminist Criticism', *Sea Changes: Culture and Feminism* (London: Verso, 1986), pp. 147–76.

44. Cf. Sebastiano Timpanaro, *On Materialism*, 2nd ed. (London: Verso, 1980), p. 261.

45. Cited in Franco Fortini, *Verifica dei poteri* (Milan: Il Saggiatore/Garzanti, 1974), p. 158.

46. This is how I interpret Gramsci's remarks on Paul Nizan; see Gramsci, *Selections From Cultural Writings*, ed. David Forgacs and Geoffrey Nowell-Smith (London: Lawrence and Wishart, 1985), pp. 99–102; see also Nizan, *Pour une nouvelle culture* (Paris: Grasset, 1971).

47. The nostrum of 'anti-humanism' calls for particular attention. Anti-humanism is confident in rejecting the notion of a human essence (its principal definition) and the putatively bourgeois conception of the subject as self-transparent originator of meaning (its longest-running theme); yet as a contributor to radical social thought, it belongs to a broad historical tradition that affirms the possibility and value of human self-development, and is in that sense humanist. This ambiguity is more than superficial and more than contemplative; it bespeaks theoretical deficiency and promotes practical confusion. The critique of essentialism, pursued unilaterally, is itself idealist, denying our common and relatively stable reality as a natural species; and too euphoric a dissolution of the humanist subject may reduce all programmes of emancipation to a Babel in which ideas of 'need' and 'right' are merely positional gambits. Anti-humanism

is defiantly historical – but historical understanding is practised whole or not at all. Human time is complex, syncopated but also regular, rapid but also unobservably slow; and even if our history does not move towards a preinscribed *telos*, it does not follow that all ideas of development are 'modern' fictions.

48. Walter Benjamin, *Charles Baudelaire: a Lyric Poet in the Era of High Capitalism* (London: New Left Books, 1973), pp. 104–6.

Reading Althusser

1. These pages offer what, for want of a better phrase, might be called a theoretical memoir. Laying no claim to the systematic achievement of critical or historical reconstruction proper, they are more personal in background and perhaps idiosyncratic in balance and range. The text is also, and for this reason, somewhat Anglocentric – a limitation I cannot surmount here, but nevertheless wish to acknowledge.

2. Louis Althusser, *For Marx* (London: Allen Lane, 1969); idem, *Reading Capital* (London: New Left Books, 1970); idem, *Lenin and Philosophy and Other Essays* (London: New Left Books, 1971), *passim*.

3. Roland Barthes spoke of 'a quadrivium of pilot sciences', though listing economics and not psychoanalysis along with the other three; see his *Elements of Semiology* (New York: Hill and Wang, 1968), pp. 101–2, n. 55.

4. My own contribution to this culture of embarrassment, 'The Marxist Aesthetics of Christopher Caudwell', *New Left Review*, 85 (May/June 1974), was typical in its 'Althusserian' desire to raze the local theoretical heritage. Though I stand by the destructive analysis proposed there, I have long felt that Caudwell deserved a more generous and more resourceful (that is, more truly critical) reading.

5. Raymond Williams's famous judgement on Caudwell epitomized a whole structure of left literary-critical feeling: 'for the most part his discussion is not even specific enough to be wrong.' *Culture and Society 1780–1950* (Harmondsworth: Penguin, 1961), p. 268.

6. Althusser, 'The "Piccolo Teatro": Bertolazzi and Brecht', in *For Marx*; idem, 'Cremonini, Painter of the Abstract', in *Lenin and Philosophy*.

7. Althusser, 'A Letter on Art in Reply to André Daspre', *Lenin and Philosophy*, pp. 204, 207.

8. Pierre Macherey, *A Theory of Literary Production* (London: Routledge and Kegan Paul, 1978).

9. *A Theory of Literary Production*, p. 59, p. 133.

10. Etienne Balibar and Pierre Macherey, 'Dé la littérature comme forme idéologique', *Littérature*, 13 (February 1974); translated as 'On Literature as an Ideological Form', *Oxford Literary Review*, 3 (1978) and reprinted in Francis Mulhern, ed., *Contemporary Marxist Literary Criticism* (London: Longman, 1992), the text to which I subsequently refer.

11. Terry Eagleton, 'Ideology and Literary Form', *New Left Review*, 90 (March/April 1975); idem, *Criticism and Ideology* (London: New Left Books, 1976).

12. *Criticism and Ideology*, pp. 83–4.

13. See my 'Marxism in Literary Criticism', *New Left Review*, 108 (March/April 1978), which advanced this critical argument, among others – but which, as a whole, shared with Eagleton the limiting problematic discussed here.

14. The tendency of Michael Sprinker's work, in the United States, runs counter to this suggestion. For him, the relation between the aesthetic and the ideological forms our 'current horizon of understanding' and, to that extent, 'we remain determinately within the Althusserian problematic.' He would add, however, that the concept of the aesthetic is more elusive than the traditions of bourgeois and Marxist reflection acknowledge; see his *Imaginary Relations* (London: Verso, 1987), p. 2, p. 3; see also, for more general interest, E. Ann Kaplan and Sprinker, eds., *The Althusserian Legacy* (London: Verso, 1993), which includes a variety of North American and European appreciations of Althusser's work.

15. 'On Literature as an Ideological Form', p. 35.

16. *Criticism and Ideology*, p. 56. Eagleton's retrospective assessment of Althusser appears in the preface of his *Against the Grain: Essays 1975–1985* (London: Verso, 1986), pp. 2–4; in the same volume, see also his 'Macherey and Marxist Literary Theory' (1975), pp. 9–21.

17. Tel Quel, *Théorie d'ensemble* (Paris: Editions du Seuil, 1968).

18. Balibar and Macherey associated *Tel Quel* with a vision of art as 'anti-nature' and 'violation of order' – a 'reversal . . . characteristic of conservative ideology' ('On Literature as an Ideological Form', p. 54, n. 10); see also Eagleton, *Against the Grain*, p. 4.

19. *Théorie d'ensemble*, p. 8.

20. Ibid; see Michel Foucault, 'Distance, aspect, origine', pp. 11–24; Roland Barthes, 'Drame, poeme, roman', pp. 25–40; Jacques Derrida, 'La Différance', pp. 41–66.

21. Peter Wollen, *Readings and Writings: Semiotic Counter-strategies* (London: Verso, 1982), p. 211; Stephen Heath, *Questions of Cinema* (London: Macmillan, 1981), p. 201. Wollen's version of this trinity formula was always firmly grounded in a commitment to science; he was correspondingly more distant from *Tel Quel* than Heath, who was for a time an active collaborator in the journal. *Signs of the Times: Introductory Readings in Textual Semiotics*, a collection of texts co-edited by Heath, Colin MacCabe and Christopher Prendergast (Cambridge: Granta, n. d.) marked the entry of *Tel Quel* into British left culture.

22. Rosalind Coward and John Ellis, *Language and Materialism* (London: Routledge and Kegan Paul, 1977) was widely received as a synopsis of *Screen's* thinking, but did not claim that status for itself.

23. See Penny Boumelha, *Thomas Hardy and Women: Sexual Ideology and Narrative Form* (Brighton: Harvester, 1982); see also Cora Kaplan, *Sea Changes: Culture and Feminism* (London: Verso, 1986).

24. See Tony Bennett, *Formalism and Marxism* (London: Methuen, 1979); idem, 'Marxism and Popular Fiction', first published in *Literature and History*, 7 (1981), and reprinted in Mulhern, ed., *Contemporary Marxist Literary Criticism*.

25. The sociologists Barry Hindess and Paul Hirst were the key figures here; their reading of Althusser quickly rose to quasi-canonical status in *Screen* and its literary-theoretical hinterland.

26. Tony Bennett explains his transition to 'post-Marxism' (not, he stresses, *anti*-Marxism) in his *Outside Literature* (London: Routledge, 1990), part I.

27. Anthony Easthope, *British Post-structuralism since 1968* (London: Routledge, 1988), pp. 17, 21.

28. *For Marx*, 'Glossary' (compiled by Ben Brewster and amended by Althusser), p. 252.
29. The absolute quality of this thesis was confirmed *a contrario* by Althusser's one attempt to qualify it. Ideology, he wrote, is 'an omni-historical reality, in the sense [that its] structure and functioning are immutable, present in the same form throughout what we can call history, in the sense in which the Communist Manifesto defines history as the history of class struggles, i.e. the history of class societies' *Lenin and Philosophy*, pp. 151–2. If this purported qualification is valid, then the substantive thesis fails.
30. Göran Therborn, *The Ideology of Power and the Power of Ideology* (London: Verso, 1980).
31. For a compact summary, see Raymond Williams, *Marxism and Literature* (Oxford: Oxford University Press, 1977).
32. See, for example, Paul Hirst, *On Law and Ideology* (London: Macmillan, 1979), pp. 52–3, 71–2, *passim*; see also, for the settled retrospect, Anthony Easthope, *British Post-structuralism*, pp. 213–14.
33. Cf. in this volume p. 50.
34. Stephen Resnick and Richard Woolf appear to me to be trying to evade this unaccommodating conclusion – or to bowdlerize it – when they maintain, first, that for Althusser there can be no one social truth, only a plurality of truths; but, second, that Marxism should accept or reject exogenous theoretical claims following an assessment of their 'social conditions and consequences'; see their 'Althusser's Liberation of Marxian Theory', in E. Ann Kaplan and Michael Sprinker eds., *The Althusserian Legacy* (London: Verso, 1993), pp. 65, 67.

Intelligentsias and Their Histories

1. Initiative Solidarität mit den Intellektuellen der Türkei, Hrsg., *Diktakatur* (Duisberg: Kaynar Verlag, 1985).
2. Régis Debray, *Le Pouvoir intellectuel en France* (Paris: Editions Ramsay, 1979); trans. David Macey, *Teachers, Writiers, Celebrities* (London: New Left Books, 1981).
3. See the next essay here, pp. 86–93, for a definition and some elaboration of this concept.
4. See Ronald Aronson, *Jean-Paul Sartre – Philosophy in the World* (London: New Left Books, 1980), pp. 122–42.
5. See, for one case among many, Talcott Parsons's contribution to Philip Rieff, ed., *On Intellectuals* (New York, 1969); see also pp. 3–5 above, and 'Intellectual Corporatism and Socialism', pp. 85–93 below.
6. See, for example, Theodor Adorno and Max Horkheimer, *Dialectic of Enlightenment*, trans. John Cumming (London: Verso, 1979).
7. F. R. Leavis, *Mass Civilization and Minority Culture* (Cambridge: Minority Press, 1930); Q. D. Leavis, *Fiction and the Reading Public* (London: Chatto and Windus, 1932).
8. See figures in Debray, *Teachers, Writers, Celebrities*, pp. 52–3, and for the USA, Donald R. McCoy, *Coming of Age* (Harmondsworth: Penguin, 1973), pp. 116–44.
9. See Debray, chapter 2, especially pp. 58–63.

10. Quoted in Aronson, p. 226.

11. C. L. Mowat, *Britain Between the Wars, 1918–1940* (London: Methuen, 1968).

12. Thus Jennie Lee, the Labour minister responsible: see Raymond Williams, *Politics and Letters* (London: New Left Books, 1979), p. 371.

13. Dewey was an important intellectual influence on several at least of the *Partisan Review* circle, most notably Sidney Hook and James Burnham, but also James T. Farrell. The Commission on the Moscow Trials and the Committee for Cultural Freedom brought the philosopher into direct contact with the journal; see James Burkhart Gilbert, *Writers and Partisans* (New York: Wiley, 1968), pp. 201–3, *passim*; and Alan Wald, *James T. Farrell: the Revolutionary Socialist Years* (New York: New York University Press, 1978). Of course, Dewey attained a national cultural influence that *Partisan Review* could never emulate. It was very much a New York journal throughout, and New York's relationship to the USA was not at all like that of London or Paris to their respective national settings.

14. Brooks's programme was the deviant continuation of Randolph Bourne's, which had envisaged a balanced combination of nationalism and internationalism. *Partisan Review* criticized Brooks's nationalism before the war, citing Bourne's position as more acceptable and more radical in its affinities. But cultural cosmopolitanism alone was not a sufficient safeguard against nationalist attitudes, after the subsidence of its own radicalism.

15. Norman Podhoretz, *Breaking Ranks: a Political Memoir* (New York: Harper and Row, 1979).

16. Régis Debray, *Prison Writings* (Harmondsworth: Penguin, 1975), pp. 169–207.

17. Régis Debray, 'A Modest Contribution to the Rites and Ceremonies of the Tenth Anniversary'; an extract from this work was published in translation, *New Left Review*, 115 (May-June 1979), pp. 45–65, together with a reply by Henri Weber, pp. 66–71.

Intellectual Corporatism and Socialism: The Twenties and After

1. I cite Mann's title in a more literal and, I think, more appropriate translation than that of the published English version, *Reflections of a Nonpolitical Man*, trans. and introduction, Walter D. Morris (New York: Frederick Unger, 1983).

2. See, for example, Benedetto Croce, *My Philosophy and Other Essays on the Moral and Political Problems of Our Time*, trans. E. F. Carritt (London: Allen and Unwin, 1949).

3. Julien Benda, *The Treason of the Intellectuals* (1928; trans. Richard Aldington, New York: Norton, 1969).

4. F. R. Leavis, *Mass Civilization and Minority Culture* (Cambridge: Minority Press, 1930); José Ortega y Gasset, *The Revolt of the Masses* (1930; London: Allen and Unwin, 1932).

5. It is worth marking the contrast between two Manns: the book of 1918, ultranationalist, inconsolable in the face of democracy, and casually racist towards Poles and Irish, among others, has been deeply embarrassing to Anglo-American liberal good sense, which cherishes the memory of Mann the anti-fascist notable.

6. T. S. Eliot, *Notes Towards the Definition of Culture* (London: Faber and Faber,

1948); G. H. Bantock, 'Cultural Implications of Planning and Popularization', *Scrutiny*, XIV, 3 (Spring 1947), pp. 171–84.

7.   Karl Mannheim, *Ideology and Utopia* (1929), trans. Louis Wirth and Edward Shils (London: Routledge and Kegan Paul, 1936).

8.   Dmitri S. Mirsky, *The Intelligentsia of Great Britain* (New York: Covici Fried, 1935); Paul Nizan, *The Watchdogs: Philosophers of the Established Order* (New York and London: Monthly Review Press, 1974).

9.   See Annie Cohen-Solal, *Paul Nizan, communiste impossible* (Paris: Grasset, 1980). Paul Nizan, *Pour une nouvelle culture*, textes réunis et présentés par Susan Suleiman (Paris: Grasset, 1971): 'Un clerc de gauche' (1937), pp. 275–9.

10. Joseph Schumpeter, *Capitalism, Socialism and Democracy* (1942; reprinted ed., London: Allen and Unwin, 1954), ch. XIII, 'Growing Hostility', pp. 143–56.

11. Lionel Trilling, *The Liberal Imagination* (1950), (New York: Charles Scribner's Sons, 1976), p. 8.

12. Friedrich von Hayek, 'The Intellectuals and Socialism' (1949), in George B. de Huszar, ed., *The Intellectuals: a Controversial Portrait* (Glencoe, Illinois: The Free Press, 1960), pp. 371–84.

13. Jean-Paul Sartre, *What Is Literature?*, trans. Bernard Frechtman (London: Methuen, 1950).

14. Jean-Paul Sartre, 'A Plea for Intellectuals', *Between Existentialism and Marxism*, trans. John Matthews (London: New Left Books, 1974), pp. 228–85.

15. Cited in Karl Marx, *The Class Struggles in France 1848 to 1850* (Moscow: Progress Publishers, 1968), p. 39.

Towards 2000, or News From You Know Where

1.   Raymond Williams, *Modern Tragedy*, 2nd revised ed. (London: Verso, 1979), p. 208.

2.   See respectively 'Ideas of Nature', 'Social Darwinism', 'Beyond Actually Existing Socialism', and 'Utopia and Science Fiction', all in Raymond Williams, *Problems in Materialism and Culture* (London: Verso, 1980); idem, *The Volunteers* (London: Eyre Methuen, 1978).

3.   Raymond Williams, *Towards 2000* (London: Chatto and Windus, 1983).

4.   Raymond Williams, *The Long Revolution* (London: Chatto and Windus, 1961).

5.   *Towards 2000*, p. 26.

6.   Ibid., p. 100.

7.   Ibid., p. 129.

8.   Ibid., p. 143.

9.   Ibid., p. 118.

10. Ibid., p. 125.

11. Ibid., pp. 184–5.

12. Ibid., p. 188; cf. Williams's 'Problems of the Coming Period', *New Left Review*, 140 (July–August 1983), pp. 7–18.

13. *Towards 2000*, pp. 190–1.

14. Ibid., p. 184.

15. Ibid., p. 197.

16. Ibid., pp. 243–8.

17. Ibid., p. 170.

18. Ibid., pp. 173–4.
19. Ibid., pp. 260–7.
20. Karl Marx, *Capital*, Volume 1 (London: Penguin, 1976), pp. 175–6n.
21. Ibid., p. 711, and part 7 generally.
22. *Towards 2000*, pp. 172–3.
23. Karl Marx and Frederick Engels, 'Manifesto of the Communist Party', *Selected Works* (London: Lawrence and Wishart, 1970), p. 46.
24. Raymond Williams, 'The Social Significance of 1926', *Llafur: The Journal of the Welsh Labour History Society*, 1977.
25. *Towards 2000*, pp. 196–7.
26. This passage owes much to the stimulus of Göran Therborn, *The Ideology of Power and the Power of Ideology* (London: Verso, 1980); also Benedict Anderson, *Imagined Communities* (London: Verso, 1983).
27. Raymond Williams, *Politics and Letters: Interviews with New Left Review* (London: New Left Books, 1979), pp. 119–20.
28. Raymond Williams, *Keywords: A Vocabulary of Culture and Society* (London: Fontana, 1976; 2nd enlarged ed., 1983).
29. *Towards 2000*, p. 195.
30. Steven Connors would say it is already out of date, and for substantive reasons to do with Williams's deficient understanding of the 'contemporal' complexity of the present; see his 'Raymond Williams's Time', *Key Words: A Journal of Cultural Materialism*, 1 (1988), pp. 12–27.

A Welfare Culture? Hoggart and Williams in the Fifties

1. See Paul Addison, *The Road to 1945* (London: Macmillan, 1975); Perry Anderson, 'The Figures of Descent', in his *English Questions* (London, Verso, 1992), pp. 121–92; Gregory Elliott, *Labourism and the English Genius* (London: Verso, 1993).
2. W.E. Morpurgo, *Allen Lane, King Penguin: a Biography* (London: Allen Lane, 1979).
3. Stephen Spender, 'Comment: On Literary Movements', *Encounter*, vol. 1, no. 2, (1953), pp. 66–8.
4. Malcolm Bradbury, 'The Rise of the Provincials', *Antioch Review*, vol. XVI, no. 4 (1956), pp. 469–77.
5. Piloted in essays for the *New English Weekly* in 1943 and then in public seminars, the book was published in 1948.
6. Richard Hoggart, *Life and Times* vol. III: 1959–91, *An Imagined Life* (London: Chatto and Windus, 1992), p. 10.
7. Richard Hoggart, *Life and Times* vol. II: 1940–1959, *A Sort of Clowning* (London: Chatto and Windus, 1990), pp. 134–5, 141.
8. Ibid., p.78. See also his 'One Man and his Dog', review of *Michael Foot* by Mervyn Jones, *Observer*, 20 March 1994 – an elegiac reaffirmation of 'humane democratic socialism'.
9. Richard Hoggart, *The Uses of Literacy* (1957) (Harmondsworth: Penguin, 1958), p. 250.
10. Ibid., p. 344.
11. *An Imagined Life*, p. 5.

12. *Universities and Left Review,* vol. 1, nos. 1–7 (Spring 1957–Autumn 1959). The editors were Stuart Hall, Raphael Samuel, Gabriel Pearson and Charles Taylor.

13. *ULR,* vol. 1, no. 2 (Summer 1957), p. 29.

14. John McLeish, 'Variant Readings', *ULR,* 1, 2, p. 32.

15. Gwyn Illtyd Lewis, 'Candy-flossing the Celtic Fringe'.

16. 'Working Class Culture', p. 31, p. 32; Raymond Williams and Richard Hoggart (in conversation), 'Working-class Attitudes', *New Left Review,* 1 (January-February 1960), pp. 26–30.

17. Raymond Williams, *Politics and Letters: Interviews with New Left Review* (London: New Left Books, 1979), pp. 61–77; idem, 'Notes on Marxism in Britain since 1945', in *Problems in Materialism and Culture* (London: Verso, 1980), pp. 240–1.

18. Anthony Barnett, 'Raymond Williams and Marxism: a Rejoinder to Terry Eagleton', *New Left Review,* 99 (September-October 1976), pp. 47–64.

19. *Politics and Letters: Interviews,* p. 97.

20. Beginning from work in adult education classes in 1949, *Culture and Society* was written between 1952 and 1956.

21. Raymond Williams, *Culture and Society 1780–1950* (1958) (Harmondsworth: Penguin, 1961), p. 17.

22. *Culture and Society,* p. 285.

23. See Graham Martin, 'A Culture in Common', *ULR,* vol. 1, no. 5 (Autumn 1958), pp. 70–9 – the moment, if there was one, when *Culture and Society* was canonized as a founding text for a New Left. The symbolic counterpoint was Terry Eagleton, *Criticism and Ideology* (London: New Left Books, 1976), ch. 1.

24. *Politics and Letters: Interviews,* p. 112. This was Edward Thompson's reading.

25. 'Comment', *Politics and Letters,* vol. I, no. 1 (Summer 1947), pp. 32–9.

26. *Culture and Society,* pp. 258–75.

27. 'Editorial Note', *Arena,* vol. I, no. 4.

28. *Politics and Letters: Interviews,* p. 98. Graham Pechey 'Scrutiny, English Marxism, and the Work of Raymond Williams', *Literature and History,* vol. 11, no. 1 (Spring 1985), pp. 65–76, has emphasized the radically disruptive strategy of the book.

29. *Culture and Society,* p. 312.

30. Ibid., p. 313.

31. Ibid., pp. 11–12.

32. Ibid., p. 12.

33. Raymond Williams, *Resources of Hope: Culture, Democracy,* ed. Robin Gable (London: Verso, 1989), p. 3.

34. Ibid., p. 16.

35. Raymond Williams, 'Communications and Community' (1961), *Resources of Hope,* pp. 23–31.

36. *Politics and Letters: Interviews,* p. 371.

37. Three examples, each involving a senior member of the liberal-labour intelligentsia, from late 1994. The first was the late Dennis Potter's widely-discussed attack on the new regime at the BBC (*Occupying Powers,* The James MacTaggart Memorial Lecture, Edinburgh International Television Festival, 1993; broadcast on Channel 4, 23 August 1994) – a discourse in which all the themes, and more than one of the contending lines, of the later fifties were swept together in a surge of invective. There followed Melvin Bragg's defence of British television as

'a kind of national health service of the mind', whose 'general democratic availability' was now under threat from satellite and cable systems (*Independent*, 7 September 1994). A month later, John Mortimer expressed his sense of grief at 'the death of liberal England' and its traditions of public service – in his view, the work of the Conservative governments of the eighties (Laurence Marks, 'The Lost Professional', *Independent on Sunday*, 9 October 1994), p. 19.

38. See Carolyn Steedman, *Landscape for a Good Woman* (London: Virago, 1986), pp. 3–25; Elizabeth Wilson, *Only Halfway to Paradise: Women in Postwar Britain 1945–1964* (London: Tavistock, 1980).

39. For a variety of feminist responses to Williams, see Jane Miller, *Seduction: Studies in Reading and Culture* (London: Virago, 1990), ch. 2, 'The One Great Silent Area'; Jenny Bourne Taylor, 'Raymond Williams: Gender and Generation', Terry Lovell, ed., *British Feminist Thought: A Reader* (Oxford: Blackwell, 1990), pp. 296–308; Carol Watts, 'Reclaiming the Border Country: Feminism and the Work of Raymond Williams', *News From Nowhere*, 6 (1989), pp. 89–108; Lisa Jardine and Julia Swindells, 'Homage to Orwell: the Dream of a Common Culture and Other Minefields', in Terry Eagleton, ed., *Raymond Williams: Critical Perspectives* (Oxford: Polity Press, 1989), pp. 108–29.

40. *ULR* was very quick to respond to the rise of violent racism in the late fifties.

41. Williams attempted to deal with these issues, particularly the latter ones, in subsequent work, with results that have provoked as many as they have impressed. See my 'Towards 2000, or News From You Know Where', pp. 94–116 above; Paul Gilroy, *'There Ain't No Black in the Union Jack': the Cultural Politics of Race and Nation* [1987] (London: Routledge, 1992); Gauri Viswanathan, 'Raymond Williams and British Colonialism: The Limits of Metropolitan Cultural Theory' Dennis L. Dworkin and Leslie G. Roman, eds., *Views Beyond the Border: Raymond Williams and Cultural Politics* (London: Routledge, 1993), pp. 217–230; see also Williams's sharply critical review, 'The Reasonable Englishman', of *An English Temper* by Richard Hoggart, *Guardian*, 8 April 1982, p. 16.

42. See Paul Jones, 'The Myth of "Raymond Hoggart": On "Founding Fathers" and Cultural Policy', *Cultural Studies*, 8 (1994), pp. 394–416, a valuable essay which, like this one, stresses the distance between Hoggart and Williams, and illuminates the role of tendentious misremembering in the recent 'policy' controversy in Australian cultural studies; see Tony Bennett, 'Useful Culture', *Cultural Studies*, 6 (1992), pp. 395–408, which devises a Foucauldian-reformist argument for the metamorphosis of the cultural 'critic' into the cultural policy 'technician'.

English Reading

1. F. R. Leavis, 'Literary Criticism and Philosophy', a reply to René Wellek's communication of the same title, *Scrutiny*, vol. 5, no. 4 (March 1936), reprinted in *The Common Pursuit* (Harmondsworth: Penguin, 1972), pp. 214, 215.

2. My critical use of the term 'humanist' bears only on this kind of essentialism. As a Marxist, I believe simple 'anti-humanism' to be theoretically shallow and morally evasive. Here and elsewhere I have summarized material from my *The Moment of 'Scrutiny'* (London: New Left Books, 1979) – to which this essay is in some other respects a corrective.

3. Joseph Conrad, Preface, *The Nigger of the 'Narcissus', Typhoon, Falk and Other Stories* (London 1950), p. x.

4. Perry Anderson, 'Components of the National Culture' (1968), in his *English Questions* (London: Verso, 1992), pp. 98–9.

5. F. R. Leavis, *Revaluation* (Harmondsworth: Penguin, 1972), p. 146.

6. Ibid., p. 12.

7. Ibid., p. 58.

8. Ibid., pp. 19, 21.

9. Ibid., pp. 26, 29.

10. Ibid., p. 55.

11. Ibid., pp. 35, 118.

12. Ibid., p. 245.

13. Ibid., p. 160.

14. F. R. Leavis, *The Great Tradition* (Harmondsworth: Penguin, 1972), p. 19.

15. Ibid., p. 148, p. 151.

16. Ibid., p. 217, p. 218, p. 219.

17. Ibid, p. 225, p. 227, p. 241.

18 Ibid., p. 27, p. 29.

19. *Towards Standards of Criticism* (1933; reprinted ed., London: Lawrence and Wishart, 1976), pp. 19–20.

20. *The Great Tradition*, p. 214.

21. 'Caterpillars of the Commonwealth Unite!', *Scrutiny*, vol. 7, no. 2 (September 1938), pp. 210–11.

22. *Scrutiny*, vol. 7, no. 2 (September 1938), and vol. 13, no. 2 (September 1945) respectively.

23. Denys Thompson, ed., *The Leavises: Recollections and Impressions* (Cambridge: Cambridge University Press, 1984), pp. 119–20.

24. Martin Green, 'British Decency', *Kenyon Review*, vol. 21, no. 4 (Autumn 1959), pp. 505–32.

25. F. R. Leavis, *For Continuity* (Cambridge: Cambridge University Press, 1933), p. 139.

26. Marius Bewley, *The Complex Fate* (London: Chatto & Windus, 1952).

27. F. R. Leavis, 'Joyce and "the Revolution of the Word"', *Scrutiny*, vol. 2, no. 2 (September 1933), pp. 193–201.

28. F. R. Leavis, *English Literature in Our Time and the University* (London: Chatto & Windus, 1969), pp. 33–5; and cf. idem, *Nor Shall My Sword* (London: 1972), pp. 223–7.

29. G. Singh, ed., *Collected Essays, Vol. 1: The Englishness of the English Novel* (Cambridge: Cambridge University Press, 1983), p. 325.

30. Raymond Williams, *The Country and the City* (London: Chatto & Windus, 1973). For criticism of Williams's analyses of the cultural relationship between nation and Empire, cf. n. 41, p. 190 above. H. S. Mohapatra objects specifically to my citing Williams's book favourably in this critical context, arguing that it remains caught in just the 'abstract' humanism I am contesting; see his ('Residual or Emergent: Critiquing Raymond Williams's *The Country and the City*', *Journal of Contemporary Thought* (1992), pp. 23, 32.

A Nation, Yet Again: The Field Day Anthology

1. See Field Day Theatre Company ed., *Ireland's Field Day*, Hutchinson, London, 1985, reprinting six pamphlets: Tom Paulin, *A New Look at the Language Question*; Seamus Heaney, *An Open Letter*; Seamus Deane, *Civilians and Barbarians* and *Heroic Styles*; Richard Kearney, *Myth and Motherland*; Declan Kiberd, *Anglo-Irish Attitudes*; see also Terry Eagleton, *Nationalism: Irony and Commitment*; Frederic Jameson, *Modernism and Imperialism*; and Edward Said, *Yeats and Decolonisation*, Field Day Pamphlets 13, 14 and 15 respectively, Derry, 1988, now included in Seamus Deane, ed., *Nationalism, Colonialism and Literature* (Minnesota University Press: Minneapolis, 1990).

2. Seamus Deane, ed., 3 vols., Field Day Publications, Derry, 1991. The work is cited here by volume and page number, thus: III, 107.

3. I, xx, xxii, xx, xix, xxi, xx.

4. I, xix.

5. I, xxvi.

6. See, for example, Siobhan Kilfeather, 'The Whole Bustle', *London Review of Books*, 9 January 1992, and, in the same issue, Edna Longley, 'Belfast Diary'; Nell McCafferty, 'Written Out of History', *Everywoman*, February 1992. British Channel 4's *Rear Window* series devoted a programme to the anthology and its critics (*Bright Through the Tears*, July 1992); the discussion, chaired by Tariq Ali, included Tom Paulin, Eavan Boland, Siobhan Kilfeather, Nell McCafferty and myself.

7. 'Written Out of History'.

8. III, 1316.

9. Quoted by McCafferty.

10. See Kilfeather.

11. 'Constructing the Canon: Versions of National Identity', II, 950–1020.

12. II, 953.

13. 'Challenging the Canon: Revisionism and Cultural Criticism', III, 561–680.

14. III, 567.

15. 'Poetry in the Wars' (1986), III, 648.

16. III, 568.

17. See W. J. Mc Cormack, introduction to 'Language, Class and Genre (1780–1830)', I, 1070–1172.

18. III, 563.

19. As the novelist Colm Tóibín wrote, reviewing the anthology in the Dublin *Sunday Independent*: 'Unreconstructed Irish nationalists have always had real difficulty with the 26 Counties . . . [which] are limbo, they believe, waiting for the day when our island will be united and the British will leave. This leaves out any idea that Southern Ireland has been forming its own habits and going its own way' (quoted by Longley, 'Belfast Diary'). Although lazy as a characterisation of Field Day's project (which is precisely not an unreconstructed nationalism) and rather blithe in its phrasing of Southern ways and days, Tóibín's protest has undeniable force.

20. Seamus Heaney, 'Open Letter', *Ireland's Field Day*, p. 27.

21. Eamonn McCann, *War and an Irish Town* (Harmondsworth: Penguin, 1974).

22. I had in mind Morrison's Belfast elegies – 'Madame George', which I mentioned,

'Cyprus Avenue' and 'Cleaning Windows' – not the thing since canonized by Northern officialdom, 'Days Like This' [1996].

23. This sub-heading, repeating my main title, is borrowed from a poem by Tom Paulin, who bears no responsibility for my use of it. The poem appears in III, 1408.

24. Seamus Deane, 'Heroic Styles', *Ireland's Field Day*, p. 58.

Postcolonial Melancholy

1. Luke Gibbons, 'Dialogue Without the Other? A Reply to Francis Mulhern', *Radical Philosophy* 67 (Summer 1994), pp. 28–31.

2. The General Editor's own reflections on the controversy have since appeared in Dympna Callaghan, 'Interview With Seamus Deane', *Social Text*, 38 (Spring 1994), pp. 39–50.

3. 'Dialogue', p. 29, p. 30.

4. 'The bourgeois viewpoint has never advanced beyond this antithesis between itself and this romantic viewpoint, and therefore the latter will accompany it as its legitimate antithesis up to its blessed end': Karl Marx, *Grundrisse: Foundations of the Critique of Political Economy (Rough Draft)*, trans. Martin Nicolaus (Harmondsworth: Penguin, 1973), p. 162.

5. Ibid., p. 101.

6. Roberto Schwarz, *Misplaced Ideas: Essays on Brazilian Culture*, trans. introduction by John Gledson (London: Verso, 1992). The essay 'Brazilian Culture: Nationalism by Elimination' (pp. 1–18) is particularly relevant to the controversy between us.

7. 'Dialogue', p. 29, p. 31.

8. However, not having seen the paper from which Gibbons quotes (his n.10), I cannot claim that my interpretation of Willemen's formulation conforms with his own.

9. 'A Nation, Yet Again', p. 156 above.

10. See, for one compilation among others of his writings on the topic, V .I. Lenin, *Questions of National Policy and Proletarian Internationalism* (Moscow: Progress Publishers, 1964). For a very useful conspectus of the history of Marxist debate over nations and nationalism, see Michael Löwy, 'Marxists and the National Question', *New Left Review*, 96 (March-April 1976), pp. 81–100.

11. 'Dialogue', p. 28, p. 29.

12. Compare, on this point and generally, Aijaz Ahmad's splendid *In Theory: Classes, Nations, Literatures* (London: Verso, 1992), p. 11, p. 171; see also his 'Nationalism, Postcolonialism, Communism' (an interview), *Radical Philosophy* 76 (March/April 1996), pp. 29–38.

13. I adapt this phrase from Walter Benjamin; see his 'Left-wing Melancholy', *Screen*, vol. 15, no. 2 (Summer 1974), pp. 28–32.

14. Gibbons says very little about Northern Ireland, for reasons I cannot presume either to know or to judge. Nothing in these closing paragraphs necessarily applies to him.

15. Unlike the Anglo-Irish, who were a colonial ruling class raised over a native peasantry whom they ruled and exploited, the Ulster Protestants came to constitute a whole society, staffing all the class positions in their regional

social formation in rough (normally privileged) proportion to their numbers there.

16. 'A Nation, Yet Again', p. 157 above.

Translation: Re-writing Degree Zero

1. Lawrence Venuti, *The Translator's Invisibility: A History of Translation*, Translations Studies, general editors Susan Bassnett and André Lefevere (London and New York: Routledge, 1995).

2. Alexander Tytler, *An Essay*, cit. Venuti, p. 68.

3. E. A. Nida, *Towards a Science of Translation. With Special Reference to Principles and Procedures Involved in Bible Translating* (Leiden: Brill, 1964).

4. For Arnold's critique of Newman, see the excerpts from 'On Translating Homer' in Arnold, *Selected Prose*, ed. and introduction by P. J. Keating (Harmondsworth: Penguin, 1970), pp. 76–84, 85–90.

5. T. S. Eliot, 'Baudelaire In Our Time' (1928), *For Lancelot Andrewes*, cit. Venuti, p. 189.

6. For the context, see 'Poetry and Song 1800–1900', Seamus Deane, ed., *The Field Day Anthology of Irish Writing*, II (Derry: Field Day Publications, 1991), pp. 1–114. See also David Lloyd, *Nationalism and Minor Literature: James Clarence Mangan and the Emergence of Irish Cultural Nationalism* (Berkeley: University of California Press, 1987).

7. Tony Harrison, *Selected Poems*, 2nd ed. (London: Penguin, 1987).

8. John Nott, *Select Odes From the Persian Poet Hafez, Translated Into English Verse* (1787), quoted by Venuti, p. 94.

9. Paul Blackburn, ed. and trans., *Proensa: an Anthology of Troubadour Poetry* (1978), edited by G. Economou (New York: Paragon House, 1978).

A European Home?

1. See 'Towards 2000, or News From You Know Where', pp. 94–116 above.

2. I have let this pre-Maastricht nomenclature stand, along with later references to 'the Soviet Union', as the lesser of two kinds of anachronism, with no bearing on the general lines of my argument.

INDEX